# Welcome to
## THE
# EVERYTHING
## — Family Guides —

THESE HANDY, PORTABLE BOOKS are designed to be the perfect traveling companions. Whether you're traveling within a tight family budget or feeling the urge to splurge, you will find all you need to create a memorable family vacation.

Use these books to plan your trips, and then take them along with you for easy reference. Does Jimmy want to go sailing? Or maybe Jane wants to go to the local hobby shop. *The Everything® Family Guides* offer many ways to entertain kids of all ages while also ensuring you get the most out of your time away from home.

Review this book cover-to-cover to give you great ideas before you travel, and stick it in your backpack or diaper bag to use as a quick reference guide for activities, attractions, and excursions you want to experience. Let *The Everything® Family Guides* help you travel the world, and you'll discover that vacationing with the whole family can be filled with fun and exciting adventures.

 **TRAVEL TIP**

Quick, handy tips

 **RAINY DAY FUN**

Plan ahead for fun without sun

≡**FAST FACT**

Details to make your trip more enjoyable

 **JUST FOR PARENTS**

Appealing information for moms and dads

# THE EVERYTHING
## — Family Guide —
## to the Caribbean

Dear Reader,

Thanks for picking up this copy of *The Everything® Family Guide to the Caribbean*! This book will help you and your family get the most out of your upcoming vacation, no matter how large or small your travel budget happens to be. Not only will you find detailed information about all there is to see and to do throughout many of the popular Caribbean islands, you'll also learn about popular Caribbean cruises and discover dozens of useful money-saving tips.

Like all the titles in the *Everything® Family Guide* series, this book was written for the entire family, a quality that sets it apart from other travel guides. You'll soon learn all about the best ways to spend your time while in the Caribbean. Plus, you'll find out what activities are most suitable for you and your kids or teens as you explore all that the Caribbean islands have to offer.

All of the attractions and activities described in this book are also rated. These ratings are based not just on the quality and overall value of the entertainment or services offered, but on age appropriateness as well. This will help you quickly identify the best, most exciting, and most appropriate things for the whole family to see and do during your vacation.

I have been very careful to ensure that all of the information contained in this guide is accurate and up to date. Still, it is always possible that some contact details will have changed by the time this guide goes to press. Be sure to check any Web sites provided for such changes. In addition, if you would like to share your own vacation experiences or opinions about any aspect of the Caribbean covered in this guide, please visit my Web site at *www.jasonrich.com* or drop me an e-mail at *jr7777@aol.com*. My goal has been to provide the most comprehensive, informative, and fun-to-read travel guide possible. After reading this book and comparing it to other travel guides available, I hope you'll find that I've achieved my objective.

Have a wonderful, memorable, and safe trip!

*Jason Rich*
(✎*www.JasonRich.com*)

# THE
# EVERYTHING®
## FAMILY GUIDE TO THE
# CARIBBEAN

A complete guide to the best resorts,
beaches, and attractions—island by island!

Jason Rich

Adams Media
Avon, Massachusetts

Publishing Director: Gary M. Krebs
Managing Editor: Laura M. Daly
Copy Chief: Brett Palana-Shanahan
Acquisitions Editor: Gina Chaimanis
Development Editor: Luann Rouff,
   Jessica LaPointe
Associate Production Editor: Casey Ebert

Director of Manufacturing: Susan Beale
Associate Director of Production:
   Michelle Roy Kelly
Cover Design: Paul Beatrice, Matt LeBlanc
Layout and Graphics: Colleen Cunningham,
   Holly Curtis, Erin Dawson, Sorae Lee

• • •

An Everything® Series Book.
Everything® and everything.com® are registered trademarks of F+W Publications, Inc.

Published by Adams Media, an F+W Publications Company
57 Littlefield Street, Avon, MA 02322 U.S.A.
*www.adamsmedia.com*

ISBN: 1-59337-427-5

Printed in the United States of America.

J I H G F E D C B A

**Library of Congress Cataloging-in-Publication Data**
Rich, Jason.
The Everything Family Guide to the Caribbean / Jason Rich.
     p. cm. — (An everything series book)
     ISBN 1-59337-427-5
   1. Caribbean Area—Guidebooks. 2. Family recreation—
Caribbean Area—Guidebooks. 3. Children—Travel—Caribbean
Area—Guidebooks. I. Title. II. Series: Everything series.

F2165.R53 2005
917.2904—dc22
                    2005015469

This publication is designed to provide accurate and authoritative information with regard to the
subject matter covered. It is sold with the understanding that the publisher is not engaged in ren-
dering legal, accounting, or other professional advice. If legal advice or other expert assistance
is required, the services of a competent professional person should be sought.
         —From a *Declaration of Principles* jointly adopted by a Committee of the
         American Bar Association and a Committee of Publishers and Associations

Many of the designations used by manufacturers and sellers to distinguish their products are
claimed as trademarks. Where those designations appear in this book and Adams Media was
aware of a trademark claim, the designations have been printed with initial capital letters.

Maps©Map Resources

**Visit the entire Everything® series at www.everything.com**

# Contents

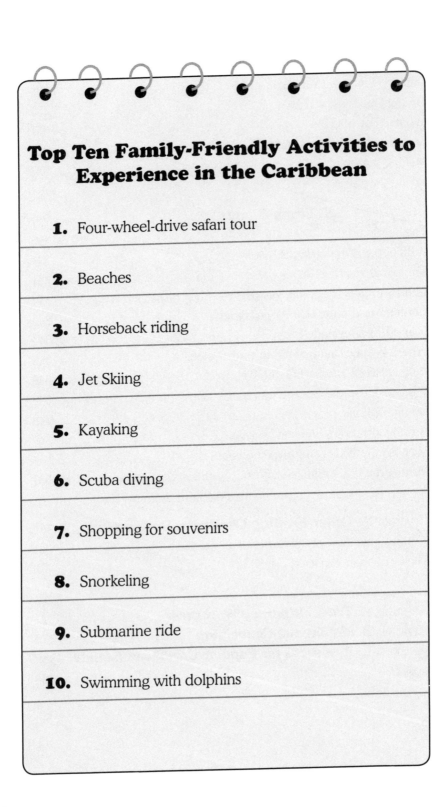

# Top Ten Family-Friendly Activities to Experience in the Caribbean

**1.** Four-wheel-drive safari tour

**2.** Beaches

**3.** Horseback riding

**4.** Jet Skiing

**5.** Kayaking

**6.** Scuba diving

**7.** Shopping for souvenirs

**8.** Snorkeling

**9.** Submarine ride

**10.** Swimming with dolphins

# Acknowledgments

Thanks to everyone at Adams Media, especially Gina Chaimanis, for inviting me to work on this exciting book. On a personal note, the love and support I receive on an ongoing basis from my closest and dearest friends is extremely important to me. For this, I am truly grateful.

Thanks to Ferras AlQaisi, who shared in my Caribbean travel adventures and who provided some of the photographs for this book. I'd also like to extend my love and eternal gratitude to Mark Giordani, the Bendremer family (Ellen, Sandy, Emily, and Ryan), and to my own family. I'd also like to acknowledge "Rusty," my newly adopted Yorkshire Terrier puppy (*www.MyPalRusty.com*), who has added a whole new level of challenge and excitement to my life and travels.

# Introduction

As the title of this book suggests, *The Everything® Family Guide to the Caribbean* is a information-packed resource written specifically for families. The goal of this book is to help you plan the ultimate vacation to any popular Caribbean destination, plus save you some money in the process! You will read about all things you can see and do on each of the popular Caribbean islands, as well as aboard the cruise ships that sail the Caribbean.

What sets this travel guide apart from others is that it has been written for families, *not* honeymooners, business travelers, college spring breakers, senior citizens enjoying their retirement, or couples looking for a romantic getaway. This book defines a family as any of the following:

- Parents traveling with infants or kids
- Parents traveling with teenagers
- An adult couple traveling with parents or in-laws
- Parents, kids, and grandparents traveling together as an extended family unit

Individual chapters provide detailed information about the most popular Caribbean islands, including the following: what makes the island a perfect family-oriented vacation destination; a little history about the island; how to get to the island and choose the best accommodations while you're there; information you need to know about that island to help you prepare for your trip; information about how to best get around the island; details about the top ten must-see activities and attractions offered on the island; and strategies for saving money during your vacation.

Because this book is targeted to families, all the attractions, activities, restaurants, shops, spas, and cruises are rated according to value as well as overall family friendliness and age appropriateness. This will enable you to make intelligent vacation-planning decisions before you leave home, based upon whom you'll be traveling with. These ratings are aimed to help you and your family to make the best decisions about where to stay, how to plan your itinerary, and how to choose the most exciting ways to spend your time. These ratings will help you decide what activities and attractions are appropriate for the people you're traveling with, whether they're toddlers, kids, teens, adults or senior citizens. They also help you decide whether the attractions are worth the money, based on the entertainment value they provide.

If you're traveling with kids or teens, please note that some of the attractions, activities, and destinations are clearly described as suitable for adults only. Many casinos, day spas, and nighttime activities and attractions, for example, are simply not suitable for kids or even teenagers. Still, they will provide plenty of entertainment to parents who decide to leave their children with a babysitter or in one of the supervised youth programs offered at many resorts and on the popular cruise ships.

# Understanding the Ratings System

To help you decide which activities and attractions you want to experience while visiting any of the Caribbean islands, you'll find detailed descriptions of what there is to see and do. This book also offers a ratings system to help you determine what activity, attraction, or tourist destination is most appropriate for various age groups: young children (up to five years old), children (ages six to fifteen), teenagers and young adults (ages sixteen to twenty), adults (twenty-one and up), and senior citizens. The rating charts use stars to show the suitability of each activity, attraction, or destination for the specific age groups, as follows:

One star (★): Fair value/interest level for that age group

Two stars (★★): Good value/interest level for that age group

Three stars (★★★): Excellent value/interest level for that age group

N.S.: Very poor value or not at all suitable for that age group

For example, an activity that's an excellent value and a lot of fun for teens or adults would receive three stars in those two age group categories. But that same attraction might only receive one star under the senior citizen and young children categories, if that activity isn't suitable for those particular age groups.

## Let's Get Started!

Your vacation-planning process begins in Chapter 1 with an overview of the Caribbean and what makes this part of the world so special. You'll also find information about the best and worst times to travel to the Caribbean, along with other useful information about currency, language, and using local services. Chapter 2 includes important information about the Caribbean that you'll want to know *before* making your travel plans and when packing your bags. In Chapter 2, you'll also discover some strategies for saving time and money as you plan your vacation, including information about package deals, the pros and cons of cruises, and much more.

Chapter 3 offers advice on choosing the ideal accommodations for your family while in the Caribbean. While there are countless traditional hotels to choose from on all the Caribbean islands, some also have a wide selection of rental cottages, apartments, or timeshare villas that are especially well suited for families. These options offer a different type of vacation experience than what you'll find at a traditional hotel. You'll also discover that some islands offer all-inclusive, full-service resort packages that are ideal for families. This chapter is meant to help you find the best deals possible for this type of vacation package. Chapter 4 describes how to book a Caribbean cruise. It includes details about the popular cruise-ship companies that sail the Caribbean and offer special services and programs for kids and teens.

No matter what island(s) you choose to visit, once you get to the Caribbean, you'll need to plan your daily itinerary and decide which of the many indoor and outdoor activities you'd like to experience, plus which of the popular attractions you'd most like to visit. Chapter 5 provides a general overview of the many family-friendly activities the various Caribbean islands offer.

Starting with Chapter 6, you'll begin learning all about the specific popular Caribbean destinations, including: Aruba (Chapter 6), the Bahamas (Chapter 7), Jamaica (Chapter 8), Puerto Rico (Chapter 9), Bermuda (Chapter 10), the British Virgin Islands (Chapter 11), Cancun (Chapter 12), the Cayman Islands (Chapter 13), St. Maarten/St. Martin (Chapter 14), the Dominican Republic (Chapter 15), the U.S. Virgin Islands (Chapter 16), and other popular Caribbean destinations (Chapter 17). Each of these chapters provides a list of the top ten must-see attractions and activities for that island. Most of these are family-friendly and worth incorporating into your vacation itinerary.

By the time you're done reading *The Everything® Guide to the Caribbean,* you will have the knowledge you need to plan and experience the ultimate family vacation!

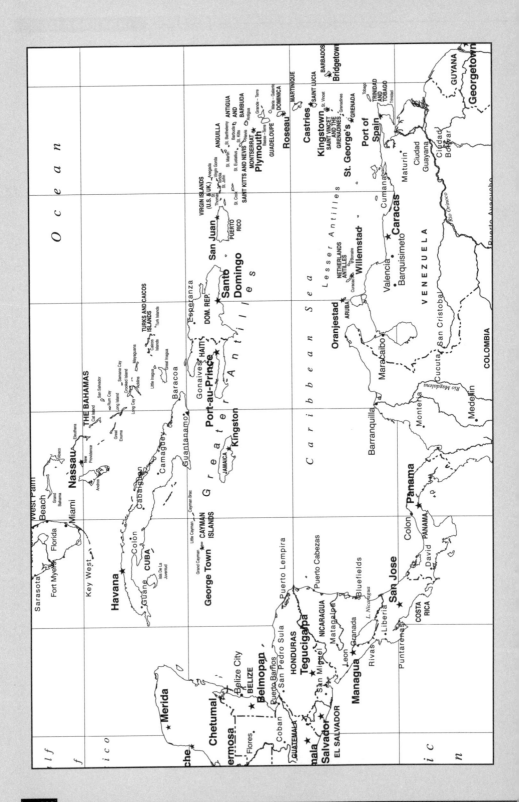

# CHAPTER 1

# *Discover the Caribbean*

COVERING THE NEARLY 2,000-MILE expanse of ocean from Cuba to South America, the Caribbean you're about to discover is an extremely popular tourist destination. The area is comprised of about thirty nations that occupy approximately 7,000 islands. While the population of the entire Caribbean region is about 38 million, many of the individual islands have relatively small populations. Tourism continues to be the biggest business in the region, with between 15 and 20 million visitors per year flocking to the Caribbean for a tropical getaway. Every island in the Caribbean has its own unique history, heritage, and culture. Influences from Africa, America, Spain, Britain, France, Holland, and India can all be found somewhere in the Caribbean. Your vacation experience will vary depending on where in the Caribbean you travel, how much exploration you do, and how long you stay.

## What's So Great about the Caribbean?

You probably already knew that millions of tourists and vacationers visit the Caribbean every year to experience a true tropical getaway. One thing virtually all the Caribbean islands have in common is their natural beauty. Surrounded by vivid blue ocean waters, the islands feature pristine beaches and breathtaking tropical landscapes. With the exception of hurricane season, the weather throughout the Caribbean is typically ideal for a vacation getaway. Because the

Caribbean offers such diverse vacation experiences, depending on where you travel, there's something for everyone here. Here is a partial list of what the Caribbean offers:

- Ideal weather virtually year-round
- Plenty of activities, day and night
- Beautiful beaches where you can simply relax
- Unique shopping
- Restaurants featuring local cuisine
- Tourist destinations and activities you don't typically find within the continental United States
- A wide range of local cultures to experience (depending on where you visit)
- The ability to participate in a wide range of water sports
- A large selection of land-based activities

Whether you're looking for peace and quiet or an exotic adventure, a pristine beach to relax on, or the ultimate spot to scuba dive, you'll find it somewhere in the Caribbean. You'll also find exciting activities, unique places to explore, top-notch hotels and resorts, countless shopping opportunities, and an array of dining options—not to mention plenty of friendly and welcoming locals. All these options make the Caribbean an ideal vacation destination. To make your planning even easier, the Caribbean islands offer many full-service resorts with countless activities available right on-site, plus accommodations suitable or even tailor-made for families.

While the adults are enjoying one set of activities, kids and teens can participate in supervised youth programs offered at many of the resorts or aboard the popular cruise ships. It is important to spend quality family time together. Still, allowing all family members to go their own ways and explore their own interests will provide for a more enjoyable and less stressful vacation for everyone.

Of course, it's impossible to experience all that the Caribbean has to offer during a single or even a dozen visits. Thus, it's important to decide what you want out of your vacation early on in the vacation-planning process. *The Everything® Family Guide to the Caribbean* introduces you to a handful of the more popular Caribbean vacation destinations and explains what each has to offer. Ultimately, you get to decide where your interests lie, what types of experiences you want to have, and what's suitable for your family.

## ≡FAST FACT

Some of the popular water-based sports in the Caribbean include scuba diving, "snuba" diving (a cross between scuba and snorkeling), snorkeling, swimming, Jet Skiing, parasailing, fishing, boating, sailing, water-skiing, swimming with dolphins, and submarine rides. Land-based activities include golf, horseback riding, hiking, tours, sightseeing, all-terrain vehicle adventures, day spas, and helicopter tours.

Regardless of how much time you have or your budget, you can create a fabulous vacation plan for you and your family. You may choose to fly to a single Caribbean island and stay at one resort and enjoy all of its amenities and activities. You might choose to island-hop (either by airplane or boat) and experience several Caribbean islands during your vacation, perhaps staying at several different hotels or resorts. Yet another alternative is to take a five-, seven-, or ten-day cruise to the Caribbean, which will allow you to explore a different Caribbean port of call with every stop the ship makes. All of these vacation options are fully explored in this book, allowing you to decide what makes the most sense for your family.

## ≡FAST FACT

The process for dialing a Caribbean island from the U.S. varies by island. In some cases, you'll need to dial the international access code (011), followed by the country code, city code and local phone number. In other cases, simply dial 1 plus the phone number. For detailed dialing information from the U.S. to specific Caribbean islands, point your web browser to ✍ www.countrycallingcodes.com.

# Deciding When and Where to Visit

Two of the most important factors that will affect your travel plans to the Caribbean are when you plan to visit (your travel dates) and where you'd like to go. Family travel is often constrained by school schedules, so you may not have much flexibility in that regard. Your destination, however, is up to you. With so many popular tourist destinations to choose from—Aruba, Jamaica, the Bahamas, Puerto Rico, the British Virgin Islands, the U.S. Virgin Islands, and Bermuda among them—you'll want to choose one or more destinations that cater to what you're looking for out of your vacation.

### Popular Times to Visit the Caribbean

For the majority of the Caribbean tourist destinations, the busiest time of year is during the Christmas and New Year's holiday period (mid-December through early January).

In general, early January through mid-April is considered the high season for tourism. If you're planning your trip for this period, you'll need to book your travel reservations early, and you can expect the beaches and tourist attractions to be crowded. In addition, this is when prices will be at their highest. Spring and summer (late May through late August) are the times when popular Caribbean destinations are the least crowded. During this off-season, prices for accommodations, all-inclusive resorts, and cruises all drop considerably. This is also when you can find excellent travel vacation bargains throughout the Caribbean.

**TABLE 1-1**

## POPULAR TIMES TO VISIT THE CARIBBEAN

| Travel Season | Dates |
| --- | --- |
| Peak holiday season (most crowded) | Mid-December through early January |
| High season (most crowded) | Early January through mid-April |
| Mid-season (average crowds) | Mid-April through late May; early September through mid-December |
| Low or off-peak season (least crowded) | Late May through late August |
| Hurricane season (the Caribbean's rainy season) | Early June through late November |

### Temperature and Climate

The Caribbean is a lovely tropical paradise and an excellent choice of family vacation destination. Throughout almost the entire year, you can expect to experience warm weather, both day and night. The average temperature is typically between 78 and 84 degrees, seldom dropping below 65 degrees or rising above 90. (The chapters on the individual islands describe their year-round weather conditions.)

There are times, however, when the weather isn't always perfect. Hurricane season in the Caribbean is generally between early June and late November. During this time, it's common for tourists to encounter rain and even severe storms. Unless you're experiencing an all-out hurricane, however, the rainstorms you encounter during hurricane season won't last too long and probably won't disrupt your outdoor plans too much.

To determine the weather forecast for the dates you plan to travel, visit any of these Web sites:

- **Caribbean Hurricane Reports**: *www.gobeach.com/hurr.htm*
- **The National Hurricane Center**: *www.nhc.noaa.gov*
- **The National Weather Service**: *www.nws.noaa.gov*
- **The Weather Channel**: *www.weather.com*
- **Yahoo! Weather**: *http://weather.yahoo.com*

 **TRAVEL TIP**

If you'll be traveling to the Caribbean during hurricane season, be sure to determine the exact hurricane- and other weather-related policies of the airlines, hotels, resorts, and/or cruise ships you'll be using before booking your reservations. You need to know in advance whether you can change or cancel your reservations due to a hurricane. It's also an excellent idea to purchase travel insurance (described in Chapter 2) to protect your family against unforeseen events when traveling overseas.

### Where to Visit

Most of the Caribbean islands belong to one of thirteen independent countries. Some island groups are part of France, the Netherlands, the United Kingdom, or the United States. Because of this diversity, you should do a little homework before planning your itinerary. In addition to the sights and services offered, be sure to consider other information about each locale, including any special entry requirements, medical care available in the event of illness (especially if you or anyone in your family has special medical needs), crime statistics, currency regulations, and even civil unrest.

Chapters 6 through 17 focus individually on the most popular Caribbean islands and will help you choose those that offer the activities and accommodations best suited for your family. No matter when you travel or what your ultimate destination, the proper advance planning will ensure you have a fun and memorable vacation experience.

## Currency Considerations

Once you arrive in the Caribbean, you'll quickly discover that the U.S. dollar and most major credit cards (and debit cards with the Visa or MasterCard logo) are accepted almost everywhere.

## ≡ FAST FACT

Thomas Cook is a currency exchange service with branches in virtually all U.S. airports as well as throughout the Caribbean. For details on local currencies and on current exchange rates, call ✆800-287-7362 or visit the company's Web site at ✍www.us.thomascook.com.

The easiest way to obtain local currency is through an ATM. You can use your debit card or any credit card affiliated with the Cirrus or Plus networks. You'll find these ATMs throughout the Caribbean. The funds you withdraw will be in local currency. Your bank will automatically offer you a competitive exchange rate, and ATM fees will apply.

For a small transaction fee, any bank or currency exchange service will also exchange U.S. dollars for the local currency. You'll find that for the majority of your purchases—at resorts, hotels, restaurants, and shops, for example—Visa and MasterCard are the most widely accepted credit cards, followed by American Express.

You can always bring traveler's checks to the Caribbean and cash them in at your hotel or resort for U.S. dollars or the local currency. At major hotels and resorts, traveler's checks are also welcome; however, traveler's checks aren't always accepted at local shops, in taxis, or at other small establishments. Thus, it's an excellent idea to carry about $100 in cash at all times, plus to have access to additional cash if you decide to make a purchase from a local shop or merchant that doesn't accept credit cards.

## 🧳 TRAVEL TIP

Should you decide to use traveler's checks, be sure to keep a written record of their serial numbers in a separate location from the traveler's checks themselves. This will enable you to replace them more easily if they're lost or stolen.

If you have questions about using your credit cards while in the Caribbean, the following numbers may be helpful, especially if you need to report a lost or stolen credit card or debit card (with the Visa or MasterCard logo):

- **Visa** (☎800-VISA-911 or ☎410-581-9994). You can call the toll number collect from overseas.
- **MasterCard** (☎800-307-7309 or ☎636-722-7111). You can call the toll number collect from outside the United States.
- **American Express** (☎800-992-3404 or ☎336-393-1111). You can call the toll number collect from outside the United States.

# Understanding the Local Language

The languages spoken throughout the Caribbean are as diverse as the cultures you'll find on the islands. English is spoken either as a primary or secondary language on many of the Caribbean islands; however, depending on where you go, expect to hear the locals speaking Dutch, Spanish, French, or one of a handful of other languages. Once you decide where you'll be traveling to, you can check to see what official language is spoken there. You may consider purchasing a phrase book or digital language translator to help you better communicate with the locals, especially if you plan on sightseeing and exploring without an English-speaking tour guide.

The Sharper Image (☎800-344-4444, *www.sharperimage.com*), for example, offers a small, pager-sized English/Spanish talking translator for under $40 as well as a ten-language talking translator (which looks like a folding personal digital assistant) for about $200.

You can also purchase easy-to-use language translator software for all Palm OS personal digital assistants from the PalmOne Web site (*www.palmone.com*). Small Talk, from Landware, Inc. (*www.landware.com*), is an excellent Palm OS-compatible, two-way translating program designed for travelers. It supports English, French, German, Italian, and Spanish. The program is priced under $20.

# Electrical Issues

In the majority of the Caribbean islands, standard 110–120-volt alternating current (AC) is used, which means the electrical wall plugs and outlets take the same type of two- or three-prong plugs used in the United States. There are some exceptions, however. If you'll be using sensitive electronic or computer equipment, it's important to make sure appropriate electrical power is available. Call the hotel or resort where you'll be staying to determine if any special electrical adapters or power converters will be required.

While many hotels and resorts will lend or sell you the necessary adapters, it's always a good idea to arrive prepared. Stores such as RadioShack, Brookstone, and the Sharper Image all offer electrical power adapters suitable for travelers.

# Making Calls to the United States from the Caribbean

Many long-distance providers offer calling cards that can be used from overseas. Before you leave, contact your long-distance provider to obtain a calling card and make sure international calling privileges are active. You should also ask whether any special procedures are necessary, such as dialing access phone numbers in certain destinations. Prior to using a calling card, be sure to inquire about the per-minute rate for calls from the Caribbean to the United States, and ask about any extra per-call fees. You'll definitely want to shop around for the most competitive calling-card plans.

With a calling card from your existing long-distance provider, for example, you will only be billed for calls actually made. International prepaid calling cards are also available that let you purchase a certain amount of telephone time from the Caribbean to the United States for a per-minute fee. These prepaid calling cards can be purchased once you arrive in the Caribbean and often offer the most competitive rates for calling home to the United States.

## ≡FAST FACT

Depending on where in the Caribbean you're calling from, you'll probably need to dial the country code for the United States, then the area code and phone number. After getting an outside line (if you're calling from a hotel, for example), you'd dial 001 + (area code) + (phone number).

# International Roaming Using Your Cell Phone

When it comes to using your cellular phone overseas, you'll find that some service providers offer international roaming for a flat per-minute fee to their customers. While this per-minute international roaming fee isn't necessarily cheap, it's often less expensive than calling home to the United States using a hotel or public phone. Also, you can often receive calls on your cell phone with your existing cell phone number.

Depending on where you travel within the Caribbean, some places—Puerto Rico, for example—are covered by most U.S. cellular service providers. If you have a national service plan, calls from Puerto Rico to anywhere in the United States may be included in your existing plan.

Some cellular service providers offer special international roaming plans and options that need to be activated before you leave the United States. Prior to your departure, contact your service provider to determine if international roaming rates are available for your destination(s).

You can reach the most popular cellular service providers through these phone numbers and Web sites:

- Cingular (✆800-331-0500, ✎*www.cingular.com*)
- Nextel (✆800-639-6111, ✎*www.nextel.com*)
- Sprint PCS (✆888-788-4727, ✎*www.sprintpcs.com*)
- T-Mobile 9✆800-T-MOBILE, ✎*www.t-mobile.com*)
- Verizon Wireless (✆800-922-0204, ✎*www.verizonwireless.com*)

The more technologically advanced traveler might have another option. If your cellular phone is an "unlocked" GSM-compatible model, you may be able to purchase a local, prepaid SIM chip and install it in your phone once you arrive at your Caribbean destination. (Your service provider can tell you whether your phone is of this type.) This will provide you with a local phone number for your cell phone, plus prepaid minutes which can be used to call domestically or internationally, depending on the prepaid plan. In addition to the convenience of having a cellular phone with you, this option is typically cheaper than calling the United States from a hotel or public pay phone while overseas.

 **TRAVEL TIP**

Making international calls from any Caribbean hotel or resort is extremely expensive. You'll often be charged even for toll-free calls. You'll save a lot of money using an international prepaid phone card, which are sold throughout the Caribbean.

## Dining Throughout the Caribbean

No matter which Caribbean island becomes your vacation destination, a multitude of dining options are available to you. In addition to local cuisine, you'll find restaurants serving American food, as well as menus influenced by Italian, French, Mexican, and Asian cuisine. Family-friendly seafood and steak restaurants are also plentiful, especially if you're interested in upscale fine dining.

If you're traveling by cruise ship, virtually all of your meals will be consumed aboard the ship. As you'll have several dining options on the ship, you won't have to seek out any restaurants unless you're at a port of call and choose to sample the local cuisine.

If you'll be staying at an all-inclusive resort, all of your meals will be included, so you probably won't have the need to venture out to find dining options. In many cases, an all-inclusive resort offers several dining options right on the property. These dining options change periodically, so as you're making your resort reservations, ask about the restaurants and meals that are available.

For an added fee, you might want to upgrade to a premium meal plan (highly recommended). This allows you to dine at the resort's finer restaurants, as opposed to the main dining room and/or buffets. In most cases, this strategy will let you enjoy meals of a much higher quality.

On virtually all of the Caribbean islands, you'll find plenty of fast food and very inexpensive dining options. In fact, the famous chain restaurants (like McDonald's, Burger King, KFC, Wendy's, and Subway, for example) have a strong presence throughout the Caribbean. While fast food may keep your kids happy, you'll probably want to experience some of the local cuisine or even a handful of fine-dining options on the Caribbean island(s) you'll be visiting.

Most restaurants located in high-traffic tourist areas feature local as well as Americanized menu options, plus special kids' menus. When it comes to fine dining, you'll discover a wide range of specialty restaurants serving meals prepared by world-renowned chefs. To find restaurants that meet your needs and budget, your best bet is to consult with your hotel's concierge or other tourists if you'll be eating away from your hotel or resort.

Because many Caribbean travelers dine at the resort where they're staying, and because independent restaurants come and go, this guide doesn't focus too much on specific restaurant suggestions. If you're looking to sample the local cuisine or want to find a specific type of restaurant, figure out what kind of food you're looking for and then define your budget. You'll then be able to seek out suitable dining options, no matter where you're vacationing.

# CHAPTER 2

# Jump-Start Your Caribbean Vacation Planning

THE PERFECT FAMILY VACATION to the Caribbean (or any other destination) naturally requires a bit of research and plenty of planning before you leave home. Proper planning will not only save you money, it will also help ensure that your whole family enjoys a great vacation to be remembered for a lifetime. This chapter will help you tailor your vacation to your own needs and interests, whether you want to fly to the Caribbean and stay at a resort or take a Caribbean cruise.

## Pre-Trip Planning Questions

Once you and your family have decided on the Caribbean as your vacation destination, you'll need answers to the following questions before moving forward with the vacation-planning process:

- What is your overall travel budget?
- What part(s) of the Caribbean do you plan to visit?
- Will you stay on one island, such as Aruba, or do you plan to visit and explore multiple islands? (It's important to choose the destination that's most suited to your interests, budget and personal tastes.)
- How many adults, children, and senior citizens will be traveling with you?
- How do you plan to get there (airplane or cruise ship)?

- How much time (days and nights) can you spend on vacation?
- What type of hotel, resort, or cruise-ship accommodations do you require for yourself and your family?
- Are you looking for a hotel, resort, all-inclusive resort, villa, time-share property, apartment-style accommodations, or guesthouse?
- If you'll be on a cruise ship, what type of cabin accommodations will you need?
- Does anyone in your family have special dietary, medical, or physical needs that must be dealt with while traveling?
- What types of activities are you looking to participate in once you arrive?
- Many resorts and cruise ships offer special organized activity programs for kids and teens. Is this important to you when planning your vacation itinerary?

## TRAVEL TIP

As you'll read in Chapter 3, it's important to consider the number of people who will be traveling, the number of beds and bedrooms required, and privacy issues.

Based on your answers to these questions, you can begin researching the best vacation opportunities available. As you do your research, make sure what you're planning fits within your travel budget, the first consideration on the preceding list. By using the worksheet provided in the next section, you can ensure that you have considered all of the costs associated with booking a vacation, including airfare, accommodations, ground transportation, airport parking, food, drinks, activities, tips, souvenirs, and travel insurance. Even if you're booking an all-inclusive vacation package, chances are good you'll have additional expenses above those included in the package, so plan accordingly. The worksheet in **TABLE 2-1** will help you anticipate all of the costs associated with the Caribbean vacation you're about to begin planning.

# Calculating Your Travel Budget

Use the following worksheet to help you calculate a budget for your Caribbean vacation before leaving home. If you're booking an all-inclusive vacation at a resort or a cruise, keep in mind that some expenses will not be included. In addition to the cost of the vacation package, determine what you'll still need to pay for, and calculate those expenses into your budget.

TABLE 2-1
**CALCULATING YOUR TRAVEL EXPENSES**

| Expense | Cost Per Person, Per Day | Total Cost |
|---|---|---|
| Adult airline tickets | $ | $ |
| Child airline tickets | $ | $ |
| Island-hopping airfares or transportation costs | $ | $ |
| Hotel/resort accommodations | $ | $ |
| Rental car, gas, and insurance | $ | $ |
| Ground transportation (airport transfers, taxis, etc.) | $ | $ |
| Meals | $ | $ |
| Snacks and drinks | $ | $ |
| Souvenirs | $ | $ |
| Tours/sightseeing | $ | $ |
| Travel insurance | $ | $ |
| Activity/attraction | $ | $ |
| Activity/attraction | $ | $ |
| Activity/attraction | $ | $ |
| Activity/attraction | $ | $ |
| Activity/attraction | $ | $ |
| Baby-sitting/child programs | $ | $ |
| Kennel costs | $ | $ |

*continued*

| Expense | Cost Per Person, Per Day | Total Cost |
|---|---|---|
| Airport parking or transportation to/from airport in your home city | $ | $ |
| Nighttime entertainment | $ | $ |
| Day spa treatments | $ | $ |
| Tips and gratuities | $ | $ |
| Passport application or renewal fees | $ | $ |
| Other: | $ | $ |
| Other: | $ | $ |
| Other: | $ | $ |
| Other: | $ | $ |

# Choosing Your Destination

Because you'll be traveling with your other people, it's an excellent idea to have everyone help select which attractions and activities you want to check out as a group. If everyone gets the opportunity for input during the itinerary planning stage, you're all more likely to have a relaxing and enjoyable experience. Once you know when your trip will begin, where you'll be staying, and how many days you have to enjoy yourself, you can begin to plan your daily itinerary and choose which of the Caribbean's many islands, beaches, resorts, casinos, day spas, restaurants, and family-oriented attractions and activities you want to experience firsthand.

You may notice that some other travel books suggest specific three-, four-, five-, and seven-day itineraries; however, these itineraries don't take into account people's individual interests. As you'll soon discover, the Caribbean islands offer tremendous variety—plenty of exotic places to visit and explore, beautiful beaches, water-based activities, land-based activities, shopping, dining, gambling, day spas where you can pamper yourself, and countless other things to see and do.

Based on the descriptions in this book, you should be able to plan an itinerary that is ideal for you and your family. You'll find descriptions of just about *everything* that's suitable for families to see, do, and experience in the Caribbean, so grab a pen and paper and prepare to take notes as you plan the ultimate trip!

# Flying to the Caribbean

All of the airlines that fly to the Caribbean offer competitive rates and travel packages, so be sure to shop around for the best airfares and flights. You have several alternatives available when it comes to securing the best airfares:

- Contact the airline directly by phone.
- Visit the airline's Web site.
- Surf the Internet and visit the various travel-related Web sites (such as Hotwire.com, Travelocity.com, or Orbitz.com).
- Call a travel agency, and have them do the busywork for you.

### Booking with Airlines Directly

If you want to fly on a specific airline, you can contact an airline directly and book your airfares either over the telephone, in person, or via the airline's Web site. Virtually all of the major airlines have reduced their customer service staff to cut costs, so it's typically faster and easier to plan your travel online as opposed to calling an airline directly. Many airlines now charge an extra per-ticket booking fee if you make your travel arrangements in person or over the phone. This fee, however, is waived if you book online, which is typically where you'll find the lowest airfares and travel packages.

**TABLE 2-2** lists the major airlines that fly between popular Caribbean destinations and various U.S. cities. Contact the airline directly to see if your home city and your destination city are served by the individual airlines.

You can also check the flight schedules and rates for multiple airlines simultaneously using any of the travel-oriented Web sites, such as Travelocity.com, Hotwire.com, Priceline.com, Cheaptickets.com, or (for AOL subscribers) AOL Travel.

**TABLE 2-2**

## MAJOR AIRLINES THAT SERVICE THE CARIBBEAN FROM THE UNITED STATES

| Airline | Reservations Phone Number | Vacation Package Information and Reservations | Main Web Site | Vacation Package Web Site |
|---|---|---|---|---|
| Air Jamaica | (800) 523-5585 | (800) LOVE-BIRD | www.airjamaica.com | www.airjamaicavacations.com |
| American Airlines | (800) 433-7300 | (800) 321-2121 | www.aa.com | www.aavacations.com |
| Bahamas Air | (800) 222-4262 | (800) 222-4262 | www.bahamasair.com | www.bahamasair.com |
| Continental Airlines | (800) 525-0280 | (800) 634-5555 | www.continental.com | http://continental.covacations.com |
| Delta | (800) 221-1212 | (800) 755-4224 | www.delta.com | www.deltavacations.com |
| JetBlue | (800) JET-BLUE | (800) JET-BLUE | www.jetblue.com | www.jetblue.com |
| Northwest Airlines | (800) 225-2525 | (800) 727-1111 | www.nwa.com | www.nwa.com/travel/vacationswv.html |
| United | (800) 241-6522 | (800) 328-6877 | www.united.com | www.unitedvacations.com |
| US Airways | (800) 428-4322 | (800) 455-0123 | www.usairways.com | www.usairways.com (follow links for Travel Planning) |

By calling the airline directly, you can often hold a reservation for up to twenty-four hours without having to pay for the ticket. It can be a good idea to hold a reservation and then shop around by calling additional airlines and surfing the Web. As a general rule, you want to book your flight as far in advance as possible. Many airlines offer their best prices if you book and pay for your tickets at least twenty-one days in advance. You can, however, also obtain good fares if you make your reservations (and pay for your airline tickets) fourteen or seven days ahead of time. When making travel plans, try to have the most flexible schedule possible. If your schedule permits, you'll almost always get a better airfare if your stay includes a Saturday night.

Keep in mind that with discounted or special airfares, the tickets are usually not refundable or changeable. If you *can* change the flight, you will generally be charged $50 to $100 or more per ticket, plus the price difference in the airfare itself. Tickets purchased from a discount online service, such as Travelocity.com or Hotwire.com, for example, cannot be changed or refunded.

If you want to use frequent-flier miles to book your airline ticket(s) to the Caribbean, keep in mind that seats may be difficult to reserve during peak travel periods, so make your reservations early. Not only is it free to use a frequent-flier ticket, most airlines allow you to change your travel plans at the last minute with no penalties or fees (although your chances of getting a last-minute frequent-flier seat on a flight to a popular destination is slim to none).

Ask the airline if they have less expensive flights to and from the Caribbean at about the same time. You can also check the travel section of your local newspaper for advertised special fares and promotions. Again, keep in mind that many airlines now charge a booking fee for making reservations by phone, so make your reservations online if possible.

## Using a Travel Agent or Service

Because the Caribbean is such a popular destination, travel agents and travel services have a lot of helpful experience in planning a trip to the Caribbean destination. Travel agents have computer systems that allow them to search for flight availability on all airlines at once. Most travel agents will be happy to work with you over the telephone, so it's not necessary to take time out of your busy schedule to visit a travel agent's office.

When choosing a travel agent, find someone who comes highly recommended by someone you trust. Travel agents can be extremely helpful, and they can save you money, but they do work on commission based on the price of the tickets they sell. Thus, some may purposely quote you higher airfares.

You may have access to a full-service, reliable, national agency through travel service companies like AAA (✆800-222-7448, ✑*www. csaa.com*) or American Express (✆800-346-3607, ✑*http://travel. americanexpress.com*).

If you're looking for a local travel agent that specializes in planning Caribbean vacations, the Caribbean Tourism Organization (✆212-635-9530, ✑*www.doitcaribbean.com*) is an excellent referral service. Click on the "Find An Agent" icon on the main Web page. This Web site also offers a travel planner and other useful information about specific Caribbean islands and vacation destinations.

### Tour Operators

An alternative to the all-inclusive resorts (described in Chapter 3) is to work with a tour operator that offers vacation packages. For a flat fee, these packages often include airfare, resort accommodations, ground transportation, a meal plan, tours, and activities. By working with a tour operator, you get to leave many of the vacation-planning details to someone else. If you decide to go this route, be sure to provide the tour operator with ample information about your family's needs and preferences. You should still answer the questions in this chapter on page 13 and fill out the budget worksheet on page 15 to ensure that the person helping you can match your interests and needs to the best package.

Some of the popular tour operators include the following:

- American Express Vacations (✆800-241-1700, ✑*www. americanexpress.com/travel*)

- Caribbean Concepts (📞800-777-0977, ✉*www.caribbeanconcepts.com*)
- Caribbean Journeys (📞888-343-2101, ✉*www.caribbeanjourneys.com*)
- Caribbean Tours (📞800-920-7070, ✉*www.caribbeantours.com*)
- Delta Vacations (📞800-654-6559, ✉*www.deltavacations.com*)
- Leisure Time Travel (📞800-771-2202, ✉*www.leisuretimetravel.com*)
- Suntrek (📞800-SUN-TREK, ✉*www.suntrek.com*)
- TNT Travel (📞617-262-9200, ✉*www.tntvac.com*)
- Tradewind Tours (📞800-860-8013, ✉*www.tradewindtours.net*)
- US Airways Vacations (📞800-454-0123, ✉*www.usairways.com*)

### Flight Status

To get your trip off on the best foot possible, be sure before you leave home that your flight is on schedule. This is also a good idea if you're planning to meet people in the Caribbean (or if someone is picking you up at the airport when you arrive home). If you give them your appropriate airline, flight number, and departure time/date information, you can be sure everyone meets up as planned. With this information, anyone can contact your airline, visit your airline's Web site, or use one of the following Web sites to obtain up-to-the-minute details about your flight and learn about any delays.

 **TRAVEL TIP**

Security is extremely tight at all U.S. airports as well as abroad. Be sure to arrive at the airport at least two hours prior to your scheduled departure time and have your passport, driver's license, and/or military ID ready to show multiple times at various security checkpoints, including the airline ticket counter.

The more popular flight-tracking Web sites include these:

- ✐*http://flighttracker.lycos.com*
- ✐*www.travelocity.com* (choose the Flight Status option under the Flights pull-down menu)
- ✐*www.orbitz.com* (choose the Flight Status option)

# Island-Hopping Tips

As you know, the Caribbean is comprised of many islands, some big and some small. If your vacation plans include visiting multiple islands (a practice known as "island-hopping"), you have several ways of traveling among the islands. If you're taking a Caribbean cruise, your itinerary will most likely include stops at several Caribbean destinations. If you're flying directly to the Caribbean, transportation among the islands is possible using smaller local, inter-island airlines or by boat. **TABLE 2-3** lists several of the inter-island airlines.

**TABLE 2-3**
**POPULAR INTER-ISLAND AIRLINES**

| Airline | Phone Number | Web Site |
|---------|-------------|----------|
| Air Caraibes | (877) 772-1005 | www.aircaraibes.com |
| American Eagle | (800) 433-7300 | www.aa.com |
| Air Jamaica Express | (800) 523-5585 | www.airjamaica.com |
| BWee Express | (800) 538-2942 | www.bwee.com |
| Caribbean Star | (268) 461-7827 | www.flycaribbeanstar.com |
| LIAT | (888) 844-5428 | www.liatairline.com |
| SVG Air | (784) 457-5124 | www.svgair.com |
| Trans Island Airways | (246) 418-1650 | www.tia2000.com |
| Winair | (599) 545-4237 | www.fly-winair.com |

When contacting these airlines, ask about special promotions and travel packages for tourists. Several offer Caribbean "hopper passes," which enable you to take a certain number of trips to any of the Caribbean islands the airline services within a certain time period, such as a week or thirty days. These passes are an excellent way to explore the Caribbean relatively inexpensively.

Island-hopping via ferry and other kinds of boats is a much less expensive way to visit various Caribbean islands. This mode of transportation, of course, takes longer than flying, so it may not be an option for you if your vacation is a short one. Reservations for these boats are recommended during the peak travel season, but they aren't always required.

Additional information about hopping to and from specific islands is included in Chapters 6 through 17, each devoted to a particular island.

 **TRAVEL TIP**

When traveling to the Caribbean, you must have a valid passport as well as all necessary travel documentation. If you're arriving by air, you must be able to present a return airline ticket or a ticket showing you'll be going on to visit additional destinations upon your departure.

## Caribbean Travel Packages

You can find travel packages among the offerings of travel agents, tour operators, major airlines, and resorts. These packages typically include round-trip airfare plus hotel/resort accommodations for a flat, per-person fee. For an additional fee, you may also choose to add extras like travel insurance, a rental car, tours, and other options when you make your reservations.

A package might include accommodations at an all-inclusive resort, which typically includes meals, drinks, activities, and entertainment. An optional money-saving meal plan may also be available to you when purchasing a travel package. While a meal plan limits where you can eat, it'll help keep your travel expenses down and ensure you eat well during your vacation.

## ≡FAST FACT

In addition to all-inclusive options described in this book, you can find plenty of good information at the Web site ✐*www.all-inclusive.com.*

Travel packages cost less than you can expect to spend if you book your airfares and hotel/resort accommodations separately. As you're comparing package deals, make sure you understand exactly what's included and what additional expenses you should expect as you calculate the cost of your overall vacation.

##  TRAVEL TIP

Many U.S. airlines have separate reservation numbers, Web sites, and travel departments that sell discounted Caribbean travel packages. You'll also find travel packages offered by virtually all of the popular travel-related Web sites (such as Hotwire.com, Travelocity. com, or Priceline.com).

Consider several types of travel packages when planning a Caribbean trip. These packages might include airfare and resort accommodations or airfare and cruise-ship travel. Some packages might also include ground transportation (such as airport transfers), food and drink, and activities. These are typically referred to as all-inclusive vacation packages. You pay one flat fee, and then everything (or almost everything) is included. When evaluating an all-inclusive package, you want to determine what's not included. In some cases, food, snacks and drinks (nonalcoholic or alcoholic) will only be available during meal times in the dining room, not throughout the day and night by the pool or beach, for example. While "water sports" might be included, you may discover that popular activities, like scuba diving or any type of boating that involves a motor (such as Jet Skis) cost extra. Any activities or excursions that take place off of the resort property will also typically cost extra and not be included within the all-inclusive price.

## Caribbean Cruises: A Resort At Sea

Imagine having all of the amenities, services, and activities of a full-service resort aboard a ship that cruises from one Caribbean island to the next. At night, while you're asleep in your cabin or dancing the night away in one of the ship's nightclubs, you'll also be traveling to your next port of call. During your full days at sea (a part of almost every Caribbean cruise), you can relax, work out, enjoy the pools on the ship's deck, and take full advantage of the ship's many other onboard activities and amenities.

Even though you have the opportunity to see and experience multiple islands, while aboard the cruise ship there's no need to pack and unpack your luggage, go through the hassle of changing hotel rooms multiple times during your vacation, or get stressed out trying to coordinate inter-island transportation (or going through immigration and customs multiple times) as you attempt to go island-hopping.

The cruise ship you select is designed to be a full-service resort at sea, offering guestrooms of varying levels of luxury (depending on whether you book a cabin, stateroom, or suite), multiple dining options, Broadway– or Las Vegas–style shows, entertainment, activities, sports, and a crew that caters to your every need. While aboard the ship, you'll find many organized group activities suitable for the entire family, along with countless activities to experience at your own pace and plenty of opportunities to simply relax. How you spend your time while aboard a cruise ship is entirely up to you. While daily activity schedules are offered aboard cruise ships, they're totally optional and you are always welcome to ignore them.

A cruise ship also offers plenty of opportunities to engage in family-oriented activities, providing numerous options for enjoying quality time together. When you've had enough of one another, however, all of the popular ships offer supervised activities and programs for youngsters and teenagers, allowing families to have ample time apart as everyone pursues the activities that most interest them. In other words, while the kids are engaged in organized and supervised activities created just for them, you can enjoy the ship's other amenities, such as the day spa, casino, shopping, wine tastings, auctions, or the various bars, lounges, and nightclubs, for example.

When you leave the ship at each new port of call, you have a wide range of new, optional activities and sightseeing opportunities available, some of which you will only find on that particular Caribbean island. All cruise ships have an activities desk, where passengers can learn about and make reservations for optional land excursions from reputable, locally operated tour companies on each of the various islands.

These companies work directly with the popular cruise lines to offer passengers everything from optional land tours and sightseeing trips to horseback riding, jeep safaris, swimming-with-dolphin programs, submarine rides, scuba diving, snorkeling, hiking, and shopping tours.

When it comes to choosing a cruise-ship experience, there are several things to consider. While Disney Cruise Lines offers the ultimate in family-oriented cruise vacations to the Caribbean, other major cruise lines, such as Royal Caribbean, also cater nicely to families. If cruising the Caribbean sounds like your idea of a dream vacation, Chapter 4 offers a wide range of information about many family-friendly Caribbean cruise vacations.

# Pros and Cons of Cruising

One of the greatest things about a cruise is that everything you could possibly want to experience during your time aboard the ship is available to you within a short walk. Contrary to some people's assumptions about cruises, they are not merely floating swimming pools. Many of the ships have indoor and outdoor activities, such as movie theaters, shops, full-service salons, big gyms with state-of-the-art equipment, basketball courts, rock-climbing walls, and even ice-skating rinks, along with Broadway-quality nightly shows, gourmet restaurants, and multiple swimming pools to help you pass the time.

Most people can find ways to enjoy all their time aboard a cruise ship and would be perfectly content not to leave at all, even to explore the ports of call. But a basic benefit of cruising is that each time the ship docks at a Caribbean island, you have a chance to spend up to a full day exploring what that island has to offer. At the end of the day, you get back on board the ship and set sail for your next tropical destination. By the time you wake up the next morning, you'll probably have arrived at your next port of call.

While visiting each Caribbean island where your ship docks, you can choose to visit the local beaches, go shopping, or engage in a wide range of optional land or water-based activities. As you'll read in later chapters, each island offers its own unique set of things to see and do. Because your time is limited on each island, it's important to spend your time wisely. Focus on what interests you the most, while paying attention to your vacation budget.

As a cruise-ship passenger, almost everything you do while aboard the ship (with the exception of certain activities, like treatments at the day spa, shopping, and gambling at the casino) is included in the price of your cruise. This means you can enjoy all-you-can-eat meals at a variety of restaurants aboard the ship, participate in as many activities as you wish, and see live shows nightly, for example. On the down side, mealtimes tend to be crowded and may involve waiting in line, and your ports of call are all chosen for you. If these two factors don't bother you, however, a cruise may be just the thing for you.

Not included in the price of your cruise are the activities you sign up for on land. These are optional and can cost anywhere from $35 to $200 per person, per activity. All land excursions and tours should be booked in advance. While you can save a little money booking your own tours and activities on each island you'll be visiting, it's easier to work through the land excursion or tour desk aboard your cruise ship. This method will also help ensure that you deal with reputable independent tour companies.

In terms of cost, taking a cruise can be cheaper than flying to a Caribbean island, staying at a resort, and having to pay for activities and meals separately. Many different cruise lines cater to families and leave regularly from major ports within the United States for travel to the Caribbean. The majority of the cruise vacations described within this book depart from Miami, Fort Lauderdale, or other East Coast port cities and last for three, five, seven, or ten days.

## Buyer Beware: Obtaining Travel Insurance

Regardless of whether you fly or cruise, travel insurance is a worthwhile expense. Just ask the nearly 3,000 passengers aboard the Premier Cruise Line ships who were suddenly stranded in September of 2000 when that company abruptly suspended its operations. Travel insurance can protect you from a number of calamities, not just airline and cruise-line bankruptcies. Even if you purchase nonchangeable, nonrefundable airfares or travel packages, having travel insurance will enable you to recoup some or all of your travel-related expenses if you or another family member becomes ill or an emergency prevents you from taking your trip. You will, however, have to document a legitimate reason for your inability to travel; last-minute changes of plans do not qualify.

Especially if you're traveling with kids, investing in optional travel insurance is often a good idea. Some travel insurance will also give you added financial coverage if your luggage is lost or stolen or if you experience any type of emergency (medical or otherwise) during your trip. Some insurance will also provide assistance resulting from natural disasters, such as a hurricane, for example.

Travel Guard (☎800-826-1300, ✐*www.travelguard.com*) is one popular travel insurance company. Travel Guard International and its affiliate companies provide integrated travel insurance, assistance and emergency travel services throughout the world. Travel Guard offers customer service, available 24 hours a day, 7 days a week through its service center.

There are several ways to find the best travel insurance for your family vacation. Any travel agent can also help you purchase travel insurance. TripInsuranceStore.com (☎888-407-3854, ✐*www.tripinsurancestore.com*) is a good online source. At this Web site, you can shop for travel insurance online and obtain price quotes from over 100 insurance companies. You can get a free, no-obligation price quote in just minutes. A third option is the travel-related Web sites, which allow you to purchase insurance from specific companies when making your airline ticket purchase.

# Obtaining or Renewing Your Passports

If you're an American citizen you'll need a valid U.S. passport any time you travel overseas. The purpose of a passport is to verify your identity and nationality whenever you enter or leave a foreign country. American passports are issued exclusively by the U.S. Department of State.

### Applying for a New Passport

You can apply for a new passport by several means, such as making a visit to the nearest passport office or filling out a form and mailing it in. You'll have to apply in person if any of the following cases applies to you:

- You're applying for a passport for the first time.
- Your U.S. passport expired and is no longer in your possession.
- Your previous passport was lost, stolen, or damaged.
- Your previous U.S. passport expired more than fifteen years ago.

- Your previous U.S. passport was issued when you were under age sixteen and has since expired.
- Your name has changed since your passport was issued and you have not legally changed your name.

To obtain a passport for the first time, you'll need to visit one of over 6,000 passport acceptance facilities located across the country. Unless you live in a very small town, your local post office will probably have passport applications and be able to process them for you. This must be done in person and often requires an advance appointment. In order to have a new passport issued, you'll need to bring with you two photographs of yourself (each two inches square) taken within the past six months. Many film-processing locations will take passport photos for a small fee. You'll also need one of the following official forms of identification:

- A valid driver's license
- Previously issued U.S. passport
- Birth certificate (which contains a registrar's raised, embossed, impressed, or multicolored seal, registrar's signature, and the date the certificate was filed with the registrar's office, which must be within one year of birth)
- Naturalization certificate
- Certificate of citizenship

## TRAVEL TIP

If you do not have at least one of these forms of identification, call the passport acceptance office in your area to determine how to proceed with the passport application process.

If time is of the essence and you need a new passport quickly, you'll need to visit one of the thirteen regional passport agencies in person. To determine where you can apply for a passport, go online to *http://iafdb.travel.state.gov* to locate the nearest office of passport services. You can also call the National Passport Information Center (NPIC) at ☎877-487-2778. Automated information is available from this service twenty-four hours a day.

When applying for a new passport, it will be necessary to complete an application for passport (Form DS-11), which can be downloaded from the Internet (*http://travel.state.gov*) or picked up at any passport agency or acceptance facility. This form is also available from many travel agents that specialize in overseas travel.

To complete the DS-11 form, you need your full name, mailing address, sex, place of birth, date of birth, Social Security number, height, hair color, eye color, home telephone number, business telephone number, occupation, plus information about your parents, spouse, and other names you've used in the past.

## 💼 TRAVEL TIP

Do not sign your passport application (Form DS-11), until you're in the presence of a passport acceptance agent and you're instructed to do so.

Once you complete your application, it usually takes up to six weeks to receive your new passport. You can also pay for expedited service and have your application processed in under two weeks. See **TABLE 2-4** for the standard and expedited passport fees.

### Renewing Your Existing (Expired) Passport

For U.S. citizens who already have a passport but have let it expire, the renewal process can be completed by mail. A form specifically for renewal of expired passports (DS-82) is available from any passport office or can be downloaded from the Internet (*http://travel. state.gov*). You can also find additional information about passport renewal at this site or by calling ☎877-487-2778.

Complete this form and enclose it in a padded envelope along with your expired passport, two new passport photos, and a $55 renewal fee. It's an excellent idea to send this package via certified mail. Allow up to six weeks for delivery of your new passport unless you request and pay for the expedited service.

**TABLE 2-4**
**PASSPORT APPLICATION AND RENEWAL FEES**

| Application Type | Standard Fee | Expedited Fee |
|---|---|---|
| New passport application (Form DS-11) | $85/$70 (adults/under 16) | $60 additional per application, plus overnight shipping charges |
| Passport renewal (Form DS-82) | $55 | $60 additional per application, plus overnight shipping charges |

## Obtaining a New Passport Quickly

Even if you pay the expedited service fees to have your new passport issued or renewed, the process can still take up to two weeks. If you're really under the gun, you can hire an independent service to process new passport applications and renewals within twenty-four hours. These services can also help you obtain visas or copies of a birth certificate. Expect to pay a hefty fee ($179 and up) for each passport renewal application.

 **TRAVEL TIP**

You can download any of the passport application or renewal forms you need directly from the U.S. Department of State Web site (*http://travel.state.gov*) or from the American Passport Express Web site (*www.americanpassport.com*).

Here's the contact information for a couple of the more popular twenty-four-hour passport services:

- Passport Express (℡800-362-8196, ✎*www.passportexpress.com*)
- American Passport Express (℡800-455-5166, ✎*www. americanpassport.com*)

## Customs and Duties

Once you have your passport in hand, you're ready to travel. And once you start traveling, you'll probably find it's time to shop! While in the Caribbean, you'll be tempted into lots of shops to peruse the many exotic items and crafts available. As you shop for newfound treasures and souvenirs, keep copies of all your receipts. Upon re-entering the United States, it'll be necessary to show U.S. customs officials what you've purchased. Don't gift-wrap any of your purchases until you get home since the contents of your luggage (including your new purchases) are subject to search. Remember, all your vacation purchases must be declared.

As long as you spend at least forty-eight hours on your Caribbean vacation, you and all your family members are allowed to return with up to $800 worth of foreign goods without having to pay additional taxes or duties. These duty-free goods may include up to one liter of alcohol and up to 100 cigars (as long as they don't come from Cuba). If you plan to spend more than $800 on jewelry, artwork, or other expensive goods, it's a good idea to check the rules ahead of time and see whether there's a way to avoid having to pay duty to get your purchases home.

## ═FAST FACT

As a general rule, you are not permitted to transport any type of pre-pared food, fruits, vegetables, animals, weapons, drugs, or plants into the United States from overseas. The U.S. Customs & Border Protection Web site, at *www.cbp.gov*, includes information about items that can and cannot be transported into the United States.

What are duties, anyway? According to U.S. Customs & Border Protection Web site (*www.cbp.gov*), "*Duty* is the amount of money you pay on items coming from another country . . . Most items have specific duty rates, which are determined by a number of factors, including where you got the item, where it was made, and what it is made of . . . The duty-free exemption, also called *the personal exemption*, is the total value of merchandise (usually $800) you may bring back to the United States without having to pay duty. You may bring back more than your exemption, but you will (probably) have to pay duty on it."

# CHAPTER 3

# Choosing Hotel
# or Resort
# Accommodations

LIKE ANY TOURIST DESTINATION, the Caribbean offers plenty of hotels, resort properties, inns, villas, cottages, and guesthouses at a wide range of prices. Once you've chosen your Caribbean vacation destination(s), your next step is deciding where you'd like to stay and what type of accommodations are best suited for your family, based on your needs, budget, and desires.

## Find Accommodations That Fit Your Family's Needs

While most of us would enjoy staying in the finest suite of a luxurious beachfront resort, not everyone can afford it. Moreover, it wouldn't be suitable for every type of traveler. Your job is to decide how to get the most from your accommodations, depending on what you and family want out of your vacation.

At one end of the spectrum is the resort, which might offer so many amenities and activities that you would never have to (or want to) leave the property. More traditional hotels, on the other hand, might give you little more than a cheap place to sleep and perhaps a location convenient to the activities, beaches, and attractions you and your family have chosen to enjoy.

Keep your budget in mind as you're planning your Caribbean getaway, along with the needs and abilities of other family members.

You should also pay attention to the availability of activities your family will enjoy. Knowing this information will help you choose the very best (and most economical) accommodations for your family.

This chapter will help you define your accommodation needs. Later chapters provide detailed information about some of the most popular places to stay on the various Caribbean islands. Before choosing where you want to stay, however, it's a good idea to focus on your accommodation needs. Ask yourself these questions:

- How many adults are in your party?
- How many kids or teens?
- How many beds and bedrooms will you need? (A basic hotel or resort room generally has two queen-size beds per room.)
- If you need multiple bedrooms (say one for the parents and one for the kids), do you want connecting rooms?
- If you're traveling with teenagers, would they be more comfortable having the privacy of their own room? Would such an arrangement allow for adequate supervision?
- Would your family be more comfortable staying in a multi-room suite?
- What special amenities do you and your family require? These might include extras like a refrigerator, full kitchen, multiple bathrooms, multiple televisions, Internet access, extra space for a crib, in-room dining (with a full room-service menu), and laundry facilities.
- Do you want/need a smoking or nonsmoking room?
- Do you need a room that's handicap accessible?
- What is your nightly budget for accommodations?

## Room Considerations When Traveling with Kids or Teens

Depending on the age of your kids, chances are they'll have special needs and interests. You can make their vacation much more pleasant (and thus less stressful) by talking to them ahead of time about their expectations. For a family of four that includes two kids, for example, the following sections describe a variety of suitable accommodations.

### One Room with Two Queen-Size Beds

You can usually request that an additional cot be placed in your room if you have two or more kids who can't or won't share a bed. You can also bring along or request a crib for the room, if necessary. The drawback to this plan is lack of space. While the extra-cot option is the least expensive, remember that things can get very crowded in the relatively confined space of a hotel room, especially if you're constantly stepping over luggage or several people need to use the bathroom at once.

### Two Connecting Guestrooms

With this arrangement, you might request one room with a single king-size bed (for the parents) and a connecting room with two queen-size beds (for the kids). This option offers more living space and privacy, while still keeping the kids under constant parental supervision. It also gives the kids their own television and bathroom, plus extra space for luggage. This type of room configuration is perfect for a family traveling with an infant or young child. At night, the parents can watch television or socialize in one room, while the child sleeps undisturbed by the noise in the adjoining room.

### Multiroom Suite

Available in all of the major resorts and many traditional hotels, a multiroom suite typically contains two or more bedrooms, a living room, and two or more bathrooms. Some also offer a separate dining area and/or a kitchenette. This option offers the parents and the kids some privacy, yet allows the family to stay together. A suite is also perfect for a family traveling with an infant or young child. At night, the parents can watch television or socialize in one room, while the child sleeps undisturbed by the noise in the adjoining room. Expect to pay more for this arrangement, of course.

### Apartment-Style Accommodations

If you're willing to pay a bit extra, you can find apartment-style accommodations at some resorts and private complexes with prices ranging from the economical to the luxurious. You can also find private villas and time-share communities that offer apartment-style accommodations to visiting vacationers. (The Internet is a great resource when it comes to searching out private owners or time-share owners interesting in renting out their properties.) Whether they are a single unit of a larger building or separate bungalows, these apartments usually have multiple bedrooms, a living room and dining area, as well as a kitchen and several bathrooms. For a family, this type of accommodation offers the advantages of space, convenience, and privacy.

 **TRAVEL TIP**

Many resort and hotel rooms within the Caribbean have televisions but very few available channels. Thus, don't rely on a television to entertain your kids when you're trying to relax or sleep late. Make sure you bring along ample activities that your kids can occupy themselves with while in the room.

## Other Arrangements

If you're interested in experiencing more of the local Caribbean culture, you'll usually find an intimate, individual setting in a guest-house or bed-and-breakfast (B&B). This type of accommodations is usually more suitable for adult couples traveling alone, or perhaps with their parents or in-laws. Sometimes furnished with antiques or other one-of-a-kind crafts and collectibles, guesthouses and B&Bs aren't usually the best choice if you're traveling with kids or teens. Some don't allow children at all.

### Traveling with Senior Citizens

If you're traveling with senior citizens, perhaps your parents or in-laws, there are some additional considerations to be made when selecting accommodations. Especially if you're traveling with kids or teens as well, you'll definitely want multiple bedrooms to give everyone some privacy. In this situation, connecting rooms aren't as important as making sure your rooms are close to one other (on the same floor of the hotel, for example.) You'll also want to avoid rooms that are a long walk from the main lobby or that involve negotiation of steps, uneven footing, or other uncertain terrain.

Here are some questions to consider when traveling with senior citizens:

- Do you need a room close to the entrance or main lobby (requiring limited walking)?
- Do you require a room that's handicap accessible?
- Will you need a refrigerator in the room to store medications?
- Does the restaurant in the hotel need to cater to special dietary needs?
- What hotel amenities and activities will the senior citizens want or need? For example, are they interested in a having access to a beach, golf course, casino, or swimming pool?

# Consider the Activities and Amenities Available

The pleasure you get from your vacation will be determined, in part, by how comfortable you are with the accommodations. Although the quality of the time you spend in your room is important, keep in mind that you'll probably be outside most of the time, pursuing all those fun activities you planned to occupy your vacation time. When weighing various accommodation options by cost, you should also consider the distance of various hotels and other properties from your chosen activities. You might find that a cheap room isn't worth the savings if it means spending a fortune (and a lot of precious time) on transportation. Therefore, when selecting a hotel or resort, you also want to consider the following:

- Distance from the airport and from popular activities and attractions
- Included amenities
- Amenities that cost extra
- Included activities
- Activities that cost extra
- Whether property will allow you to experience the local culture
- Luxury and comfort of rooms and overall accommodations

Many of the full-service and all-inclusive resorts located throughout the Caribbean offer all the amenities and activities you could possibly want. You'll find multiple restaurants and lounges, a wide range of guest accommodation options, swimming pools, fitness centers, day spas, tennis, golf, and plenty of shopping. With many located right on the water, Caribbean resorts are also known for their beautiful beaches and their wide range of water-based activities. Some also offer casinos, shows, and other forms of entertainment.

If you're traveling with kids or teens, you might appreciate the special activities that many resorts plan for kids and teens. These options give parents time alone to experience adult-oriented activities, and they provide kids with the opportunity to meet and spend time with others in a supervised, structured, fun environment.

If the resort claims a specific activity is available, you should find out ahead of time whether it's offered on the property or close by. You should also ask about additional charges that might apply. You don't want to arrive at your hotel or resort and learn that all you favorite activities are going to cost you extra, especially if these additional costs weren't calculated into your initial travel budget.

Very few resorts offer access to every activity you might want to enjoy on your Caribbean vacation. Thus, it's important to shop around and choose accommodations that either offer the activities you want on-site or that are located close to the activities you're interested in experiencing. Here's a list of the most popular activities, amenities, and services you'll find offered at Caribbean hotels and resorts:

- All-terrain-vehicle sightseeing tours
- Beaches and sunbathing
- Biking
- Boat rentals
- Bus sightseeing tours
- Car rentals
- Casino
- Day spa (massages, pedicures, etc.)
- Fishing/deep-sea fishing
- Golf
- Hiking and jogging
- Horseback riding
- Jet Skiing
- Moped rentals
- Plenty of dining options
- Nightclubs, bars, lounges, and/or organized night-time activities
- Parasailing
- Sailing
- Scuba diving and snorkeling; snuba diving (a combination of the two)
- Shopping
- Special events
- Structured and supervised activities for kids and teens
- Submarine rides
- Swimming pool/Jacuzzi/hot tub
- Swimming with dolphins
- Walking tours
- Water-skiing
- Windsurfing

# Getting the Cheapest Room Rate

Throughout the Caribbean, the year is divided into tourist seasons. The peak tourist season goes from mid-December through April. Room rates are at their highest during these months, especially during the holiday periods and on weekends.

During the off-peak season, you can often find the same rooms at savings of 40 to 50 percent, particularly on weekdays. As with any other product anywhere in the world, room prices are set by demand. When hotels and resorts are close to or at capacity, rates increase. You'll might be able to find better rates if you shop around and have somewhat flexible travel dates. If you can leave on a Wednesday or

Thursday and return on a Monday or Tuesday, for example, you'll miss the high-traffic travel days. This might end up saving you a fortune when it comes to booking hotel/resort accommodations, not to mention on your airfare.

Once you know what kind of accommodations you're looking for, you can make a list of places you'd like to stay. At that point, you're ready to start shopping for the best bargain out there. To find the lowest room rates, you can try several things.

If you know exactly where you want to stay, you can call the hotel or resort directly. Tell them when you'll be visiting and ask for the room rate. Be sure to ask for any special discounts available. Don't be surprised if you're quoted different rates for different nights during your stay. For example, if you're staying in the same room on Thursday, Friday, and Saturday night and checking out on Sunday morning, the rate on Thursday might be lower than what you're quoted for Friday and Saturday. Some places require you to stay for a full weekend (Friday through Sunday). While you're on the hotel or resort's Web site, be sure to hunt down any special "Internet only" rates or special promotions that may be offered during the dates you'll be visiting. Be prepared to take advantage of those immediately, as they may expire without warning.

If you don't have a particular property in mind, try visiting the discount-travel Web sites to shop for the best deals online. These Web sites—which include Hotwire.com, Travelocity.com, Orbitz.com, Expendia.com, and Priceline.com—usually offer special package deals if you book your airfare and hotel/resort reservations at the same time. Some travel-related Web sites, such as Hotels.com, focus exclusively on finding the lowest hotel rates possible. You probably won't find much price variation among those sites for rooms at any given hotel or resort. You might be able to get a bargain, however, by doing a "blind" booking—you get to choose the hotel by rating only (from economy to luxury), not by name or even precise location. In exchange for this leap of faith, you can sometimes get a fabulous deal at the perfect place!

Other sources of possible bargains include the travel section of your local newspaper as well as travel magazines. Be on the lookout for ads that promote specials and discounted package deals. Don't overlook the resources offered by your local travel agent, either. If you're not having any luck finding price breaks, or if you don't have the time to investigate all your options, call a travel agent and let a professional do all that legwork. Ask for the best room rates for a variety of options, based on your specific needs.

You can also visit the department of tourism Web site for the Caribbean island you plan to visit. Search for accommodations based on your needs, paying special attention to any package deals and promotions being offered. Appendix C includes a listing of these official Web sites.

# Resort Types

Throughout the Caribbean, there are two main types of resorts. At regular or traditional resorts, guests pay a per-night fee for accommodations, plus extra for meals, tips, and activities. For most families, however, an all-inclusive resort often makes more financial sense. Depending on the resort you choose and the package you purchase, you'll pay a flat fee that includes the cost of your room, all meals (often featuring all-you-can-eat menus), unlimited drinks (often including alcoholic beverages), activities, and tips. This is not only easier on your pocketbook, it makes budgeting easier for extras.

## What Traditional Resorts Offer

Traditional resorts, located throughout the Caribbean, are basically large, full-service hotels offering a wide variety of amenities, dining options, and activities located right on the property. These amenities and activities might include a private beach, an eighteen-hole golf course, a large selection of water sports, organized activities, a day spa, and a youth program.

However, in order to experience these activities and services as a guest, you'll pay for each thing separately, sort of like ordering from an a-la-carte menu at a restaurant. Your guestroom accommodations are the main entrée, while everything else you do at the resort would be considered optional side orders. At a traditional resort, all of your meals and drinks, for example, would also be paid for separately or added to your hotel bill.

If you're planning on doing a lot of sightseeing and dining at local restaurants, a traditional resort is a good idea from a convenience and financial standpoint. Be sure, however, to calculate the cost of the traditional resort accommodations, plus meals, drinks, and activities you'd be participating in at the resort, as well as necessary ground transportation (rental car or taxis, for example). You might be surprised to find that the cost of paying for each thing separately adds up to much more than you would pay at an all-inclusive resort.

## The All-Inclusive Resort Alternative

As the name suggests, an all-inclusive resort offers guestroom (or suite) accommodations, all meals, drinks, activities, entertainment, and a wide range of amenities, for one flat fee per guest.

While airport transfers within the Caribbean are often included, what's typically *not* included in these deals are airfares. For an additional fee, airfares can be coordinated through the reservations office of the various all-inclusive resorts.

The per-person price of an all-inclusive resort is based on the duration of your vacation. Some all-inclusive resorts have a minimum stay of three, five, or seven days. They might also offer specially priced packages for longer stays, with additional days costing extra should you choose to add them.

When investigating all-inclusive resorts, keep in mind that not everything is always included in your package, despite what the "all-inclusive" title suggestions. The following sections describe things to ask about in advance.

### Unlimited Beverages

Your flat fee might include an "unlimited beverages" option. This does not always mean unlimited alcoholic beverages. If alcohol is included, moreover, it might only include tropical drinks, such as piña coladas, as opposed to mixed drinks. In some cases, bottled water is not included, while sodas, teas, and coffees are. Drinks might also be included only at designated meals, as opposed to throughout the day.

### Unlimited, All-You-Can-Eat Meals

This sometimes means that guests can dine only at one or two restaurants or dining areas within the resort. If you're interested in experiencing the higher-end restaurants located on the resort's property, there's often an additional charge, per person and per meal (or per day). Ask in advance if you'll be expected to purchase an upgrade or premium meal package when you actually arrive at the resort. This additional fee could add between $10 and $30 a day for each family member to your vacation expenses.

### Activities and Entertainment

In many instances you can expect to pay extra to enjoy the resort's more luxurious amenities, such as day-spa treatments, golf, tours, activities outside of the resort's property, scuba diving, and motorized boating activities. Some all-inclusive resorts advertise unlimited water sports, for example, but boat rentals or equipment rentals (such as snorkeling gear) cost extra. Make sure you understand exactly what's included when it comes to activities and on-property entertainment.

One reason that families tend to choose all-inclusive resorts for their Caribbean vacation is because they plan to stay on the resort's property for the majority of their vacation. This means they don't plan to do too much exploring (sightseeing) or eating at restaurants located off of the resort's property. When staying at an all-inclusive resort, there's seldom a need to carry your wallet, because everything you'll be doing is included in the price. Another plus is that no tipping is allowed at these resorts.

If you're traveling with kids or teens, make sure you choose a resort that caters to younger people and offers structured activities, children's menus at the restaurants (featuring kid-friendly foods), and baby-sitting services. After all, the adults in your family will most likely want to experience the resort's nightlife, without the kids.

A family-friendly all-inclusive resort is usually more than adequate to meet any family's needs. However, you'll often find that all-inclusive resorts that cater specifically to families with kids are lower-end resorts with fewer luxuries and amenities. The quality of the food and service might not be as high as at an all-inclusive resort that caters to people of all ages. Keep in mind that some all-inclusive resorts cater to adults only, so if you're traveling with kids or teens, choose a place that offers the services, guestroom accommodations, and activities you want and need.

If you decide to stay at an all-inclusive resort, make sure the resort offers enough in the way of activities to keep you and your family entertained for the duration of your stay. The one drawback to many of the all-inclusive resorts throughout the Caribbean is they're often designed to keep guests on the property. As a result, they aren't typically located very near the main tourist areas. Only a handful of the all-inclusive resorts succeed in offering a true all-inclusive vacation, where the whole family can enjoy all their favorite activities without ever having to leave the property. It's likely, therefore, that you and your family will want to explore other local entertainment, shopping, and activities. If you do decide to leave the property for some sightseeing or to experience the tourist attractions on the Caribbean island you're visiting, it'll often require either renting a car, spending a lot on a taxi, or paying an additional fee to participate in an organized tour or day-trip coordinated by the resort.

Plan on venturing out for at least one or two days during your stay to see the local tourist attractions on the island you're visiting. After all, what's the point of traveling all the way to Aruba, Jamaica, or another popular Caribbean getaway if you don't want to experience the local culture and attractions? If you don't plan on leaving the resort's property, it hardly matters which Caribbean island you choose to visit, because your experience on the resort's property will be pretty much the same wherever you stay.

# Popular All-Inclusive Resorts

This section offers details about several popular all-inclusive resort operators in the Caribbean. As you'll see, each of these companies has multiple properties. When shopping for the perfect all-inclusive resort, consider the following:

- **Location**: Is the resort located in a part of the Caribbean you want to visit? How far is it from the airport, major tourist destinations, shopping, and other attractions you'll want to see?
- **Price**: What is the per-person price? Are discounts offered for kids? What special discounts are you eligible for? Will you need to pay extra to upgrade your meal plan or activities package in order to experience everything offered by the resort?
- **Activities**: Specifically what land- and water-based activities are included in the price? Are these activities you and your family will want to participate in?
- **Dining**: How many different dining options are offered? Does the resort offer special kids' menus/meals?
- **Accommodations**: What are the available room configurations for guestrooms or suites? Will the resort guarantee the type of room configuration(s) you want or need?
- **Additional fees**: What isn't included with the price?

As your quest for the ultimate all-inclusive resort begins, call each of the popular resort operators described in the following sections and request free brochures and trip-planning videos. You'll also find an abundance of information online.

### Club Med

☎800-CLUB-MED

✐*www.clubmed.com*

Club Med resorts tend to be more upscale. Many of the popular Club Med resorts cater to families, although some specifically cater only to adults. The all-inclusive packages include breakfast, lunch, and dinner; snacks and beverages (premium alcohol with open bar, as well as sodas, teas, and coffees); over sixty water and land sports (with all necessary equipment and instruction); and all on-property entertainment and tips.

The typical Club Med property occupies at least fifty acres. The resorts offer guestroom accommodations at a variety of price points and in several different guestroom/suite configurations. Club Med locations in the Caribbean can be found in Cancun, the Bahamas, Guadeloupe, and the Dominican Republic, as well as Turkoise, Turks, and Caiscos.

### Divi Resorts

✆800-367-2484

✎www.diviresorts.com

Throughout the Caribbean, Divi Resorts operates both traditional and all-inclusive resorts. If you're staying at one of the company's all-inclusive resorts, you may also be able to take advantage of the amenities and activities offered at the company's nearby traditional resorts. You'll find these mid- to upper-priced resorts to be well equipped, clean, and extremely comfortable. Divi Resorts has all-inclusive properties in places like Aruba, Bonaire, St. Maarten, Barbados, St. Croix, and Cayman Brac.

### Iberostar Hotels & Resorts

✆888-923-2722

✎www.iberostar.com

With a handful of locations in and around the Caribbean, particularly Cancun, Cozumel, Paraiso Beach, and Paraiso del Mar in Mexico, these mid-priced, all-inclusive resorts offer comfortable guestrooms, junior suites and suites, all meals, beverages, and a wide range of land- and water-based activities. Most of the resorts also have special kid-oriented programs, designed for the four-to-twelve age group. Baby-sitting services are also available.

### Sandals

✆800-SANDALS

✎www.sandals.com

With multiple locations in Jamaica, St. Lucia, Antigua, and the Bahamas, Sandals resorts are family friendly. This resort company boasts, "At Sandals, there are no compromises and no surprises. The best of everything is included at one up-front price." This includes activities such as golf, water-skiing, and even scuba diving, for which many all-inclusive resorts charge extra. Airport transfers are also included with packages from Sandals.

Specifically for families, Sandals operates several Beaches Resorts. These properties are also all-inclusive, but they cater more to kids and teens in terms of the menu options and activities offered.

## SuperClubs

✆800-GO-SUPER

✑*www.superclubs.com*

SuperClubs operates a large number of all-inclusive resorts that cater to very different types of travelers. The mid-priced Breezes Resorts are family friendly, while the Grand Lido Resorts & Spas cater to a more upscale, primarily adult clientele. The Hedonism Resorts are definitely for adults only.

The company's Starfish Resorts offer the ultimate in competitively priced (lower-end) resorts targeted to families with kids and teens. The guestrooms at the Starfish Resorts tend to be more generic with limited in-room amenities. For information about the Starfish Resorts, visit ✑*www.starfishresorts.com.*

While the SuperClubs resorts offer all of the activities and amenities you'd typically want, the company does impose surcharges for a handful of popular activities, and they encourage guests to upgrade their meal plan (for an additional fee) in order to enjoy the nicer restaurants and dining areas offered at the various resorts. You'll find SuperClubs has multiple locations in several popular vacation destinations, including Jamaica, the Dominican Republic, the Bahamas, Curacao, and St. Kitts.

# CHAPTER 4

# Cruising the Caribbean

IF YOU HAVE ALREADY decided that taking a cruise will be the ideal way for you and your family to enjoy the Caribbean, this chapter will provide you with all the information you need to get started. Whether you plan to take a three-day, five-day, or two-week Caribbean cruise, you want to maximize your time and money. A little planning will go a long way toward ensuring that everyone in the family enjoys your eagerly anticipated vacation.

## Things to Consider When Choosing Your Cruise

The trick to finding the best cruise for your family is to select a ship that travels to the destinations you most want to visit, sets sail during the dates you want to travel, offers the activities you want, and fits within your budget. The cruise best suited to your family will depend on several factors, including the following:

- What's included in the cruise package
- Cost of the cruise (including all extras, such as tips, taxes, and optional expenses for activities)
- Length of the cruise
- Cruise ship's itinerary and ports of call
- Available activities for the entire family and adults

- Selection of activities specifically for kids or teens
- Selection and prices of optional land excursions and activities at the various ports of call
- Time of year you plan to take the cruise
- Type of accommodations
- Where cruise ship departs (and whether airfare to that city is included)
- How far in advance you make your reservations

Caribbean cruises tend to last three, four, five, seven, or ten nights and depart from Florida (typically Miami or just outside of Orlando) or from San Juan, Puerto Rico.

 **TRAVEL TIP**

When planning your costs, whatever you budget per person for the cruise itself, plan on spending an additional 50 to 75 percent of that amount per person on optional activities and add-ons during the cruise. Land-based tours, certain activities and shopping, for example, are not included in the cruise price.

Some cruise ships cater to families, while others attract senior citizens, single travelers, or newlyweds. Especially if you're traveling with kids or teens, it's important to choose a ship that offers onboard activities that will appeal to your whole family. Look carefully at the onboard activities each specific ship offers before booking your cruise.

As you'd expect, Disney Cruise Lines definitely appeals to family travelers, and offers many activities specifically for kids. In fact, if you'll be traveling with young kids, Disney Cruise Lines is clearly the best option in terms of the kid-oriented programs, activities, and available baby-sitting services. Royal Caribbean caters to everyone, with its special kid and teen-oriented programs and activities, plus adults-only activities, such as an upscale day spa, multiple nightclubs, bars, and a casino aboard each ship.

Once you know when you'd like to set sail and how long you want to spend at sea (the number of days and nights), consider the destinations the ship will visit during the cruise and how you'll spend your time on land at each port of call. As you look at the ship's itinerary, consider how many full days are spent at sea versus how much time is spent at various ports of call. Some passengers eagerly anticipate each new port, while others are content to stay aboard the ship.

Many of the Caribbean cruises include at least one full day visiting a private island owned by the cruise line. On this island, you'll typically find multiple beaches, an all-you-can-eat lunch, and plenty of water sports activities. While the ship is docked at the private island or at any of the ports of call, many of the activities, shops, and dining rooms aboard the ship itself will be closed. If the itinerary doesn't include plenty of destinations you're interested in visiting, choose another cruise with a more appealing itinerary.

## ≡FAST FACT

If you're traveling with kids, make sure the ship offers both supervised activities for young people during the day and baby-sitting services at night. This way you can enjoy the late-night, adults-only activities aboard the ship without worrying about your children. Private, in-room baby-sitting services are typically available on a per-hour, per-child basis.

## Cabins Versus Hotel Guestrooms

Traditional, land-based resorts and hotels typically offer spacious guestrooms in a variety of room configurations to accommodate families. Cruise ships offer cabins, staterooms, and suites in a variety of sizes and configurations, but these accommodations tend to be much smaller than typical hotel guestrooms or suites. If you're traveling with children or teens (or your in-laws), booking two adjoining cabins will make a lot more sense than trying to fit three, four, or five people into a standard cabin with one queen-size bed and perhaps a bunk bed or a fold-out sofa.

Due to the small size of most cabins aboard the ships, there's minimal closet space or room to store luggage. Thus, if the cruise line brochure recommends no more than one suitcase per passenger, it's important to stick to those guidelines.

The larger staterooms or suites on a cruise ship are more expensive than basic cabins. For two people or a couple traveling with an infant, a basic cabin is usually adequate. The price you'll ultimately pay for accommodations on a ship are also based upon whether the cabin has an outside (ocean) view and/or a terrace or veranda. Inside cabins, with no ocean view, are typically the cheapest, while cabins, staterooms, or suites with terraces or verandas tend to be more expensive. The spectacular ocean view, additional in-cabin amenities, and additional living space make staterooms or suites overlooking the ocean worth the extra money, if you can afford it.

## Cabin Considerations

Knowing that cabins, staterooms, and suites aboard cruise ships are relatively small, it's important to choose accommodations that are adequate for your family. After all, you don't want to trip over three people and luggage if you need to use the restroom in the middle of the night. Also, being cooped up for days in tight quarters with too many people will add stress to what should be a carefree, relaxing vacation.

On most ships, a traditional cabin is much smaller than a hotel room. A cabin typically offers two twin-size beds (which can be combined to create one queen-size bed), a small bathroom with a shower (no bathtub), a small closet, and some additional furnishings, such as a couch (which can be transformed into a fold-out sofa), a desk, and a television. You'll typically have less than 200 square feet of total living space (including the bathroom) when staying in a basic cabin.

When it comes to choosing accommodations, you'll find that every ship has a multitude of options at various price points. The cruise lines also use fancy names to describe accommodations, such as "deluxe stateroom," "grand suite," "royal suite," or "family suite." Ignore the fancy labels, and focus instead on what the room actually offers, its layout, the in-room amenities offered, and the square footage of available living space.

Aboard a Royal Caribbean cruise ship, for example, you'll typically find suites in six different configurations, balcony suites in two configurations, ocean-view sites in four configurations, and interior suites in five configurations. The room configuration is determined by its size (measured in square feet), the number and size of the beds, and the number of people the cabin accommodates. Also, the size of the bathroom and its amenities are determining factors when it comes to price. Smaller, less expensive cabins typically offer just showers, as opposed to a bathtub and shower (as you'd find in many hotels.)

## ≡FAST FACT

A larger stateroom typically offers more amenities than a traditional cabin, including a separate sitting area, a small refrigerator and mini bar, larger closets, a terrace or veranda, a larger bathroom, fold-out bunk beds, a fold-out sofa bed, and 300 or more square feet of living space. These rooms can accommodate four people. While two adults and two children will be comfortable in a standard cabin, four adults will often feel a bit cramped due to limited living and storage space.

Some cabins have a small sitting area that's separate from the sleeping area, plus in-room amenities like a television (with pay-per-view movies), high-speed Internet access (for an additional fee), a telephone, and a small refrigerator or mini bar. Closet space and room to store luggage is typically limited.

For example, a family interior stateroom aboard a Royal Caribbean ship measures between 265 and 320 square feet and offers two twin beds (which can be merged to create a single queen-size bed), twin-size bunk beds, and a sofa bed.

## ▐▊ TRAVEL TIP

A multiroom suite offers a living room that's separate from the sleeping areas. Many ships offer one-, two-, or even three-bedroom suites. These suites are designed for larger or extended families. They typically offer more than one bathroom, at least one terrace or veranda, and ample space for four, six, or even eight people.

When choosing accommodations, consider the size of the cabin and personal privacy issues. While it may cost a bit more, reserving two smaller adjoining cabins will offer added personal space and privacy for everyone. You'll also have two bathrooms to share among family members. Many teens would prefer the added privacy of their own cabin, to avoid having to change clothes, for example, in front of their parents. It is important to consider the cabin accommodations, especially when traveling with kids. But don't get too bogged down in these details; most people who choose to go on a Caribbean cruise spend little time in their cabins, except to sleep.

## Activities Aboard the Ship

You can find literally hundreds of things to do aboard a cruise ship at any time of day or night. Some are organized group activities, and others you can experience whenever you want, at your own pace. Every evening you will receive a printed itinerary with activities happening on the ship the following day. Read this schedule carefully to determine what activities you're interested in participating in, and then plan your day accordingly.

One decision you'll need to make early on is the time you'll eat dinner. Most ships have an early and late seating (typically around 6:00 and 8:00 P.M.). Most families traveling with young children opt for the early seating. The time you eat dinner each evening will also determine when you get to enjoy the live theatrical entertainment that's presented on the ship nightly. There is typically an early and later edition of each night's show. (The performances themselves are identical.) Throughout the day and night, just some of the many activities you'll find on most popular cruise ships include the following:

- Auctions (adults only)
- Bars, sports bars, lounges, and nightclubs (adults only)
- Basketball
- Bingo (with cash prizes)
- Supervised activities and programs for kids and teens
- Casino (adults only)
- Classes and discussions
- Dance instruction
- Day spa and salon services
- Elaborate all-you-can-eat meals
- Gym/workout facilities
- Jogging/running track
- Karaoke and talent competitions
- Miniature golf (or golf simulators)
- Movies (plus in-room television)
- Shopping
- Sunbathing, swimming, and hot tubs
- Wine tastings (adults only)

##  RAINY DAY FUN

On Royal Caribbean's ships, two popular activities include a rock-climbing wall and an indoor ice-skating rink.

## Choosing the Cruise That's Right for You

Once you know your travel budget, how much time you can spend on vacation, and what activities you'd like to participate in, finding the best cruise simply requires a bit of research. Ideally, you want to find a cruise that caters to your interests, based on the activities offered, and that offers a competitive price that fits within your vacation budget.

As you're pricing cruise vacations, focus on what's included in the package. Most cruises include meals aboard the ship, for example, but they might charge extra for drinks and to participate in some onboard activities.

Land-based excursions and activities at the various ports of call usually cost extra. Some cruise packages include airfare from your home city to the ship's departure port, such as Miami. In some cases, however, you'll need to book your airfare and ground transportation separately, for an additional fee.

## Selecting the Right Ship and Itinerary

As you begin researching cruise lines and potential travel itineraries, you'll discover that each cruise line has its own approach to offering the perfect high-seas vacation. Beyond that, each individual ship in a cruise line's fleet offers a unique cruise experience unto itself.

Some ships and itineraries are specifically family oriented, meaning you'll find an abundance of separate activities and programs specifically for kids, teens, and adults, plus additional activities and programs that families can enjoy together. Other ships welcome young people, but they don't necessarily offer specialized programs or activities for them. Especially if you're traveling with younger kids, you'll appreciate the extra effort some cruise lines, like Disney Cruise Lines, make in order to cater to young travelers. Some ships are definitely more adult-oriented, catering more to honeymooners, senior citizens, or upscale travelers looking for a quieter, more elegant cruise experience. **TABLE 4-1** lists several popular cruise-ship lines that would be suitable for families. (Detailed information about several of these cruise lines can be found in the individual listings on page 67).

**TABLE 4-1**
**POPULAR CRUISE-SHIP LINES**

| Cruise Line | Phone Number | Web Site |
|---|---|---|
| Carnival Cruise Lines | (888) 227-6482 | www.carnival.com |
| Celebrity Cruise Lines | (800) 647-2251 | www.celebritycruises.com |
| Disney Cruise Lines | (800) 951-3532 | www.disneycruise.com |
| Holland America Line | (800) 426-6593 | www.hollandamerica.com |
| Norwegian Cruise Lines | (800) 327-7030 | www.ncl.com |
| Princess Cruises | (800) 774-6237 | www.princesscruises.com |
| Royal Caribbean International | (800) 398-9819 | www.royalcaribbean.com |

By contacting the cruise lines directly or working with a travel agent, you'll be able to identify cruise lines, specific ships, and even specific cruise dates that most appeal to your family. Many cruise ships offer periodic themed cruises on which fans of popular television shows, like *Star Trek,* might be able to cruise with their favorite stars. Other themed cruises are structured around famous lecturers, celebrity performers, charity benefits, special interests, or specific lifestyles. While these themed cruises are very appealing to their target audiences, families might not find them quite so interesting.

# Finding the Best Cruise Deals

The first rule when booking a cruise is to determine the list price of the cruise (the one advertised in the cruise line's brochure) and throw it out the window. Throughout the year, even during the peak holiday season, you can always find amazing cruise deals and discounted packages if you shop around.

Without a doubt, the online travel sites (like Travelocity.com, Hotwire.com, Orbitz.com, and Priceline.com), offer some of the best discount cruise packages you'll find anywhere. Still, you can sometimes do better working with a travel agent or responding to an ad in your local newspaper. This section focuses on how to find the best deals on the most popular, family-oriented cruise ships that sail the Caribbean.

As you review cruise packages and offers, determine exactly what the price includes. Make sure you aren't comparing apples to oranges. Some packages are "cruise only," which means airfare between your home city and the ship's departure city is not included. Thus, you're on your own to book your airfares separately, and you must make sure you'll arrive with ample time before the ship's departure. "Land and Sea" packages include round-trip airfare, the cruise itself, and often ground-based transportation to and from the airport to the ship's departure port.

In some cases, a cruise package will include one or more days on land before or after the cruise. Disney Cruise Lines, for example, has packages that enable you to enjoy several days at the Walt Disney World Resort in Orlando (with hotel accommodations and theme-park tickets included) before embarking on your cruise. Some cruises, such as those that depart from San Juan or Miami, for example, allow you to spend a day or two in the departing city (with hotel accommodations included) before and after your cruise.

All cruise ships include unlimited food, but not all ships include unlimited drinks. In some cases, drinks (including bottled water and soda) are only included in the dining rooms during meal periods. If you want a drink while sunning on the ship's deck, for example, that'll cost extra. Those charges are billed directly to your cabin, so carrying cash while aboard the ship isn't necessary. You will, however, want to carry cash (and perhaps a credit card) when you go on land at the various ports of call during your cruise.

## ≡FAST FACT

For a flat fee, many of the cruise ships offer special deals for unlimited soda and nonalcoholic drink refills for the duration of the cruise. Especially if you're traveling with kids, this option can save you money if you take advantage of this offer at the start of the cruise.

## Contacting the Cruise Lines Directly

As your quest to find the perfect cruise begins, contact each of the popular cruise lines and request brochures or a free vacation-planning video. The information from the cruise lines will provide a detailed overview of each ship, what's offered, the types of cabins available, profiles of the ports of call, plus information about some of the optional land excursions. This information is also available on each cruise line's Web site and from many travel agents. The more you learn about what each ship offers, the better your chances are of finding the best match for you and your family. Once you board the ship and begin your cruise, you don't want any unwelcome surprises.

 **TRAVEL TIP**

When you book your cruise, keep in mind that many popular activities aboard cruise ships, such as treatments at the day spa, book up within several hours of the cruise's departure. If you know what you want to do in advance, make the appropriate reservations early on to ensure you'll have the opportunity to experience everything you'd like to while cruising.

Booking your cruise directly with the cruise line by calling the toll-free reservations number or visiting the company's Web site is convenient, but you'll almost never get the lowest possible price for your cruise package. Optional activities and land excursions coordinated through the cruise line need to be booked directly with the cruise line, however, after your actual cruise reservation is made. Use the cruise line's toll-free number to get your questions answered about a specific ship or itinerary once you receive the brochures or visit the cruise line's Web site.

### Working with a Travel Agent

Many travel agents are specially trained to help clients plan cruise vacations. These are travel professionals who are familiar with the major cruise lines and each of the individual ships. A travel agent can suggest a type of cabin for your accommodations and assist you in planning your complete itinerary, including helping you book round-trip airfares and ground transportation. While you won't always get the lowest available prices from a travel agent, what you will often receive is personalized vacation-planning advice.

### Booking Your Travel Online

The way to save the most money on a cruise, whether you book months in advance or just days before your scheduled departure, is to go online and visit the various travel-related Web sites. Each of these sites includes a special "Cruises" link that enables you to narrow your cruise options, based on duration, cruise line, a specific ship, or by destinations.

The majority of the cruise packages available from the popular travel-related Web sites are for cruise-only packages, so plan on booking airfares and possibly hotel accommodations and ground transportation separately.

Some of the travel-related Web sites offer details about specific cruise lines and ships, plus their itineraries, and some offer links to travelogues posted by previous customers, both satisfied and unsatisfied. Your best bet is to first contact the cruise lines directly or consult with a travel agent to pinpoint the exact cruise you're looking for, and then go online to seek out the lowest possible price for that sailing. By shopping online, you can often shave between 40 and 70 percent off the published rates for a cruise. If you have flexibility, you can often save a fortune on a cruise package simply by adjusting your sail dates.

## Cruise Insurance

Once you book a cruise, the reservation usually can't be cancelled or changed for any reason. However, if you miss your cruise, or your cruise experience gets cut short due to illness, an unexpected emergency, bad weather, or for a handful of other reasons, having travel insurance can save you from a financial loss. Over sixty insurance companies offer cruise insurance. Some of the cruise lines and travel agents offer this as an optional benefit for an additional fee at the time you book your cruise. In some cases, you'll need to obtain this insurance on your own.

The cost of travel insurance will depend on several factors, including these:

- Age of the traveler(s)
- Number of people traveling who need insurance coverage
- Cost of the cruise
- Duration of the cruise
- Level of coverage you select

According to InsureMyCruise.com, travel insurance specifically for cruises includes "trip cancellation, baggage, medical, dental, emergency evacuation, twenty-four-hour traveler assistance, baggage delay, travel delay, and accidental death coverage. Some policies also have options for collision/damage coverage for rented cars, flight insurance (a form of accidental death coverage while flying only) and added emergency evacuation insurance. Some package policies include coverage for children at no extra charge."

The following independent brokers can help you find the best cruise insurance:

- **Insure My Cruise**: (800) 487-4722, *www.insuremycruise. com*
- **Trip Insurance Store**: (888) 407-3854, *www.tripinsurancestore. com*
- **Travel Guard:** (800) 826-4919, *www.travelguard.com*

# Choosing Your Shore Excursions

The shore excursions offered at each port of call are designed to offer you additional, exciting, unique, and fun vacation experiences. Your cruise line will provide you with a full-color catalog describing all of the different activities, tourist attractions, and tours available at each stop on your cruise. Of course, your participation in any of these activities is entirely optional. Depending on the destination and what your interests are, you might choose to skip participating in an optional shore excursion and simply enjoy a day of duty-free shopping or visiting the beautiful local beaches.

Chapter 5 provides detailed descriptions of many popular, family-friendly shore excursion options available on the various Caribbean islands, including the following, to name only a few:

- Bus tours of the island
- Glass-bottom boat rides
- Golf
- Hiking or biking tours
- Horseback riding
- Jeep or four-wheel-drive safari tours
- Parasailing
- Scuba diving
- Snorkeling cruises
- Submarine rides
- Swimming with dolphins
- Trips to specific tourist attractions and historical sights

As you read the descriptions of the shore excursions available on each island, keep three things in mind: cost, scheduling, and appeal. Participating in one or more optional shore excursions at each port of call will increase the cost of your trip dramatically, especially if you're a family of four or more.

When booking your land-based activities, also pay careful attention to scheduling. Always allow for delays. If you only have a few hours to visit and explore a particular Caribbean island, don't plan too many activities or travel too far from the port, or you could wind up missing the boat—literally. Allow ample travel time between activities, and pace yourself. The reservations you make through the cruise line for land excursions are often nonchangeable and nonrefundable.

Finally, choose shore excursions that will appeal to the whole family. In Jamaica, for example, climbing Dunn's River Falls is a popular activity among cruise-ship passengers, but if you're traveling with young kids, this activity won't be suitable.

 **TRAVEL TIP**

When you make a reservation for a shore excursion, you'll be told what to bring with you. Following these recommendations is important. For many outdoor activities, wearing the appropriate shoes and protecting yourself from the sun is critical. Don't plan on buying what you need when you get there. And no matter what shore excursions you sign up for, bring a camera!

Booking your shore excursions through the cruise line is the most convenient and easiest way to coordinate and schedule the activities you'd like to do (although it's not always the cheapest). If you choose this method, make your reservations early. Most cruise lines allow you to book shore excursions several weeks before your actual cruise. You can also book these excursions once you're aboard the ship.

You will find that space for some activities is limited and will fill up quickly. If you get shut out of an activity at one port of call, find out if a similar shore excursion is available at one of the ship's other stops.

One of the best ways to choose shore excursions is to seek out recommendations from other travelers. You'll often find many people aboard your cruise ship who are repeat passengers. Many of the crew members aboard your ship have also experienced most or all of the optional shore excursions offered at each Caribbean port of call and will be happy to share their recommendations. You can also get online before you leave for your cruise and do some preliminary research. In addition to customer reviews, find out what is included in each excursion, how physically challenging it is, and whether tips are expected.

During the day, when you're exploring various ports of call, you'll be eating breakfast and/or lunch on land. Any meals you don't eat aboard the ship are not included in your cruise price, so this will be an additional expense. On virtually all of the Caribbean islands, you'll find a wide range of dining options at many different price points. On many islands, you'll also typically find all of the popular fast food chains, including McDonald's, Subway, and KFC, which your kids will appreciate.

## Packing for a Cruise

The atmosphere aboard most cruise ships is that of an informal, casual resort, so dress accordingly. That said, however, at least one night of the cruise will often be formal, with black tie optional in the dining room. A regular dress suit, however, is perfectly acceptable.

As you're getting ready for your cruise, the trick is to avoid overpacking! Several casual outfits, along with bathing suits, workout gear, one formal outfit, at least one pair of comfortable walking shoes, one pair of sneakers/hiking shoes, and one pair of dress shoes will be adequate. If you have beach shoes, those will come in handy as well. A light jacket or waterproof windbreaker and a sweatshirt will also be useful.

A great Web site with excellent packing tips and lists can be found at *www.cruisediva.com*. The packing lists are divided into three separate categories, for women, men, and babies, so you're sure to find your own needs represented. Two items that should be on everyone's list are a hat and sunscreen.

## Gathering Your Travel Documents

Upon booking your cruise, you'll be provided with a portfolio of travel documentation, which includes multiple forms that'll need to be filled out before you board the ship. Before leaving home, make sure you have all of the required documentation for each passenger, which will typically include the following:

- Cruise tickets and related paperwork/forms
- Airline tickets
- Ground-transfer vouchers
- Passports and government-issued IDs (such as a driver's license)
- Baggage tags (provided by the cruise line)

The baggage tags provided by the cruise line should be attached to each piece of luggage that you'll be bringing aboard the ship (except for your carry-on bags). These tags are in addition to the luggage tags already on your suitcases. They're preprinted with your cabin and ship information.

After you board the ship, your luggage will be delivered to your cabin. This can take several hours, so anything you'll need during the first few hours of your voyage should be packed in a carry-on and brought on the ship personally. In your carry-on, consider packing a change of clothes, medications, sunglasses, and a bathing suit for each person. This will allow you to begin enjoying your cruise from the moment the ship departs.

# Your Caribbean Cruise Options

Well, are you ready to pack your bags for a fun-filled high-seas adventure? Start your vacation planning by contacting these popular cruise lines, all of which offer multiple Caribbean and Bahamas cruises.

## Carnival Cruise Lines

☎(888) CARNIVAL

✎*www.carnival.com*

Carnival Cruise Lines offers a fleet of family-friendly ships that sail throughout the Caribbean on four-, five,- seven-, eight-, and ten-day cruises. In addition to offering a wide range of activities for adults—like a casino, day spa, and various bars, lounges, and night-clubs—Carnival Cruise Lines offers four separate, supervised "Camp Carnival" programs for these age groups: toddlers (ages 2–5), juniors (ages 6–8), intermediates (ages 9–11) and teens (ages 12–15).

These programs, which are included with the cruise, are run by specially trained counselors and offer age-specific activities. Kids' menus are also available at most of the ship's restaurants and dining facilities. Optional in-room baby-sitting service is available at night for an additional fee.

**CARNIVAL CRUISE LINES**

| Ages up to 5 | Ages 6–15 | Ages 16–20 | Adult | Senior Citizens |
|---|---|---|---|---|
| ★ | ★★ | ★★ | ★★★ | ★★★ |

## Celebrity Cruise Lines

☏800-647-2251

✍www.celebrity.com

Celebrity Cruise Lines also offers a casual, resort-style environment that is family friendly. These fully equipped ships feature specialized and supervised children's programs for kids and teens in various age groups. Private, in-room baby-sitting services are also available for an additional fee. Aboard the ships, a wide range of family-oriented activities, suitable for both parents and kids, are readily available.

**CELEBRITY CRUISE LINES**

| Ages up to 5 | Ages 6–15 | Ages 16–20 | Adult | Senior Citizens |
|---|---|---|---|---|
| ★ | ★★ | ★★★ | ★★★ | ★★ |

## Crystal Cruises

☎ 866-446-6625

✎ *www.crystalcruises.com*

The focus of Crystal Cruises is definitely on catering to upscale adults, with its casino, world-class day spa, the ships' Creative Learning Institute, and onboard shopping, for example.

Each ship in its fleet, however, offers special Junior Activities Programs for kids ages 3–7, ages 8–12, and ages 13–17. Activities offered vary based on the time of year and number of kids participating. Parents with infants are not encouraged to sail with Crystal Cruises. Private, in-room baby-sitting services are available.

**CRYSTAL CRUISE LINES**

| Ages up to 5 | Ages 6–15 | Ages 16–20 | Adult | Senior Citizens |
|:---:|:---:|:---:|:---:|:---:|
| ★ | ★ | ★★ | ★★★ | ★★★ |

## Disney Cruise Lines

☎ 800-951-3532

✎ *www.disneycruise.com*

Without a doubt, the most family-oriented cruise line sailing the Caribbean waters is Disney Cruise Lines, which offers its famous hospitality and family-themed fun on each of its ships.

Specialized kids' programs are only the beginning of what Disney Cruise Lines offers to families. With no casino on board, virtually everything there is to do on the ship (with the exception of the day spa, bars, lounges, and nightclubs) is suitable for young people.

Even meals become magical, when kids get to interact with their favorite Disney characters. While kids of all ages are welcome aboard the ship and are truly catered to, adults traveling without kids (or who need time away from their own kids) can enjoy peace and quiet in several areas of the ship that are designated for adults only. Adults have their own sun deck, pool, nightclubs, day spa, and fitness facility, for example.

While older teens may think they're too cool to enjoy a Disney cruise, once they get on board, they'll often come around quickly. Parents, grandparents, and kids, however, will love it, especially if they've been to a Disney theme park in the past.

Everything from the menus served in the dining areas to the layout of the cabins, staterooms, and suites is designed with families in mind and offers a Disney theme. Thus, you'll find spacious cabins with separate bunk beds for kids and kid-oriented programming readily available on television. Throughout the day and night, the movie theater aboard the ship offers family-friendly movies. In addition, all the live shows aboard the ships are Broadway-style, musical shows that'll appeal to people of all ages.

**DISNEY CRUISE LINES**

| Ages up to 5 | Ages 6–15 | Ages 16–20 | Adult | Senior Citizens |
|:---:|:---:|:---:|:---:|:---:|
| ★★★ | ★★★ | ★★★ | ★★★ | ★★★ |

## Norwegian Cruise Lines

☎800-327-7030

✍www.ncl.com

Norwegian Cruise Lines offers several Caribbean cruising options, including five-, seven-, and ten-day trips vacations to the western Caribbean, southern Caribbean, and the Bahamas. These cruises cater more to adults, but special Kid Crew and Teen Passport programs are offered for younger travelers. Hours of operation for these programs are 9:00 A.M. to noon, 2:00 P.M. to 5:00 P.M. and 7:00 P.M. to 10:00 P.M. daily during sea days, and between 7:00 P.M. and 10:00 P.M. on days when the ship is docked at a port of call. Group sitting and private in-room baby-sitting services are available for an extra fee.

**NORWEGIAN CRUISE LINES**

| Ages up to 5 | Ages 6–15 | Ages 16–20 | Adult | Senior Citizens |
|:---:|:---:|:---:|:---:|:---:|
| ★ | ★★ | ★★ | ★★★ | ★★★ |

## Princess Cruises

✆800-PRINCESS

✐www.princess.com

Like Carnival Cruise Lines and Royal Caribbean, Princess Cruise Lines caters to families with a wide range of family-friendly activities available aboard each ship in its fleet. The cruise line also offers specialized and supervised programs for young passengers, ages three to seventeen. The Princess Fun Zone and the Teen Center both offer organized, age-specific activities. In the dining rooms, kid-friendly menu selections are readily available, plus you'll always find suitable programming on the television in your cabin.

**PRINCESS CRUISE LINES**

| Ages up to 5 | Ages 6–15 | Ages 16–20 | Adult | Senior Citizens |
|:---:|:---:|:---:|:---:|:---:|
| ★ | ★★ | ★★★ | ★★★ | ★★ |

## Radisson Seven Seas Cruise Lines

✆(877) 505-5370

✐www.rssc.com

Whether you're looking for a luxurious four-, seven-, eight-, or even an eleven-day Caribbean cruise that's ideal for older teens, adults, and seniors, Radisson Seven Seas has a lot to offer. While this cruise line offers some programs and activities catering to younger travelers (over the age of six), the ships in this fleet offer an entertainment experience that's more upscale, sophisticated, and luxurious than some of the other cruise lines sailing the Caribbean.

**RADISSON SEVEN SEAS CRUISE LINES**

| Ages up to 5 | Ages 6–15 | Ages 16–20 | Adult | Senior Citizens |
|:---:|:---:|:---:|:---:|:---:|
| N.S. | ★ | ★★ | ★★★ | ★★★ |

### Royal Caribbean Cruise Lines

☎800-398-9819

✍*www.royalcaribbean.com*

Imagine the perfect, family-friendly, land-based resort and think about everything it would offer. Now, take all of those activities, amenities, and services, and pack 'em all into a cruise ship. Royal Caribbean offers top-notch entertainment, comfortable cabins, many dining options (with kid-friendly menus), plenty of family-oriented activities, plus separate, specialized, and supervised programs and activities for younger travelers (starting at age three).

Royal Caribbean ships all offer some activities suitable only for adults, like the casino, night clubs, bars, lounges, and the day spa, but kids and teens will find plenty to do on the ship to keep thoroughly entertained.

What's great about Royal Caribbean is that the cruise rates are reasonable and a wide range of onboard activities are included. As with any cruise ship, however, there are upgrades and optional activities, all of which have additional fees associated with them.

**ROYAL CARIBBEAN CRUISE LINES**

| Ages up to 5 | Ages 6–15 | Ages 16–20 | Adult | Senior Citizens |
|---|---|---|---|---|
| ★★★ | ★★★ | ★★★ | ★★★ | ★★★ |

# What to Know Before You Go

A cruise vacation is unlike any other type of vacation. Even if you've already visited a few Caribbean destinations, there's nothing like sailing between Caribbean islands and experiencing life for a few days at sea. If you're traveling with kids or teens, however, the trick to ensuring you'll have the best cruise vacation possible is to select the best cruise ship and itinerary. It's also important to choose the right cabin accommodations for the whole family.

If you've never been anywhere in the Caribbean, taking a cruise will allow you to explore several different Caribbean islands during one exciting trip. Each island offers a unique culture and its own assortment of things to see and do. The rest of this chapter offers information that'll be helpful once you set sail and start enjoying your Caribbean cruise adventure.

## Tips on Tipping Aboard a Ship

In addition to the cost of the cruise itself and any optional tours or activities, at the end of your voyage it's customary to tip several of the ship's crew with whom you've had a lot of contact. It's important to calculate tips into your travel budget, as they add up quickly.

Throughout your voyage, the same cabin attendant will attend to your needs as they relate to anything having to do with your cabin or stateroom. You'll also have the same waitstaff for every meal in the ship's main dining room. Tips and gratuities are traditionally distributed on the final evening of your voyage. You will be provided with preprinted envelopes for these tips and gratuities, which are optional.

Keep in mind that on some ships, the crew relies on the tips for their income, and tips are often pooled with other crew members you don't see as a passenger. You'll typically find that the crew aboard the ship will provide excellent and highly personalized service.

The following are general tipping guidelines:

- **Cabin steward**: $3 per person/per day of the cruise
- **Waiter**: $3 per person/per day of your cruise
- **Assistant waiter**: $2 per person/per day of your cruise
- **Busser**: $3 per person/per day of your cruise
- **Maitre d' and/or headwaiter**: $1 per person/per day of your cruise

For a family of four traveling on a five-day cruise, tips will add an additional $235 or more to the overall cost of your vacation if you follow recommended tipping guidelines.

##  JUST FOR PARENTS

On most ships, any drinks you order from a bar (that get charged to your cabin/stateroom) will automatically include a gratuity for the bartender and server. Thus, additional tipping at the bars, clubs, and lounges aboard the ship isn't necessary.

### Phone Calls and Internet Use

All ships are equipped with satellite phones that enable you to make and receive calls, typically from your cabin or stateroom. The per-minute fees associated with making calls from ship to land, however, are hefty. Expect to pay upwards of $3 to $5 per minute, plus an initial connection fee for each call.

High-speed internet access is also available on most cruise ships, also at a premium rate. On some ships you can play a flat fee for unlimited Internet access per day or for the duration of your cruise. While aboard the ship, this is typically the least expensive way of communicating with friends, family, and coworkers back home.

Cell phones usually don't work at sea, unless when you're very close to land or docked at certain ports of call. In these situations, if your cell-phone service provider offers international roaming, your phone will work, but roaming fees will apply when you visit most Caribbean islands.

The cheapest way to place a call to the United States during a cruise is to use a prepaid calling card from a public pay phone while visiting any of the ports of call. Near most ports, you'll often find an Internet café that also offers inexpensive calling to the United States. Prepaid calling cards are available at shops near virtually all ports (except on the private islands operated by the cruise lines.)

### Souvenir Photos

Your cruise experience will create many lasting memories. To help you share these memories with others, while aboard the cruise ship, you'll have your photo taken on multiple occasions by professional photographers. In some cases, these will be candid photos, however—as you enter the dining room on the formal evening, for example, the photographers will have mini portrait studios set up.

Once your photo is taken by one of the ship's photographers, it will typically be put on display in a photo gallery aboard the ship later that day or the following day. Prints can then be purchased in a variety of sizes. Passengers are not obligated to purchase any photos taken. You can have your photo taken as often as you wish, then purchase only the photos you like in whatever quantity you choose. If you're interested in having a formal family portrait, you'll have several opportunities during your cruise. Of course, you're also welcome to shoot your own photos using your own equipment and can get them developed aboard the ship or once you get home.

## Celebrate a Special Occasion at Sea

One thing that the crew aboard virtually every cruise ship specializes in is helping people celebrate special occasions. If you have an event you want to celebrate, be sure to contact the ship's activities director and/or your headwaiter to assist you in coordinating the details. In addition, at any time during your cruise, you can arrange to have a wide range of items delivered to your cabin, such as flowers, balloons, or champagne.

# Family-Friendly Activities in the Caribbean

THIS CHAPTER DESCRIBES MANY of the activities offered on each Caribbean island, typically for an extra fee. Many of these activities will allows you to experience new things, take full advantage of your tropical outdoor surroundings, and, in many cases, get some exercise while having fun.

## Unlimited Pleasures Await You in the Caribbean

No matter where you travel in the Caribbean, you can pretty much count on finding beautiful weather, sandy beaches, a selection of attractions to visit, countless activities to participate in, great shopping opportunities, and many unique places to explore. One of the main reasons that families go to the Caribbean to vacation is the abundance of things to see and do. Some of these attractions are land-based, while others are related to the beautiful beaches or the ocean.

Depending on where you choose to stay, some activities may be offered directly by your hotel or resort. In many cases, however, you'll need to hire a local tour operator in order to experience some or all of these activities. Not all of the Caribbean islands or resorts offer all the activities described in this chapter, so it's important to pick the ones that are of the most interest to you and your family. Before you book your travel arrangements, you should also determine their availability and cost.

As you read about each activity, you will also find useful information about items to bring along. The ratings will help you determine the age groups for which specific activities are best suited. In some cases, you may want to leave your kids with a baby-sitter. Better yet, get them involved with your resort's supervised kids' program if there's one available. Either option is preferable to dragging the young ones along to experience something they won't enjoy.

 **TRAVEL TIP**

No matter what outdoor Caribbean activity you choose, it's extremely important to protect yourself and your family from the strong sun. It's impossible to overstate the importance of using a strong sunscreen and wearing a hat, sunglasses, and other protective clothing. The Caribbean sun can be intense and cause serious sunburn relatively quickly if you're not careful.

## What to Bring Along

In many cases, the activities you participate in while in the Caribbean won't be at your hotel or resort. Thus, it's important to bring along the gear and clothing you'll need to ensure your comfort throughout the day or evening. The following is a basic checklist of items you should have with you most of the time, especially if you're traveling with kids. It's a good strategy to pack a backpack with these items whenever you venture away from your hotel or resort for an extended period.

- Bathing suits
- Beach/water shoes
- Bottled water
- Bug repellent

- Camera, camcorder, batteries, film, and related supplies
- Cell phone (if applicable)
- Change of clothes
- Hats
- Hotel room key/card
- Light jacket
- Map and/or guidebook
- Plastic bag to carry wet clothing and bathing suits
- Snacks
- Sneakers or hiking shoes
- Sunscreen and sunglasses
- Towels
- Wallet (ID, along with cash, traveler's checks, and/or credit cards)

# Choosing Your Activities

The activities described in this section reflect the most popular options offered throughout the Caribbean. To determine whether specific activities are offered at or near your hotel or resort, contact the concierge or tour desk where you'll be staying.

If you're taking a Caribbean cruise and you're planning your land-based excursions at each port of call, your cruise line will provide you with a catalog of optional activities (shore excursions) available at each stopover. It's a good strategy to book these activities as far in advance as possible. Visit your ship's tour desk or the cruise line's Web site for more information.

Remember that participating in optional activities can dramatically increase the cost of your vacation. If you're not staying at an all-inclusive resort, the average activity will cost between $25 and $100 (or more) per person, plus the cost of transportation. Thus, it's important to decide what activities interest you the most and make sure they fit within your travel budget and itinerary.

##  TRAVEL TIP

> For each activity you choose, make sure the tour provider gives you experienced, licensed, or certified guides and instructors, as well as high-quality equipment. This is particularly important for potentially dangerous activities like scuba diving.

Your Caribbean vacation will offer you plenty of time to relax and enjoy the sunshine. At the same time, your vacation is a golden opportunity to experience many new things. Open your mind. Challenge yourself, and consider this to be a unique opportunity to expose yourself and those you're traveling with to new experiences. Try things you've never tried before! You may find yourself embarking on activities that have some element of danger to them. However, if you use plenty of common sense and participate in organized tours (from reputable companies with knowledgeable and highly skilled instructors or guides), chances are that you'll be in good hands. You can use your vacation experience to improve the skills you already have. For example, if you enjoy playing golf or tennis, in addition to just participating in these sports, consider taking lessons from pros who can help you improve your game.

If you want to participate in an activity that involves an element of danger, such as scuba diving, but the dive master you'll be working with doesn't offer you proper instruction, the equipment doesn't seem to be in good shape, or the instructor doesn't instill the necessary confidence you need, seek out another tour company to work with. If you'll be relying on someone else to help keep you and your family safe, it's important that you feel 100-percent comfortable with that instructor or guide, no matter what activities you're engaging in. Again, talk to other guests or passengers. You're almost certain to find someone else who has participated in that activity already and can give you some advice.

# Popular Beach-Related Sports and Activities

If you'll be spending some quality time at the beach, this section offers ideas about activities you and your kids can engage in while enjoying the Caribbean's sun and pristine sandy beaches.

### Building Sand Castles and Collecting Shells

Whether it's part of a resort-wide competition or just a fun way to pass the time, as you walk along almost any beach where kids and teens are at play, you're bound to find sand castles being built. This is an activity your kids will probably want to participate in as well. Children, especially if they are somewhat shy, can often make friends while building an elaborate sand structure.

Not all of the beaches will have an abundance of seashells, but if you find a beach with lots of shells, kids will enjoy collecting them. Be aware, however, that many nations now regulate the collection or export of shells. You might consider purchasing a guidebook to shells before leaving home, and then explain to your children why they are welcome to collect shells but must put them back before leaving for home.

For your kids (or the kid in you), bring along your own shovels, buckets, and any other beach toys. These toys are often sold at hotel or resort shops, but you'll pay a hefty premium.

**BUILDING SAND CASTLES AT THE BEACH**

| Ages up to 5 | Ages 6–15 | Ages 16–20 | Adult | Senior Citizens |
|:---:|:---:|:---:|:---:|:---:|
| ★★★ | ★★★ | ★ | ★ | ★ |

### Fishing

If hooking a forty-pound mackerel is your idea of a great time, you can find plenty of opportunities to fish in the Caribbean. Fishing is a popular activity offered by many resorts and hotels on or near the beach, and some cruise ships also offer fishing excursion options. Fishing rods and supplies can often be rented. If you do go fishing, be sure to following the local guidelines. Half-day or full-day fishing trips are generally available.

**FISHING**

| Ages up to 5 | Ages 6–15 | Ages 16–20 | Adult | Senior Citizens |
|:---:|:---:|:---:|:---:|:---:|
| N.S. | ★ | ★★ | ★★ | ★★★ |

## Sunbathing

Most people who visit the Caribbean hope to return home with an awesome tan to show off to their coworkers, friends, and relatives. While it's easy to get a nice tan, it's even easier to get a nasty sunburn anywhere in the Caribbean. At least for the first few days of your vacation, limit your exposure to the sun in order to slowly build a base tan. Carefully follow the directions printed on your favorite brand of sunscreen or sunblock, and don't forget to reapply it after swimming or taking a shower.

Things to remember when trying to prevent sunburn are that the sun is strongest between 10:00 A.M. and 2:00 P.M., and that even on overcast days, it's possible to get burnt relatively quickly. The ultraviolet rays of the sun will bounce off the sand and water and can intensify the burn you receive and speed up the process if you're not properly protected.

Sunscreens are rated for their effectiveness according to their sun protection factor (SPF). This is a measure of how much longer someone wearing sunscreen can stay exposed to the sun before they start to burn (as opposed to someone not wearing sunscreen). You'll find many companies offer sunscreen with SPF numbers ranging from 2 to 50 (with 50 being the strongest.) The American Academy of Dermatology and the Sun Safety Alliance (SSA) recommend an SPF of 15 or higher for adults. To protect your kids, apply sunscreen with an SPF of 30 or higher, depending on how fair their skin is and how much time they'll be spending in the sun. Adults who are not fair-skinned can often get away with a sunscreen with a lower SPF rating.

You'll find that sunscreens and sunblocks come in creams, sprays, and in a variety of strengths and formulas. It's a good idea to purchase the right type of sunscreen or sunblock for all the skin types in your family before you leave home. This way, you'll ensure you have the best formulation when you're actually exposed to the sun in the Caribbean. For tips on choosing the right sunscreen or sunblock, consult with a pharmacist or visit the Coppertone Web site (⊘*www.coppertone.com*). When purchasing your sunscreen or sunblock, it's also a good idea to purchase some type of cream or spray designed to relieve sunburn pain, plus some type of aloe cream or gel which can help prevent peeling. The best protection, of course, is a wide-brimmed hat or cap, and it is a good idea to pack two of these for each member of your family.

 **TRAVEL TIP**

Always keep infants out of the direct sun, and apply special sunscreen designed for infants to all exposed areas of their skin. Infants should be kept in the shade and wear a hat whenever they're brought outdoors.

If you're planning to sunbathe at the beach or by a pool, apply the appropriate type of sunscreen or sunblock for your skin. If you'll be sunbathing alone, always bring an alarm of some kind or have someone check in on you periodically to ensure that you don't accidentally fall asleep and get badly burned. While not life-threatening, a serious burn can all but ruin an otherwise great vacation.

Other items that'll help you enjoy your sunbathing time include:

- Beach towel
- Bottled water
- Cash or your hotel room key/resort charge card (to purchase drinks or snacks, if beach service is offered)
- Magazines or a book
- Sunglasses
- Walkman or iPod (MP3 player) with headphones

**SUNBATHING**

| Ages up to 5 | Ages 6–15 | Ages 16–20 | Adult | Senior Citizens |
|:---:|:---:|:---:|:---:|:---:|
| N.S. | N.S. | ★★★ | ★★★ | ★★ |

### Beach Volleyball

On many beaches, you'll find volleyball nets where impromptu volleyball games tend to be played. This is a great way for people of all ages to get exercise, enjoy the Caribbean weather, and meet new people. Many hotels and resorts coordinate volleyball tournaments for different age groups, so check with the beach activities desk at your hotel or resort. A bathing suit or comfortable, loose-fitting clothes are the ideal attire for a game of beach volleyball. The net and ball(s) will typically be provided by your hotel or resort.

**BEACH VOLLEYBALL**

| Ages up to 5 | Ages 6–15 | Ages 16–20 | Adult | Senior Citizens |
|:---:|:---:|:---:|:---:|:---:|
| N.S. | ★★ | ★★ | ★★ | ★ |

# Popular Water Sports and Activities

The following is just a sampling of the many water sports and water-based activities available to vacationers in the Caribbean. Some of these activities require that participants be physically fit. In some cases, previous experience is strongly recommended, but not required.

### Boat Rentals

Sailboats, kayaks, motorboats, paddleboats, and other types of boats that you can manage by yourself can often be rented by the half-hour, hour, or by the day. All-inclusive resorts typically include unlimited use of nonmotorized boats. However, you may have to pay an additional fee to rent any type of motorized craft. Contact your hotel or resort's activities desk to determine what type of boats can be rented.

When participating in any type of boating activity, be sure to wear a lifejacket, even if you consider yourself to be a good swimmer. Kids and teens especially should always wear a lifejacket, proper sun protection, and rubber-soled beach shoes when engaged in any type of boating activity.

## BOAT RENTALS

| Ages up to 5 | Ages 6–15 | Ages 16–20 | Adult | Senior Citizens |
|---|---|---|---|---|
| N.S. | ★★★ | ★★★ | ★★★ | ★★ |

## Boat Tours, Dinner Cruises, and Party Cruises

No matter which Caribbean island you visit, you will find a wide selection of boat tours to enjoy. In addition to choosing the type of cruise, you'll also be able to select the type of boat you travel in. Boat tours typically host anywhere from twenty to 100 or more passengers. Some cruises anchor for awhile offshore and allow passengers to go snorkeling, scuba diving, or swimming off the boat.

If you're traveling with kids or teens, a traditional sightseeing boat tour or a sunset cruise will be appropriate. A dinner cruise tends to provide a romantic setting for couples and may not be suitable for kids or teens. What kids and teens will love, however, are high-speed motorboat rides and tours.

For family members over the age of eighteen (or twenty-one on some islands), party cruises can be a fun way to meet people, socialize, and enjoy the tropical climate. Party cruises typically offer loud music and an open bar (serving unlimited drinks for between one and four hours). These cruises are definitely not suitable for kids and teens.

Depending on the type of cruise or boat tour you choose, bring along a light jacket, a change of clothes, a bathing suit, and a towel. You should also consider bringing snacks and bottled water if food won't be provided aboard the ship.

## BOAT TOURS, DINNER CRUISES, PARTY CRUISES

| Ages up to 5 | Ages 6–15 | Ages 16–20 | Adult | Senior Citizens |
|:---:|:---:|:---:|:---:|:---:|
| N.S. | ★ | ★★ | ★★★ | ★★ |

### Deep-Sea Fishing

The Caribbean offers excellent deep-sea fishing. It's important to choose a tour operator that offers an experienced crew and quality fishing gear. Deep-sea fishing trips tend to last either a half-day or a full-day and typically are not included in an all-inclusive resort package. If this will be your first time fishing, be sure you sign up for an introductory fishing expedition.

Consult with the tour operator to determine what you'll need to bring on a deep-sea fishing excursion. Snacks, drinks, and all necessary fishing gear are typically provided.

### DEEP-SEA FISHING

| Ages up to 5 | Ages 6–15 | Ages 16–20 | Adult | Senior Citizens |
|:---:|:---:|:---:|:---:|:---:|
| N.S. | ★ | ★★ | ★★★ | ★★ |

### Jet Skiing

Depending on where you go, Jet Skis can often be rented by the half-hour or by the hour. This is an activity that typically is not included with vacation packages at all-inclusive resorts. Plan on spending at least $50 per half-hour to rent a Jet Ski. No previous experience is necessary. Many Jet Skis will hold one, two, or three passengers, but they must be driven by an adult (or someone over the age of sixteen under parental supervision).

Almost all Jet Ski rental companies will insist that all passengers on the vehicle wear a lifejacket. This is definitely something you should do regardless of the rules. Also, kids and teens can often ride as passengers on a Jet Ski, but they aren't allowed to rent one on their own without adult supervision and consent. It's best to wear a bathing suit with the lifejacket, although a light wetsuit can also be worn.

**JET SKIING**

| Ages up to 5 | Ages 6–15 | Ages 16–20 | Adult | Senior Citizens |
|:---:|:---:|:---:|:---:|:---:|
| N.S. | ★ | ★★★ | ★★★ | ★★ |

## Parasailing

Parasailing is a fun sport that is a cross between skydiving and water-skiing. As in water-skiing, you are pulled behind a boat, but instead of wearing skis you strap a parachute to your back. As the boat moves forward, the parachute fills with air and pulls you aloft. The experience is typically very smooth and exhilarating. Unless you're afraid of heights, this is a fun activity for anyone over the age of 12.

The safest way to experience parasailing is if you're launched off of a dock in the middle of the water, as opposed to off of the beach. The typical ride lasts anywhere from five to fifteen minutes (or longer) depending on the tour operator. You'll typically pay extra for parasailing, since this activity isn't included in most vacation packages offered by all-inclusive resorts. Wear a bathing suit. Otherwise, all equipment will be provided.

**PARASAILING**

| Ages up to 5 | Ages 6–15 | Ages 16–20 | Adult | Senior Citizens |
|:---:|:---:|:---:|:---:|:---:|
| N.S. | ★ | ★★★ | ★★★ | ★★ |

## Rafting

Rafting is another fun and unusual activity that lets you paddle a big rubber raft down a river, enjoying the water and all the scenery as you float by. Depending on the intensity of the water, this may be a calm and soothing ride or a very active adventure. At the very least, plan on wearing a bathing suit and lifejacket. Other safety gear, such as a helmet, may also be required. A rafting trip can last anywhere from one hour to a full day, depending on the location, the tour operator, and your experience level.

Consult with the tour operator to determine what you'll need to bring on a rafting expedition. Snacks, drinks, and all necessary gear are typically provided.

**RAFTING**

| Ages up to 5 | Ages 6–15 | Ages 16–20 | Adult | Senior Citizens |
|:---:|:---:|:---:|:---:|:---:|
| N.S. | ★★ | ★★ | ★★★ | ★★ |

## Sailing

Regardless of whether you're an experienced sailor or a lifelong landlubber, you can take sailing lessons and then rent a small one- or two-person sailboat. You can also charter a larger sailing vessel (complete with a captain), depending on your interests and skill level. Smaller sailboats are usually available for rent by the hour, although this is an activity that is included at many all-inclusive resorts. Consult with the tour operator to determine what you'll need to bring when renting a sailboat. All necessary gear, including lifejackets, is typically provided.

**SAILING**

| Ages up to 5 | Ages 6–15 | Ages 16–20 | Adult | Senior Citizens |
|:---:|:---:|:---:|:---:|:---:|
| N.S. | ★★ | ★★★ | ★★★ | ★★ |

## Scuba Diving

Scuba diving is an amazing experience that lets you see ocean life from an entirely different perspective. To experience even an introductory dive, you should be in excellent physical shape. For experienced, certified scuba divers, the Caribbean offers some of the most incredible and beautiful dive sites in the world. For people over the age of twelve who want to experience scuba diving for the first time (without getting certified), introductory classes and dives are offered by dive schools, dive operators, and some resorts.

An introductory dive typically entails in-person instruction by a dive master on land. This instruction should last about one hour. After this, participants put on the dive suit and equipment and practice the scuba technique in a pool or in very shallow water. Finally, the class includes a short dive (thirty minutes to an hour) with a certified dive master as your guide, in which you dive to depths no greater than forty or fifty feet.

Introductory scuba-diving lessons and tours tend to book up quickly, so make your reservations well in advance. Seek out a referral from your hotel or resort when looking for a qualified dive instructor or dive master. The cost of an introductory dive ranges from $50 to $200 per person. This activity, from start to finish, will take at least three to five hours. Ideally, if you'll be diving with a group, insist on no more than three or four people for each dive master/instructor.

##  TRAVEL TIP

Make sure you work with a certified dive master when embarking on an introductory scuba dive. If after your preliminary instruction, you're not 100-percent comfortable actually taking the dive, seek out another dive instructor and guide.

The dive operator will provide all of the equipment you need, including a wet suit. You should only need to bring a bathing suit, towel, and optional change of clothing, along with sunscreen, a hat, and sunglasses (for the boat ride to the actual dive site.) To ensure that you'll remember your experience, consider purchasing a disposable waterproof camera, so you can take underwater photos of your experience.

**SCUBA DIVING**

| Ages up to 5 | Ages 6–15 | Ages 16–20 | Adult | Senior Citizens |
|:---:|:---:|:---:|:---:|:---:|
| N.S. | N.S. | ★★★ | ★★★ | ★ |

## Snorkeling

A much cheaper and less challenging alternative to scuba diving is snorkeling. This is an activity that virtually all hotels and resorts offer. With just a few minutes of instruction, you can begin snorkeling, even if you're not a strong swimmer. Snorkeling involves swimming on the surface of the water with a mask and snorkel (breathing tube) that let you can keep your face underwater while looking at the underwater sights.

All of the necessary gear—including a life jacket, fins, mask, and the snorkel—will be provided by the resort, hotel, or tour operator. You can also purchase your own snorkeling gear starting at around $100 for a basic, well-made set. You'll often save money if you purchase your snorkeling equipment from a U.S. sporting goods store instead of a local shop for tourists in the Caribbean.

**SNORKELING**

| Ages up to 5 | Ages 6–15 | Ages 16–20 | Adult | Senior Citizens |
| --- | --- | --- | --- | --- |
| N.S. | ★★ | ★★★ | ★★★ | ★★ |

## Snuba Diving

Many Caribbean vacation destinations now offer snuba diving, a cross between scuba diving and snorkeling. No experience is necessary, and you need to wear very little equipment. Almost all of the gear (such as your air tank) floats on the water's surface while you dive below, giving you maximum mobility as you explore underwater. Snuba diving is ideal for anyone over the age of fifteen, even those who aren't necessarily strong swimmers. This is an activity typically offered by tour operators that also offer snorkeling or scuba diving.

Consult with the tour operator to determine what you'll need to bring when participating in a snuba diving tour. Typically, all you'll need is a bathing suit.

**SNUBA DIVING**

| Ages up to 5 | Ages 6–15 | Ages 16–20 | Adult | Senior Citizens |
| --- | --- | --- | --- | --- |
| N.S. | ★ | ★★★ | ★★★ | ★★ |

## Submarine Rides

Atlantis Adventures (*www.atlantisadventures.com*) is one of the only submarine tour operators in the world. The company has several locations throughout the Caribbean, on islands including Aruba, Barbados, Cozumel, Grand Cayman, Curacao, St. Croix, St. John, St. Maarten, and St. Thomas.

Prepare to take a unique and exotic submarine adventure as you dive 100 to 150 feet toward the ocean floor. You'll see incredible ocean life and even several sunken ships through the submarine's portals. The entire adventure from the time you board the submarine is about ninety minutes long and includes live narration by the copilot.

Built at a cost of $3.6 million, each Atlantis submarine holds forty-eight passengers and makes up to nine dives per day. The undersea journey is surprisingly smooth, although if you're claustrophobic, being enclosed within the submarine itself probably isn't the best idea. Also, there are no restrooms available on the submarine, so plan accordingly.

An Atlantis submarine ride provides a memorable and exciting experience for people over the age of four. The cost is $84 per adult and $34 per child (ages four to sixteen). To save $10 on each adult ticket, make your reservations online at *www.atlantisadventures.com*. Advance reservations are definitely required. This is an extremely popular attraction, and rides book up quickly.

You can wear normal street clothes when embarking on a submarine ride, since you'll stay totally dry. No special equipment or experience is needed. Eating and drinking are not allowed on the submarines.

**SUBMARINE RIDES**

| Ages up to 5 | Ages 6–15 | Ages 16–20 | Adult | Senior Citizens |
|:---:|:---:|:---:|:---:|:---:|
| ★ | ★★★ | ★★★ | ★★★ | ★★★ |

## Surfing

Many areas of the Caribbean offer beaches with waves the perfect size for learning how to surf. At these beaches, you'll often find surfing schools or instructors that offer lessons as well as rental equipment. Surfing is a fun and challenging activity for teens and adults who are physically fit, and it definitely takes skill and plenty of practice. To avoid injury, definitely take lessons before trying this sport on your own. For kids, body surfing (which requires no board) and boogie boarding (which requires a small board you lie on) are more popular activities. Boogie boards are often provided free or can be rented from hotels and resorts.

Depending on where you'll be surfing, either a bathing suit or a wetsuit will be required. If the water is cold or rough enough to necessitate a wetsuit, you will be able to rent one along with your surfboard. Rubber-soled beach shoes may also be worn.

**SURFING**

| Ages up to 5 | Ages 6–15 | Ages 16–20 | Adult | Senior Citizens |
|---|---|---|---|---|
| N.S. | ★ | ★★★ | ★★★ | ★ |

## Swimming

Throw on a bathing suit and take a dip in the ocean, swimming pool, or in a lagoon at the bottom of a waterfall. The opportunities for swimming throughout the Caribbean are plentiful. If you're not an experienced swimmer, stick to beaches and pools where a lifeguard is on duty and the water is calm (with little or no undertow). Of course, as a parent, you should always supervise your children when they're in the water, regardless of whether a lifeguard is on duty. This is definitely the most popular activity (aside from sunbathing) in the Caribbean.

A bathing suit, towel, and sunscreen will be all you need to enjoy hours of fun swimming at a beach, in a swimming pool, or in a lagoon.

**SWIMMING**

| Ages up to 5 | Ages 6–15 | Ages 16–20 | Adult | Senior Citizens |
|---|---|---|---|---|
| ★ | ★★★ | ★★★ | ★★★ | ★★★ |

### Swimming with Dolphins

While not offered on all of the Caribbean islands, the chance to swim with dolphins is something that kids and teens in particular will remember for a long time. The tour operators that offer this activity typically invite guests to swim in an enclosed area with one or more bottlenose dolphins. All interaction with the dolphins is carefully supervised, and participants wear provided lifejackets.

Some swimming-with-dolphin programs offer little more than a chance to pet a dolphin as you stand in waist-high water. Others allow you to interact and actually swim with the dolphins. Determine, in advance, what the program offers. This activity costs anywhere from $50 to $200 per person, depending on the program. When available, swimming-with-dolphin programs tend to be extremely popular. They book up quickly, so make your reservations early.

Aside from a bathing suit, everything you'll need will be provided by the tour operator. Be sure you leave all metal jewelry, including rings, watches, bracelets, and earrings, in your hotel room or store these items in a locker. They should not be worn when swimming with dolphins.

**SWIMMING WITH DOLPHINS**

| Ages up to 5 | Ages 6–15 | Ages 16–20 | Adult | Senior Citizens |
|:---:|:---:|:---:|:---:|:---:|
| ★ | ★★★ | ★★★ | ★★★ | ★★ |

### Windsurfing

Windsurfing is a cross between sailing and surfing. It requires skill and a lot of upper-body strength. It's also a popular activity throughout the Caribbean and one that's offered at many resorts. If you've never experienced this sport before, it's important to receive proper instruction before trying it by yourself. Boards for windsurfing (along with experienced instruction) are available by the half-hour or by the hour. This is a sport that teens and adults in particular will enjoy. It's not suitable for kids or anyone who isn't physically fit.

Plan on wearing a bathing suit and a lifejacket (provided). Rubber-soled beach shoes or a light wetsuit are optional.

**WINDSURFING**

| Ages up to 5 | Ages 6–15 | Ages 16–20 | Adult | Senior Citizens |
|---|---|---|---|---|
| N.S. | N.S. | ★★★ | ★★★ | ★ |

# Popular Land-Based Activities

Most families opt to spend the majority of their time in the Caribbean enjoying all that the beach and ocean have to offer. When you're ready to venture out and explore the island you're visiting, you'll find a wide range of land-based activities families can enjoy.

This section offers just a sampling of the land-based sports and activities available to vacationers on many of the Caribbean islands.

## Four-Wheel-Drive Safari Tours

There are many ways to get around a Caribbean island. You can drive a rental car, take a taxi, hop on a local bus, or ride a bike or scooter. You can also have some fun by participating in a four-wheel-drive safari tour, usually offered in Jeeps or all-terrain vehicles (ATVs). What sets these tours apart is that they typically start off as a traditional tour, taking you to the most popular tourist destinations and historical sites on the island. From there, your tour will leave the roads and give you a look at the island that most tourists don't get to see.

As the name suggests, safari tours allow you to go off road, exploring dirt paths and easily reaching destinations not typically accessible by car. Some of these tours allow you to drive your own vehicle, while others provide a driver.

Since these are open-air vehicles, it's common for passengers to get wet or even muddy, so dress appropriately. You'll also have extended exposure to the sun, so wear sunscreen or a hat and suitable clothing.

Safari tours are fast-paced, fun, a bit bumpy at times, and a lot more exciting than taking a traditional sightseeing tour by bus. Riding in the vehicles is an adventure unto itself. The interesting and exotic places you visit on the tour only add to the entertainment value and fun.

In addition to sun protection, consider bringing a bathing suit (for any stops where you might be able to swim), a change of clothes (if you're told you'll get wet or muddy), and bottled water and snacks. Don't forget your camera!

**FOUR-WHEEL-DRIVE SAFARI TOURS**

| Ages up to 5 | Ages 6–15 | Ages 16–20 | Adult | Senior Citizens |
|---|---|---|---|---|
| ★ | ★★★ | ★★★ | ★★★ | ★ |

## Bus Tours

Especially of interest to adults, one of the easiest and cheapest ways to go sightseeing on a Caribbean island is to take a bus tour. Depending on the size of the bus, you'll ride with a few or a lot of other tourists in an enclosed, air-conditioned vehicle. A tour guide offers informative narration as you get driven from one popular tourist destination to the next.

A bus tour allows you to sit back and relax as you travel from place to place. You'll typically be allowed to leave the bus when it makes short stops at popular attractions. The drawback to this type of tour is that you're stuck with a schedule. If you want to spend extra time at any particular stop, that's not possible on a bus tour.

Bus tours can last anywhere from a few hours to an entire day. You can often sign up for one of these tours at your hotel. They provide a great introduction and overview to the island where you'll be staying.

Unless you're told to bring additional items, when participating in a traditional bus tour, wear comfortable clothes and shoes, and bring along bottled water and a snack. A camera or camcorder will enable you to relive the experience when you get home (and it's snowing).

**BUS TOURS**

| Ages up to 5 | Ages 6–15 | Ages 16–20 | Adult | Senior Citizens |
|---|---|---|---|---|
| ★ | ★ | ★★ | ★★ | ★★★ |

## Casinos

Throughout the Caribbean, especially in many of the upscale resort hotels and on cruise ships, you'll find casinos offering popular table games (like poker, craps, roulette, and blackjack) and slot machines. These casinos are open to guests over the age of either eighteen or twenty-one (depending on the island).

Casinos provide evening and nighttime entertainment. Even if you don't typically enjoy gambling, many of the casinos offer table games with very low minimum bets, plus nickel slot machines. Thus, by gambling just a few dollars, you can typically enjoy hours of entertainment.

Some of the casinos you'll find in the Caribbean are open twenty-four hours a day, and just as in Las Vegas, they offer live entertainment, bars, and nightclubs. Others are smaller, open only at night, and offer just slot machines and table games.

The casinos typically take cash or traveler's checks. You can also obtain a cash advance from a credit card at the cashier's desk within a casino. Aside from that, bring along some luck! If you're planning to spend time at the casino, be sure to schedule in-room baby-sitting services for your kids in advance.

**CASINOS**

| Ages up to 5 | Ages 6–15 | Ages 16–20 | Adult | Senior Citizens |
|:---:|:---:|:---:|:---:|:---:|
| N.S. | N.S. | ★ | ★★ | ★★★ |

## Day Spas

Upscale day spas offer a wide selection of luxury personal care services, including massages, facials, aromatherapy, seaweed wraps, and other body treatments. These are commonly available at mid- to high-priced hotels and resorts, as well as on cruise ships. These spas offer an excellent way for adults to relax and be pampered, especially after spending a day participating in some type of rigorous sport or activity. The day spas are typically open to adults only. Reservations should be made in advance.

When choosing a day spa, make sure it's fully equipped with all of the amenities you want in order to get the most out of your experience. A sauna, steam room, hot tub, showers, and locker rooms are among the basic amenities you should look for.

One way to truly enjoy your Caribbean spa visit is to experience the spa's signature treatments. These are usually some sort of exotic body treatment or massage technique that's unique to that spa and that uses locally made massage oils or skin creams, for example.

Everything required for your spa treatments will be provided by the spa. Be sure to arrive for your appointment at least fifteen minutes early so you have ample time to change. If you plan to enjoy the sauna, steam room, or hot tub before your treatment, plan accordingly. Many spas also sell the creams and lotions they use, so be prepared to splurge.

**DAY SPA TREATMENTS**

| Ages up to 5 | Ages 6–15 | Ages 16–20 | Adult | Senior Citizens |
|:---:|:---:|:---:|:---:|:---:|
| N.S. | N.S. | ★ | ★★★ | ★★★ |

## Experience the Nightlife

No matter where you go, chances are good that within your resort or hotel (or somewhere nearby) will be an assortment of nightclubs, bars, and lounges offering nighttime entertainment, such as disc jockeys, live music, or dancing. Ask your hotel's concierge for recommendations based on the type of atmosphere you're looking for.

On many Caribbean islands, the drinking age is eighteen. The carding policies at many Caribbean nightspots, however, are somewhat lax. In other words, if you're a parent, pay attention to what your teens are doing at night.

Bring some cash or a credit card. As far as attire is concerned, many of the more upscale nightclubs require proper attire, so dress accordingly.

**EXPERIENCE THE NIGHTLIFE**

| Ages up to 5 | Ages 6–15 | Ages 16–20 | Adult | Senior Citizens |
|:---:|:---:|:---:|:---:|:---:|
| N.S. | N.S. | ★★ | ★★★ | ★★ |

## Golf

The Caribbean has become known for its world-class championship golf courses. If you're a golfer, no matter where you go in the Caribbean, you'll find at least a handful of places to enjoy the sport. Some of the things that make Caribbean golf courses highly attractive to vacationers are their landscaping and surroundings. Stunning ocean views from the golf course are common.

While golfers are welcome to bring their own equipment, you can also rent everything you need. Many of the courses also offer lessons and full-service golf shops.

To learn about some of the best golf courses in the Caribbean, go online to visit the Caribbean Golf Vacations Web site (✐*www.caribbeangolf.com*). Here you'll find course reviews, course guides, information about tournaments, and details about special golf vacation packages. This Web site offers vacation-package recommendations and offers suggestions on courses, resorts, and travel packages to meet your budget and needs.

## 🧳 TRAVEL TIP

Caribbean Golf Vacations (✐*www.caribbean-golf-vacations.com*) is a popular Web site dedicated to helping golfers plan their dream Caribbean vacations. Packages typically include hotel/resort accommodations, ground transportation, greens fees, and sometimes even meals and drinks.

If you're a golfer, you can bring your own clubs and equipment (which must be checked as luggage on the airplane). Otherwise, plan on renting everything you need. Tee time reservations should be made in advance, especially at the more popular, upscale courses. Plan on spending anywhere from $35 to well over $200 per round, depending on the location and course.

**GOLF**

| Ages up to 5 | Ages 6–15 | Ages 16–20 | Adult | Senior Citizens |
|---|---|---|---|---|
| N.S. | ★ | ★★ | ★★★ | ★★★ |

## Helicopter Tours

One memorable although expensive way to see any Caribbean island is to take a helicopter tour. While not available on all Caribbean islands, these tours usually offer spectacular views, live narration from your pilot, and a chance to experience an exhilarating helicopter ride. Sunset tours are extremely popular and visually breathtaking. Depending on the length of the tour, plan on spending at least $150 per person for this opportunity. In most cases, the cost is well worth it!

Wear comfortable clothing. Everything you need will be provided by the tour operator (except a camera, of course).

**HELICOPTER TOURS**

| Ages up to 5 | Ages 6–15 | Ages 16–20 | Adult | Senior Citizens |
|---|---|---|---|---|
| N.S. | ★★★ | ★★★ | ★★★ | ★★ |

## Hiking

The Caribbean is known for its tropical settings. Depending on what Caribbean island you visit, you may find tropical rainforests or desert surroundings. What you can count on, however, is beautiful scenery. For eco-tourists looking to experience nature at its best, a wide range of hiking trails for novice and skilled hikers alike is available on virtually every Caribbean island. In some cases, tour guides and organized hikes are offered.

Before setting off on a hike by yourself (or with fellow tourists), learn about the local environment. Study a local map, and determine if there is any dangerous wildlife in the area.

In addition to comfortable hiking shoes and appropriate clothing for the climate, be sure to bring along ample bottled water, snacks, and anything else you'll need, based on the duration of your hike and where you'll be exploring. Don't forget your camera!

**HIKING**

| Ages up to 5 | Ages 6–15 | Ages 16–20 | Adult | Senior Citizens |
|:---:|:---:|:---:|:---:|:---:|
| N.S. | ★ | ★★★ | ★★★ | ★ |

## Horseback Riding

Throughout the Caribbean, you'll find a wide range of horseback-riding tours, equestrian centers, ranches, and stables that offer riding lessons and guided tours. To experience a horseback-riding tour, no previous experience is necessary. The most memorable tours follow trails along the beach. When choosing a horseback-riding tour, be sure to determine where you'll be touring and what experience level is required.

What you wear and the items you bring with you will depend on where you'll be riding and what type of terrain you'll encounter. If you'll be riding along a beach, for example, plan on getting plenty of sun and a bit wet. If your tour will take you along forest trails, however, long pants and a light jacket might be more appropriate attire.

**HORSEBACK RIDING**

| Ages up to 5 | Ages 6–15 | Ages 16–20 | Adult | Senior Citizens |
|:---:|:---:|:---:|:---:|:---:|
| N.S. | ★★ | ★★★ | ★★★ | ★ |

## Local Shows and Entertainment

One thing to do at night is to take in the local entertainment. Many all-inclusive resorts, for example, offer live musical entertainment as a nighttime activity. In some areas, you'll find shows or other forms of live entertainment offered that are well worth experiencing. In Aruba, for example, there's the popular *Let's Go Latin* show, a Las Vegas–style variety show that's suitable for the whole family and that should not be missed!

Reserve your tickets in advance, especially during peak vacation periods. Before purchasing tickets for the whole family, though, make sure the show or entertainment is suitable for all ages.

**LOCAL SHOWS AND ENTERTAINMENT**

| Ages up to 5 | Ages 6–15 | Ages 16–20 | Adult | Senior Citizens |
|---|---|---|---|---|
| Determine suitability based on the show's content. | | | | |

## Movies

Most of the Caribbean islands offer movie theaters that show the latest Hollywood blockbusters (typically in English) throughout the day and evening. If you're staying near a movie theater, this provides an excellent option for evening entertainment with your kids. Check with your hotel's concierge for local movie listings and show times.

An alternative is to take advantage of the pay-per-view movies offered in your hotel room or to bring a portable DVD player with you on your trip, along with a small library of DVDs suitable for your kids.

Portable DVD players are now available for under $200. They have a built-in screen, and you can also connect them to many television sets. If you have kids, this is a wonderful personal electronics item for traveling. It helps keep young people entertained on airplanes, during long car trips, and at night in a hotel room. Portable DVD players are sold at consumer electronics stores, such as Best Buy, Circuit City, Wal-Mart or RadioShack.

If you're going to a local movie theater, make sure the movie you're going to see is presented in English and not with English subtitles. Also, bring along money for snacks, just as you would if you were seeing a movie within the United States.

**MOVIES**

| Ages up to 5 | Ages 6–15 | Ages 16–20 | Adult | Senior Citizens |
|:---:|:---:|:---:|:---:|:---:|
| ★★ | ★★ | ★★ | ★★ | ★★ |

## Rock Climbing

To give vacationers a taste of what rock climbing is all about, many resorts and even cruise ships offer rock-climbing walls. Participants are strapped into a safety harness and, while under supervision, can climb up a man-made wall. This is a fun, physical activity that's suitable for anyone over the age of twelve.

Sneakers or rubber-soled shoes are a must. All safety equipment is provided.

**ROCK CLIMBING**

| Ages up to 5 | Ages 6–15 | Ages 16–20 | Adult | Senior Citizens |
|:---:|:---:|:---:|:---:|:---:|
| N.S. | ★★ | ★★ | ★★ | ★ |

## Scooter and Bicycle Rentals

One way to explore many Caribbean islands is to rent a motorized scooter or a bicycle. You'll usually have to pay an hourly rate for scooters, but many all-inclusive resorts offer loaner bicycles to guests. While the motorized scooters are ideal for sightseeing and exploring the local area at your own pace, a bicycle allows you to go off-road and explore the many trails you'll find along local beaches, for example.

Be sure to wear comfortable clothing along with a safety helmet when renting a motorized scooter or bicycle. If kids or teens will be riding without adult supervision, insist for their own safety that they stay on marked trails and off the local roads. Bike riding on local roads in the Caribbean can be hazardous to anyone.

**SCOOTER AND BICYCLE RENTALS**

| Ages up to 5 | Ages 6–15 | Ages 16–20 | Adult | Senior Citizens |
|:---:|:---:|:---:|:---:|:---:|
| N.S. | ★ | ★★★ | ★★★ | ★★ |

### Shopping

Depending on where you're traveling within the Caribbean, shopping will probably be an extremely popular activity. Duty-free shopping allows you to save money on jewelry, designer watches, perfumes, liquor, and tobacco products, for example. Throughout the Caribbean, you'll also find designer clothing shops, plus souvenir shops selling T-shirts and all kinds of other relatively inexpensive items featuring the name of the island you're visiting.

Aside from shopping for discounted, duty-free items that you can just as easily find back home (though for more money), the Caribbean offers locally made crafts, jewelry, and artwork that make perfect souvenirs. Never purchase any items that are living (such as plants), since you won't get these items home again through customs.

 **TRAVEL TIP**

Never purchase any souvenirs or products made from endangered or protected wildlife. Not only are you contributing to the destruction of a species or ecosystem, any such items will be confiscated if found, and penalties are likely.

Many tour operators offer half-day or full-day shopping excursions. These are guided tours of the most popular shopping areas on the island. The advantage is you'll get an overview of what's available. The disadvantage is that you won't be able to spend too much time at any one shopping area and you'll need to stick with the tour operator's schedule.

If you're interested in purchasing duty-free items while in the Caribbean, such as a designer watch, for example, be sure to first price similar watches in the United States so you can intelligently compare prices and model numbers. Keep in mind that almost anywhere you shop in the Caribbean, negotiating is commonplace.

You can often get a discount if you pay for your expensive items in U.S. dollars, although traveler's checks, local currency, and major credit cards are also widely accepted.

### SHOPPING

| Ages up to 5 | Ages 6–15 | Ages 16–20 | Adult | Senior Citizens |
|:---:|:---:|:---:|:---:|:---:|
| ★ | ★★ | ★★ | ★★★ | ★★★ |

## Sightseeing

Every Caribbean island has its own unique history and culture. To truly experience what each island has to offer, consider taking a sightseeing tour of the local tourist attractions and historical sites. These tours will be of greater interest to adults and seniors. You can usually choose from walking tours, bus tours, or other forms of guided tours (such as horse and buggy). However you decide to travel, visiting the historic and cultural attractions of your vacation destination will provide you with a glimpse into the island's past and help you learn about the local culture.

##  TRAVEL TIP

Consult your hotel's concierge to learn about the tours that best fit your family's schedule, interest, and budget.

In addition to bringing a camera, contact the tour operator to determine what items you should bring with you and the best clothing to wear. Comfortable shoes are a must, as considerable walking is almost always required. You might also be traveling over uneven terrain or climbing a lot of hills or stairs. Depending on the ages of people in your party, it's a good idea to find out ahead of time how much physical exertion the tour will require.

**SIGHTSEEING**

| Ages up to 5 | Ages 6–15 | Ages 16–20 | Adult | Senior Citizens |
|:---:|:---:|:---:|:---:|:---:|
| N.S. | ★★ | ★★ | ★★★ | ★★★ |

## Tennis

Many of the resorts throughout the Caribbean have tennis courts on the property. If not, chances are good you can find a court or racquet club within a short distance of where you're staying. You can bring your own racquet or rent one locally. In some cases, courts can be reserved for free at your resort. Depending on where you're staying and what your package includes, you may need to pay an hourly court fee. No matter what, it's always a good idea to reserve your court time in advance.

If you'll be playing on an outdoor court, consider playing in the early morning (before 10:00 A.M.) or in the late evening to avoid the strong Caribbean sun and heat. Proper attire is required at some of the more upscale racquet clubs.

**TENNIS**

| Ages up to 5 | Ages 6–15 | Ages 16–20 | Adult | Senior Citizens |
|:---:|:---:|:---:|:---:|:---:|
| N.S. | ★ | ★★ | ★★★ | ★★★ |

# CHAPTER 6

# *Aruba*

WHETHER IT'S BECAUSE OF the island's beauty, modern amenities, comfort, ease of travel, and a wide range of activities for people of all ages, Aruba has become one of the Caribbean's ultimate family-vacation destinations.

## The Scoop on Aruba

Like all of the Caribbean islands, the vacation-oriented activities for tourists available in Aruba typically involve water sports and the beach. However, Aruba also has several upscale golf courses, plenty of shopping, day spas, land-based tourist attractions, hundreds of wonderful restaurants, and many other activities to experience.

In terms of hotel and resort amenities, Aruba offers an excellent selection of large, fully equipped resorts that are family friendly and located right on the beach. Some of these resorts are all-inclusive. Others offer money-saving packages that include accommodations, meals, and a selection of activities. There are also many smaller low-rise resorts and a growing selection of time-share properties. Thus, no matter what your travel budget, you'll be able to find accommodations to meet your family's needs. You'll also discover that several popular cruise ships include Aruba among their ports of call.

Aruba is located toward the center of the southern Caribbean, about fifteen miles off the coast of Venezuela. (It's about a two-and-a-half-hour flight from Miami.) The island itself is only about twenty miles long by six miles across, but there's a lot packed into this lovely island for vacationers. The attractions that draw many vacationers to Aruba are its pristine white sandy beaches and the near-perfect year-round weather. In conjunction with a handful of new time-share properties recently built, several world-class golf courses have also recently opened.

What Aruba shares with its Caribbean neighbors is a rich mixture of cultures and influences. You'll find much of Aruba's 100,000-person population to be well educated and eager to share their island with vacationers and tourists. Virtually everyone in Aruba speaks fluent English, and many people speak Spanish as well. The island's official language is Dutch, and the native language is called Papiamento (which is a combination of Portuguese, Spanish, Dutch, English, African dialect, and French).

Aruba is on Atlantic Standard Time (AST), which is one hour ahead of Eastern Standard Time (EST). Aruba does not observe Daylight Saving Time, so during this period the Aruba is basically on EST.

 **TRAVEL TIP**

Aruba uses standard 110-volt electrical power, identical to that used in the United States, so no power converters or adapters are needed.

The official currency is the Aruban florin, but the U.S. dollar is readily accepted everywhere. You'll find full-service banks and ATMs located throughout Oranjestad (the main city in Aruba), near most of the major hotels and resorts. If your bank is associated with the Cirrus or Plus network, you'll have no trouble using your ATM card in Aruba to make cash withdrawals.

Driving in Aruba is easy, as the rules are the same as they are in the United States. You will find plenty of opportunities to rent a car and navigate your way around the island, although many vacationers choose to use taxis, organized tours, or the local bus service to get around.

In general, casual attire is the norm everywhere in Aruba. While bathing suits are perfect for the beach, they're not acceptable at any of the indoor restaurants or shopping areas. Some of the finer restaurants, nightclubs, and casinos have a more formal dress code.

## A Bit of Aruba History

Aruba was originally inhabited by the Caquetio Indians. Back in 1636, however, the Dutch took possession of the island until 1805. The English then took control for a few years, until 1816. Since January of 1986, however, Aruba has been considered a separate entity within the kingdom of the Netherlands. Aruba has its own constitution, which is based on Western democratic ideals. As you might guess, the island's largest industry is tourism.

## The Local Weather

No matter when you visit Aruba, you can typically count on an average temperature of around 82 degrees (Fahrenheit). Unlike other Caribbean vacation destinations, Aruba is situated outside the hurricane belt, so the island seldom experiences hurricanes or tropical storms.

While Aruba can windy at times (depending on where you're staying), the island usually enjoys a warm, tropical breeze. Many of the beaches offer the perfect climate for sunbathing, relaxing, or enjoying or your favorite water sports.

## Getting to Aruba

Whether you arrive by air or cruise ship, getting to Aruba from the United States is relatively easy, as it is served by several major international airlines and most of the cruise lines. One nice convenience for American travelers is that the main airport in Aruba, the Queen Beatrix International Airport, has its own terminal for passengers coming from and going back to the United States. The terminal has an in-house U.S.

immigration and customs facility, which means that flights from Aruba can enter the United States like any other domestic flight.

As you arrive in Aruba by airplane, your flight attendant will provide you with an international embarkation/disembarkation card, which you must fill out and present as you deplane. The bottom portion of this card will be detached and returned to you, and you should keep it with your passport until you leave. A valid passport is required to visit Aruba. For U.S. citizens who were born in America, an alternative is to present an original birth certificate in conjunction with a valid, government-issued photo ID (such as a driver's license). Upon arriving in Aruba, your baggage will go through customs.

## ≡FAST FACT

When it's time to leave Aruba, be prepared to pay a departure tax of $36.75 per person. This is a common practice throughout the Caribbean.

## The Queen Beatrix International Airport

The Queen Beatrix International Airport in Aruba is a large, modern, full-service international airport, complete with all of the services you'd expect from any other international airport. The following airlines offer service between major U.S. cities and Aruba:

- **American Airlines** (✆800-433-7300, ✐*www.aa.com*) offers nonstop service from New York, Miami, San Juan, and Boston, but connections are available from virtually all major U.S. cities.
- **Continental Airlines** (✆800-525-0280, ✐*www.continental. com*) offers nonstop service from Newark and Houston, but connections are available from virtually all major U.S. cities.

- **Delta Airlines** (☎800-221-1212, ✐*www.delta.com*) offers non-stop service from Atlanta and New York (JFK), but connections are available from virtually all major U.S. cities.
- **US Airways** (☎800-428-4322, ✐*www.usairways.com*) offers nonstop service from Philadelphia, Charlotte, Boston, and New York, but connections are available from virtually all major U.S. cities.
- **United Airlines** (☎800-241-6522, ✐*www.united.com*) offers nonstop service from Chicago and Washington, D.C., but connections are available from virtually all major U.S. cities.

In addition to the major airlines that offer either nonstop or connecting flights to Aruba, a handful of popular charter and tour companies also offer vacation packages. Contact your travel agent, or get in touch with tour companies such as Vacation Express (☎800-309-4717, ✐*www.vacationexpress.com*), GWV/TNT Vacations (☎617-262-9200 / ✐*www.tntvacations.com*) or FunJet (☎888-558-6654, ✐*www. funjet.com*) for details.

Upon clearing customs, taxi service and rental car agencies are readily available to get you to your hotel or resort. The airport is located less than a fifteen-minute drive from virtually all of the popular hotels and resorts in Aruba.

## 💼 TRAVEL TIP

If you require special assistance at the Queen Beatrix International Airport, call ☎011-297-582-4800, ext. 300. There is a fully equipped medical facility on the premises. In addition, the airport is equipped to handle passengers with any type of physical disability.

# Getting Around Aruba

Whether you're taking a taxi, driving a rental car, riding a local bus (a convenient, safe, and very inexpensive way to get around) or walking, navigating your way around the tourist-oriented areas of Aruba is extremely easy.

With the exception of the popular Renaissance Resort, which is located in the middle of downtown Oranjestad (the main shopping and tourist area of Aruba), virtually all of the resorts and hotels are located either along the low-rise or the high-rise resort area of the island. Both of these areas are right on the water and offer easy access to the beaches.

Having a rental car gives you a convenient way to get around Aruba, but it certainly isn't necessary. If you'll be exploring the island, your best bet is to sign up for one of the many tours available. Otherwise, taking advantage of taxis or the bus system will get you where you need to go in a timely and cost-effective manner.

### Taking Taxis

From the airport, it'll cost about $20 each way to reach the high-rise hotel area, $17 to reach the La Cabana and low-rise hotel area, or about $13 to reach the Renaissance Beach Resort and main downtown area. For more information about taxi services in Aruba, contact the Department of Transportation at ✆011-297-582-4140. Basic taxis hold a maximum of five passengers. On Sundays, official holidays, and after midnight, there's a $2 surcharge per trip.

If you're interested in sightseeing, and you don't wish to rent a car and navigate on your own, you can hire a taxi for $40 per hour. Once you've checked into your hotel, if you need to get between your resort and the downtown area or most tourist attractions within Aruba, the bus system is inexpensive, safe, and easy to use.

### Taxi Services In Aruba

Any of the following companies can provide reliable taxi service in and around Aruba:

- **Aruba's Transfer Tour & Taxi** ☎011-297-582-2116, ☎011-297-583-2856
- **Best Taxi Services Aruba** ☎011-297-588-3232
- **Taxi Address Service** ☎011-297-587-5900

## Local Bus System

The bus system is definitely the least expensive way to get around Aruba. For just over $1 per person each way, Aruba's local buses will take you from the downtown Oranjestad area to most of the major hotels and resorts. The bus system is made up of six routes that extend throughout the island. If you're planning to stay out late, be sure to check the schedule for the last bus back to your hotel.

## Renting a Car

As you'd expect, all of the popular U.S. rental car companies have offices in Aruba. Avis (✐*www.avis.com*), Budget Car Rental (✐*www. budget.com*), Dollar Rent-A-Car (✐*www.dollar.com*), Enterprise Rent-A-Car (✐*www.enterprise.com*), Hertz Car Rental (✐*www.hertz. com*) and Thrifty Car Rental (✐*www.thrifty.com*) are among the internationally known car rental companies with branches there.

On the island of Aruba, you'll also find dozens of local car rental companies. For details, contact your hotel's concierge. Rental cars can be picked up at the airport, as well as from many popular hotels and resorts where rental-car agencies have kiosks.

##  JUST FOR PARENTS

Instead of a rental car, you can rent a Harley-Davidson motorcycle on Aruba. For details, contact Big Twin Aruba (☎011-297-582-8660, ✐*www.harleydavidsonaruba.com*) during normal business hours.

# Where to Stay

Perhaps the perfect family-oriented accommodations within Aruba can be found at the Renaissance Aruba Beach Resort & Casino (✆800-421-8188, ✑*www.arubarenaissance.com*), located in the center of downtown Oranjestad. This upscale, ultramodern resort offers a large selection of amenities and has its own private island for beach-goers, which guests can visit by taking a short boat ride from the resort's main lobby.

Just outside of Oranjestad, you'll find the two main resort areas, where the high-rise and low-rise resorts are located. Both are located along the beach. Aruba has a nice selection of all-inclusive resorts, traditional resorts, hotels, guesthouses, and time-share properties. Some of the resorts offer everything you'd possibly want right on the property, making it unnecessary to leave the premises for the duration of your stay. Other resorts and hotels offer fewer amenities and activities but are more competitively priced.

##  TRAVEL TIP

Aruba has become known for its wide selection of top-notch restaurants that serve virtually every kind of cuisine you can imagine, from steaks and seafood to Dutch, Japanese, Italian, French, Chinese, and Caribbean. Along with McDonald's, Taco Bell, Wendy's, Subway, KFC, Burger King, and many other fast-food chains, you'll find many family-friendly restaurants in downtown Oranjestad and throughout the island.

In addition to beach access, many of the resorts offer multiple restaurants, a day spa (for adults only), golf course, casino, tennis courts, an array of water-based activities, and supervised activity centers for the kids. Once you decide to visit Aruba, select your accommodations by first asking yourself the following questions:

- What type of accommodations are you looking for? (Your choices include a traditional hotel room, multibedroom suite, bungalow, or apartment-style accommodations.)
- Do you prefer an all-inclusive resort that includes your accommodations, meals, and activities at one price per person?
- Do you prefer to stay in a high-rise hotel or in a low-rise building?
- What activities, in addition to the beach, are you looking for? Golf, a day spa, workout facility, restaurants, tennis courts, and a casino are among the popular options.

## ≡FAST FACT

One way to get the most out of your vacation without incurring unexpected expenses for activities and meals is to stay at one of Aruba's family-oriented all-inclusive resorts. Divi Resorts (☎207-594-7888, ✍www.diviaruba.com), for example, offers several mid- to high-priced properties there.

### High-Rise Resorts in Aruba

On Aruba, most of the popular resorts are the mid- to high-price resorts, although money-saving travel packages are often available from travel agents, travel-related Web sites, and directly from the resorts themselves.

As the category name suggests, these resorts are comprised of one or more high-rise towers, almost all of which overlook the beach and coastline on one side and, usually, the island's large wildlife preserve on the other.

Within the high-rise resorts, you'll find traditional hotel room accommodations, along with one-, two-, or three-bedroom suites. Adjoining rooms are sometimes available. Many of these rooms have outdoor decks.

### Aruba Grand Beach Resort & Casino
☏954-427-5499 (U.S.), ☏011-297-586-3900 (Aruba)
✐www.arubagrand.com

### Aruba Marriott Resort & Stellaris Casino
☏908-302-5206 (U.S.), ☏011-297-586-9000 (Aruba)
✐www.marriott.com

### Aruba Marriott Ocean Club (Time-share)
☏908-302-5206 (U.S.), ☏011-297-586-9000 (Aruba)
✐www.vacationclub.com

### Aruba Marriott Surf Club (Time-share)
☏908-302-5206 (U.S.), ☏011-297-586-9000 (Aruba)
✐www.marriottarubasurfclub.com

### Divi Phoenix Aruba Beach Resort
☏800-367-3484 (U.S.), ☏011-297-586-6066 (Aruba)
✐www.arubaphoenix.com

### Holiday Inn Sun Spree Resort Aruba
☏800-HOLIDAY, ☏011-297-586-3600 (Aruba)
✐www.holidayinn-aruba.com

### Hyatt Regency Aruba Beach Resort and Casino
☏800-233-1234 (U.S.), ☏011-297-586-1234 (Aruba)
✐www.aruba.hyatt.com

### Occidental Allegro Aruba & Casino
☏800-858-2258 (U.S.), ☏011-297-586-4500 (Aruba)
✐www.occidentalhotels.com

### Playa Linda Beach Resort
☏800-346-7084 (U.S.), ☏011-297-586-1000 (Aruba)
✐www.playalinda.com

### Radisson Aruba Beach Resort & Casino

☎800-333-3333 (U.S.), ☎011-297-586-6555 (Aruba)

✍*www.radisson.com*

### Renaissance Aruba Resort & Casino

☎800-421-8188 (U.S.), ☎011-297-583-6000 (Aruba)

✍*www.arubarenaissance.com*

### Wyndham Aruba Resort Spa & Casino

☎800-WYNDHAM (U.S.), ☎011-297-586-4466

✍*www.arubawyndham.com*

## Low-Rise Resorts in Aruba

A low-rise resort usually features a cluster of buildings no more than two or three stories tall. Apartment-style accommodations, suites, and bungalows are commonplace. These accommodations offer a very different view and a cozier stay than the high-rise resorts.

Here's a listing of the popular, family-friendly, low-rise resorts located in Aruba. The easiest way to get in touch with most of these places is by e-mail, as most have local Aruba phone numbers only.

### Amsterdam Manor Beach Resort

☎800-932-6509 (U.S.), ☎011-297-587-1492 (Aruba)

✍*www.amsterdammanor.com*

### Aruba Beach Club

☎011-297-582-3000

✍*www.arubabeachclub.net*

### Aruba Surfside Marina

☎011-297-583-0300

✍*www.arubasurfsidemarina.com*

### Brickell Bay Beach Club

☎011-297-586-0900

✍*www.brickellbayaruba.com*

### Bucuti Beach Resort and Tara Beach Suites & Spa
☎011-297-583-1100
✎*www.bucuti.com*

### Caribbean Palm Village Resort
☎011-297-586-2700
✎*www.cpvr.com*

### Casa Del Mar Beach Resort
☎011-297-582-3000
✎*www.casadelmar-aruba.com*

### Coconut Inn
☎866-978-4952 (U.S.), ☎011-297-586-6288 (Aruba)
✎*www.coconutinn.com*

### Costa Linda Beach Resort
☎011-297-583-8000
✎*www.costalinda-aruba.com*

### Divi Aruba Beach Resort All-Inclusive
☎207-594-7888 (U.S.), ☎011-297-582-3300 (Aruba)
✎*www.diviaruba.com*

### La Cabana All-Suites Beach Resort & Casino
☎800-835-7193 (U.S.), ☎011-297-587-9000 (Aruba)
✎*www.lacabana.com/resort*

### La Quinta Beach Resort
☎800-426-5445 (U.S.)

### MVC Eagle Beach Resort
☎011-297-587-0110
✎*www.mvceaglebeach.com* (click on the British flag for English version)

### Manchebo Beach Resort & Spa

&800-223-1108 (U.S.), &011-297-582-3444 (Aruba)

✍*www.manchebo.com*

### Paradise Beach Villas

&011-297-587-4000

✍*www.paradisebeachvillas.com*

### Talk Of The Town Hotel and Beach Club

&011-297-582-3380

✍*www.talkofthetownaruba.com*

### Tamarijn Aruba All-Inclusive Beach Resort

&207-594-2008 (U.S.), &011-297-525-5200 (Aruba)

✍*www.tamarijnaruba.com*

### The Mill Resort & Suites

&800-992-2015 (U.S.), &011-297-586-7700 (Aruba)

✍*www.millresort.com*

### Tierra Del Sol Resort & Country Club

&011-297-586-7800

✍*www.tierradelsol.com*

##  TRAVEL TIP

If you're traveling with kids or teens, it will be worth any extra cost to have the convenience of staying in a resort located right on the beach. You should also make sure that it offers organized and supervised activities for young people. These activity centers offer kids the chance to meet and interact with people their own age and experience a wide range of fun activities.

# Calling Home and Surfing the Web

Aruba offers modern phone service with easy, direct-dial access to the United States or overseas. One of the cheapest alternatives is to purchase a prepaid calling card in Aruba and use a public phone when calling home. Many hotels and resorts add a surcharge on international calls. International roaming is also available with many U.S.-based cell phone carriers.

If you have an unlocked GSM phone, you can purchase a pre-paid SIM chip from one of Aruba's local cell-phone service providers and receive low per-minute rates for outgoing local and international calls. Using a prepaid SIM card with your unlocked GSM cell phone will allow you to receive calls (incoming) from anywhere for free (with no airtime charges). There is a competitive, per-minute rate for initiating calls, which starts at $.31 per minute for calls to America. Aruba Primo SETAR (✐*www.setar.com/visiting_aruba.html*) is one of the most popular telecommunications companies and GSM cell-phone service providers in Aruba. One of the newer cell-phone companies in Aruba is Digicel (which has an international roaming agreement with several U.S. based cellular phone companies, including T-Mobile.) For details, contact that company at (✆011-297-522-2200, ✐*www.digicelaruba.com*).

 **TRAVEL TIP**

You can rent a cellular phone in Aruba for $5 per day (plus airtime, with free incoming calls) from many of the Internet cafés in Oranjestad, such as Internet Planet Communications Center. You'll find this café located within the Renaissance Aruba Resort & Casino (✆011-297-588-2499).

Many of the resorts offer high-speed Internet access within their business center or lobby, and a growing number of resorts are starting to offer in-room high-speed access for travelers who bring their own laptop computer on vacation.

Within Oranjestad, you'll find several Internet cafés, offering inexpensive high-speed Internet access (for as little as $3 for thirty minutes) and the capability to call the United States for as little as $.25 per minute.

## ≡ FAST FACT

From any hotel room with a telephone, you can access inexpensive dial-up Internet access using the 123-Instant Access service provided by Setarnet (*www.setarnet.aw*). All you need is a computer, modem, and a telephone line.

# What to See and Do

One of the greatest things about Aruba is the abundance of things to see and do. In addition to offering virtually every type of water and beach-based activity you'd expect from a premier vacation destination, Aruba offers unique land-based adventures as well. For example, kids, teens, and adults alike will enjoy the Aruba Off-Road Safari Adventure offered by De Palm Tours (℅800-766-6016, *www. depalm.com*). Young kids especially will love Aruba's Butterfly Farm (page 125) and the Aruba Ostrich Farm (page 123), while the whole family will enjoy a ride in an Atlantis submarine.

##  TRAVEL TIP

Tennis at the Aruba Racquet Club (℅011-297-586-0215, *www.arc. tennist.nl*) features eight lighted tennis courts, a swimming pool, fitness center, and restaurant. The basic rental fee for a court is $10 per hour. Reservations are definitely recommended, especially during peak vacation periods. Hours of operation are 8:00 a.m. to 11:00 p.m.

Your hotel's concierge or any of the tourist information offices in Aruba can help you schedule the following activities, as well as make restaurant recommendations and reservations. Just some of the popular activities readily available in Aruba include the following:

- Boat rides
- Casinos
- Day spas
- Deep-sea fishing
- Galleries
- Golf
- Helicopter tours
- Horseback riding
- Museums

- Nightclubs, bars, and lounges
- Restaurants
- Sailing
- Scuba diving and snorkeling
- Shopping
- Tours
- Windsurfing

### Golfing in Aruba

Aruba is the home to several world-class golf courses, including the Tierra del Sol eighteen-hole championship golf course (✆011-297-586-7800, ✍ *www.tierradelsol.com*) and The Links at Divi Aruba (✆800-554-2008 (U.S.), ✍ *www.diviaruba.com/golf.html*). Both courses are open to guests and nonguests. Reservations should definitely be made in advance, especially during peak travel seasons. Equipment rentals and instruction are available.

### Movies at The Renaissance Village Cinema

This modern movie cineplex offers six theaters, all with state-of-the-art projection equipment and sound systems. Here, you'll find the most current movies from the United States playing, all in English. The movies change every Thursday. Typically, at least one or two family or kid-oriented movies will be offered. It's a great rainy-day activity, and the theater is conveniently located in downtown Oranjestad (✆011-297-583-0318, ✍ *www.seaportcinemas.com*).

# Must-See Activities and Attractions

With its diverse offerings, Aruba can offer anything from luxury to simplicity, from a place to relax to a place to have an active vacation while enjoying the natural beauty of the island. In addition to all of the tropical beach-oriented and water-based activities you could possible desire, you can enjoy a wide range of other attractions and activities.

If you're planning to tour the island, which definitely deserves a full day of your vacation, either by bus, rental car, or four-wheel-drive, one of your stops should be at Aruba's famous Natural Bridge. This is the most photographed spot on the island. This solid coral bridge rises twenty-five feet above the water and spans over 100 feet. In addition to being a great photo spot, it's an ideal place to have a family picnic.

The top ten must-see attractions and family-friendly activities in Aruba include the following:

### The Beaches

On the side of the island where the hotels and resorts are located, the water is typically calm, the beaches are nicely groomed, and the view is utterly spectacular. This is the perfect place to relax, unwind, sunbathe, swim, or participate in a wide range of beach-oriented activities and water sports.

While all of the beaches in Aruba are public, the resorts typically have their own areas where lounge chairs, towels, cabanas, bar and snack service, and other amenities are available. To participate in activities like parasailing, windsurfing, scuba diving, or sailing, contact your resort's concierge desk. You'll find that many activities are offered through private companies, such as De Palm Tours (☎011-297-582-4400, *www.depalm.com*) and cost extra.

**ARUBA'S BEACHES**

| Ages up to 5 | Ages 6–15 | Ages 16–20 | Adult | Senior Citizens |
|:---:|:---:|:---:|:---:|:---:|
| ★★ | ★★★ | ★★★ | ★★★ | ★★★ |

### Aruba Ostrich Farm

This relatively small petting zoo is a fun outdoor destination for kids. You can get up close to and interact with ostriches, while getting a behind-the-scenes look at how baby ostriches are raised.

Families can explore the five-acre farm and experience a fun and educational tour. There's also a souvenir shop and restaurant here. The location of the ostrich farm is just under thirty minutes away from the popular resorts by car. It's a great add-on activity if you're already planning a sightseeing trip of the island or on your way to the Natural Bridge. Plan on spending between an hour and ninety minutes exploring this attraction. No reservations are required. Call the farm at ☎011-297-585-9630 for more information.

Open daily 9:00 a.m. to 4:00 p.m.
Admission $10 (adults)/$5 (children)/Children under age 2 are free

**THE OSTRICH FARM**

| Ages up to 5 | Ages 6–15 | Ages 16–20 | Adult | Senior Citizens |
|:---:|:---:|:---:|:---:|:---:|
| ★★★ | ★★★ | ★ | ★ | ★ |

### Atlantis Submarine Ride

Prepare to take a unique and exotic submarine adventure as you dive 150 feet toward the ocean floor. You'll see incredible ocean life and several sunken ships through the submarine's portals. Your journey begins from Seaport Village Marina in downtown Oranjestad, where you'll take a fifteen-minute boat ride to the submarine. Upon boarding the submarine, your undersea journey lasts about one hour. The entire adventure is about ninety minutes long and includes live narration by the copilot.

Built at a cost of $3.6 million, the Atlantis submarine holds forty-eight passengers and makes nine dives per day. The undersea journey is surprisingly smooth, although if you're claustrophobic, being enclosed within the submarine itself probably isn't the best idea. Also, there are no restrooms available on the actual submarine, so plan accordingly.

An Atlantis submarine ride provides a memorable and exciting experience for people over the age of four. The cost is $84 per adult and $34 per child (ages four to sixteen). To save $10 per adult ticket, make your reservations online at ✍*www.atlantisadventures.com*. Advance reservations are definitely required. This is an extremely popular attraction, so it books up quickly. For more information, call ☎011-297-583-6090.

**ATLANTIS SUBMARINE RIDE**

| Ages up to 5 | Ages 6–15 | Ages 16–20 | Adult | Senior Citizens |
|:---:|:---:|:---:|:---:|:---:|
| N.S. | ★★★ | ★★★ | ★★★ | ★★★ |

## The Butterfly Farm

The Aruba Butterfly Farm offers an outdoor, but enclosed, walk-through attraction on a farm that is home to thirty-two different species of colorful and exotic butterflies. Guests walk through a meshed-in, lavishly landscaped, tranquil park. Flying around are literally hundreds of butterflies. Short, guided tours are offered throughout the day. This fifteen-minute tour explains and demonstrates the lifecycle of a butterfly, from egg to caterpillar to chrysalis to butterfly, in an interesting way.

Plan on spending about an hour exploring this attraction. The Aruba Butterfly Farm is conveniently located within a three- to five-minute drive from the high-rise hotels (across the street from the Wyndam Aruba and Phoenix Resorts) along J. E. Irausquin Blvd.

The entry fee is $12 per adult and $6 for children, and your ticket allows re-entry for the entire time you're in Aruba. Hours of operation are from 9:00 A.M. to 4:30 P.M. daily. For more information, call ☎011-297-586-3656 or go online to ✍*www.thebutterflyfarm.com*. The entrance to this attraction doubles as a small gift shop, which sells many unique butterfly-themed gifts, toys, and souvenirs.

**THE BUTTERFLY FARM**

| Ages up to 5 | Ages 6–15 | Ages 16–20 | Adult | Senior Citizens |
|---|---|---|---|---|
| ★★ | ★★★ | ★★ | ★★ | ★★★ |

## Experience Aruba Panorama

Shown every hour between 11:00 A.M. and 5:00 P.M. (Mondays through Saturdays) in the Crystal Theater at the Renaissance in downtown Oranjestad, this stunning, twenty-two-minute, multimedia movie presentation depicts the sights, sounds, beauty, culture, and rich history of Aruba.

While this movie will appeal more to adults, it's suitable for the entire family. It's shown on a big screen and includes state-of-the-art surround sound effects. The ticket price is $10 per person (free to Renaissance resort guests), but discount coupons are available for $2 off per ticket.

The theater holds 430 guests, so advance reservations are not required. For more information, call ☎011-297-583-6000 or go online to ✐*www.arubapanorama.com*. This movie offers a great way to break up an afternoon of shopping, if you choose to take a half-hour break and want to relax in a comfortable, air-conditioned theater. If you're visiting Aruba for the first time, this movie offers an excellent and beautifully produced overview of the island.

**EXPERIENCE ARUBA PANORAMA**

| Ages up to 5 | Ages 6–15 | Ages 16–20 | Adult | Senior Citizens |
|---|---|---|---|---|
| N.S. | ★ | ★★ | ★★ | ★★★ |

## Horseback Riding

Several stables throughout Aruba offer horseback-riding tours. Some of these tours include horseback riding along Aruba's lovely beach trails. No previous riding experience is necessary. As with other popular activities, reservations should be made in advance. Contact any of the following companies for details:

- **Rancho Deimari** ☏011-297-587-5674
- **Rancho del Campo** ☏011-297-585-0290
- **Rancho Notorious** ☏011-297-586-0508, ✐*www.ranchonotorious. com*
- **Rancho Arizona** ☏011-297-586-8686
- **Desert Rose Equestrian Center** ☏011-297-994-7806

**HORSEBACK RIDING**

| Ages up to 5 | Ages 6–15 | Ages 16–20 | Adult | Senior Citizens |
|:---:|:---:|:---:|:---:|:---:|
| N.S. | ★★ | ★★★ | ★★★ | ★ |

## Water Sports: Scuba Diving, Snorkeling, and Windsurfing

Tourists can participate in dozens of different water sports, boat tours, and adventures. Whether you're interested in experiencing a memorable scuba-diving adventure or want to take a sunset cruise, the following tour companies provide plenty of options:

- **Dive Aruba**: ☏011-297-582-7337, ✐*www.divearuba.com*
- **Aruba Water Sports Center**: ☏011-297-586-6613
- **Dax Divers**: ☏011-297-585-1270
- **De Palm Water Sports**: ☏011-297-582-4400, ✐*www.depalm.com*
- **Jolly Pirates**: ☏011-297-583-7355
- **One Happy Dive Center**: ☏011-297-583-2332
- **Tattoo Party Cruises**: ☏011-297-586-2010, ✐*www.arubaadventures. com*
- **Native Divers**: ☏011-297-586-4763
- **Pelican Water Sports**: ☏011-297-587-2302, ✐*www.pelican-aruba. com*
- **Pro Dive**: ☏011-297-582-5520, ✐*www.arubawavedancer.com*
- **Rainbow Runner**: ☏011-297-583-1689
- **Red Sail Sports**: ☏011-297-586-1603, ✐*www.redsail.com*
- **Scuba Plus**: ☏011-297-584-4292
- **SEAruba Fly 'n Dive**: ☏011-297-583-8759

- **Unique Sports of Aruba**: ☎011-297-586-0096
- **Wave Dancer**: ☎011-297-582-5520, ✎*www.arubawavedancer. com*

While scuba diving and snorkeling are the best ways to see Aruba's exotic underwater life firsthand, some companies—De Palm Tours, for example—also offer snuba diving, a combination of scuba diving and snorkeling that's ideal for beginners. There's no heavy equipment to wear and no previous experience needed. Snuba diving is suitable for anyone over the age of twelve.

For more information about the other water sports available in Aruba, contact any of the above-listed tour companies or your hotel's concierge. Especially during peak travel seasons, be sure to make your reservations in advance.

**SCUBA DIVING**

| Ages up to 5 | Ages 6–15 | Ages 16–20 | Adult | Senior Citizens |
|---|---|---|---|---|
| N.S. | N.S. | ★★★ | ★★★ | ★ |

**SNUBA DIVING**

| Ages up to 5 | Ages 6–15 | Ages 16–20 | Adult | Senior Citizens |
|---|---|---|---|---|
| N.S. | ★ | ★★★ | ★★★ | ★ |

**SNORKELING**

| Ages up to 5 | Ages 6–15 | Ages 16–20 | Adult | Senior Citizens |
|---|---|---|---|---|
| N.S. | ★★ | ★★★ | ★★★ | ★★ |

### The *Let's Go Latin* Show

Presented nightly at 9:00 P.M. in the Crystal Theater of the Renaissance Aruba Resort & Casino, *Let's Go Latin* is a live, Las Vegas–style music and variety show that's suitable for the entire family. Featuring a large cast of talented Cuban performers, lavish sets, over 180 colorful costumes, and plenty of upbeat music, this eighty-minute show is extremely fun and entertaining.

Ticket prices are $44 for adults and $22 for children, but special family packages are available. For example, a four-ticket package for two adults and two children is priced at $110. The Renaissance also offers a money-saving dinner-and-show package, which includes dinner at the award-winning L.G. Smith's Steak & Chop House for $75 per person.

*Let's Go Latin* offers top-notch entertainment and a fun-filled way to enjoy an evening in Aruba. Kids and even surly teens will enjoy this show as much as adults.

### LET'S GO LATIN

| Ages up to 5 | Ages 6–15 | Ages 16–20 | Adult | Senior Citizens |
|:---:|:---:|:---:|:---:|:---:|
| N.S. | ★★ | ★★ | ★★★ | ★★★ |

### Four-Wheel-Drive Tours

See the island of Aruba while driving your own all-terrain vehicle or Jeep. It's a much more entertaining way to see the island than a traditional bus tour. These guided tours last an entire day and feature stops at all of Aruba's most popular tourist attractions, including the California Light House, the Bushiribana gold mills, the Natural Bridge, and Arikok National Park.

These tours are most suitable for teens and adults. When participating in one of these tours, determine in advance what you should bring along. Many of the tour operators strongly recommend that you bring a bathing suit, hat, and sunblock, for example. Contact your hotel's concierge or one of the following tour companies for details:

- **De Palm Tours**: ☎011-297-582-4400, ✎*www.depalm.com*
- **Rancho Daimari**: ☎011-297-587-5674
- **Rancho Notorious**: ☎011-297-586-0508, ✎*www.ranchonotorious. com*

### FOUR-WHEEL-DRIVE TOURS

| Ages up to 5 | Ages 6–15 | Ages 16–20 | Adult | Senior Citizens |
|:---:|:---:|:---:|:---:|:---:|
| N.S. | ★ | ★★★ | ★★★ | ★ |

## Shopping

Downtown Oranjestad offers excellent shopping that goes well beyond the duty-free jewelry stores you traditionally find on Caribbean islands. If you enjoy shopping, plan on spending at least one full day exploring the lovely indoor and open-air shopping areas in Oranjestad. Within the Renaissance Mall & Marketplace, the Seaport Mall, and the Seaport Marketplace, for example, you'll find dozens of designer clothing shops, jewelry stores, boutiques, duty-free shops, and unique gift shops.

Stores are typically open between 8:00 A.M. and 6:30 P.M., but hours vary based on the season and whether a cruise ship is in port. All shopping in Oranjestad is within walking distance of the downtown area. Prices are extremely reasonable, even in the upscale shops and boutiques, and sales are held throughout the year.

### SHOPPING IN ARUBA

| Ages up to 5 | Ages 6–15 | Ages 16–20 | Adult | Senior Citizens |
|:---:|:---:|:---:|:---:|:---:|
| ★ | ★ | ★★ | ★★ | ★★★ |

##  RAINY DAY FUN

Black Hog Bash (☎011-297-587-6625, ✐www.blackhogsaloon.com) is a family-oriented entertainment complex, complete with two eighteen-hole miniature golf courses, a large game room, go-karts, paddleboats, and batting cages. Here you'll also find Alfredo's Just Like Boston's North End Ristorante. At night, there's an adults-only motorcycle bar that's makes for a fun place to enjoy Aruba's upbeat nightlife.

# Making Aruba Your Vacation Destination

If Aruba sounds like your perfect Caribbean getaway, you can find all the planning information you need at the following four excellent Web sites, including details about hotel or resort accommodations:

- **Official Aruba Tourism Web site** ✒*www.aruba.com*
- **Aruba Chamber of Commerce** ✒*www.arubachamber.com*
- **Aruba Cruise Tourism Authority** ✒*www.arubabycruise.com*
- **Aruba Channel** ✒*www.arubachannel.com*

##  JUST FOR PARENTS

Visiting a day spa is a perfect way to relax and pamper yourself while on vacation. Many of Aruba's upscale resorts offer full-service day spas where you can enjoy a massage, body wraps, a facial, and many other relaxing treatments. Prices vary, but they average about what you'd pay in the United States at a mid-priced or upscale day spa. While your kids are enjoying the supervised activities at your resort, sneak away for this memorable indulgence.

Throughout the year, a handful of the resorts in Aruba offer families money-saving "Aruba: One Cool Family Vacation" promotional vacation packages. In addition to discounts on accommodations, this program includes a coupon book offering up to $1,000 in savings on family-friendly activities, tours, and attractions. For details, ask your travel agent or check online at ✒*www.aruba.com/coolprograms/family.html.*

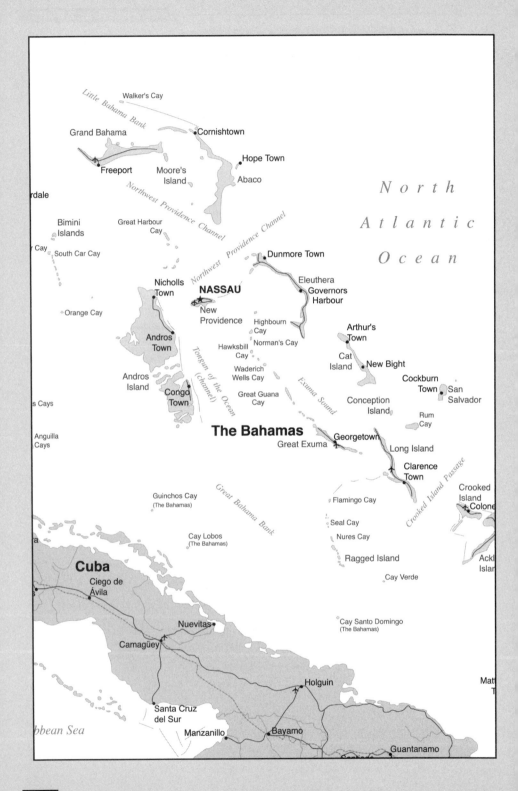

# CHAPTER 7

# The Bahamas

THE ADVERTISEMENTS FOR THIS Caribbean getaway state, "It's better in the Bahamas!" Well, there is truth in advertising, at least in this case! The islands of the Bahamas offer a wonderful, mid-priced vacation destination which is family friendly, and they're easy to get to from the United States. While the Bahamas are comprised of more than 700 islands, only a handful, like Nassau and Grand Bahama Island, are inhabited. This small selection of islands are all popular tourist destinations.

## The Scoop on the Bahamas

Every year, more than 4 million vacationers visit the islands of the Bahamas, including more than 350,000 children traveling with their parents. Because so many young tourists visit the islands, many of the hotels, resorts, and tour operators welcome young people and families by offering a wide range of package deals and special programs, including numerous kid-friendly activities.

If the Bahamas are included in your itinerary, expect to find one of the broadest selections of activities, attractions, and tourist destinations in the Caribbean. Virtually everyone in your family will easily be able to experience things to enjoy during their visit. Vacationers can often find a perfect balance between adventure and relaxation, based on the activities they choose to experience.

The islands of the Bahamas are located just fifty miles off the coast of Florida. By airplane, that translates into a roughly thirty-five-minute flight. If you're departing from New York, Boston, or another East Coast city, the flight time will be around three hours. While many guests travel to the Bahamas by air and spend time exploring the various islands and staying at resorts or hotels, these islands are also extremely popular ports of call for cruise ships.

The 700 islands that make up the Bahamas are scattered throughout a 100,000-square-mile expanse of the Atlantic Ocean. Islands such as New Providence Island, Paradise Island, and Grand Bahama Island, however, tend to be the most popular among vacationers. Nassau is the Bahamian center for commerce, tourism, and industry. Only about thirty islands in this region are widely inhabited, but most of the population lives in the cities of Nassau (on New Providence Island) and Freeport (on Grand Bahama Island). About 80 percent of the population is black, and 17 percent is white.

## ≡FAST FACT

At 2,300 square miles, Andros is among the largest of the Bahamian islands. At the same time, it is one of the least explored.

The primary language spoken in the Bahamas is English. The official currency is the Bahamian dollar, which is equal in value to the U.S. dollar. Both U.S. and Bahamian currency are accepted throughout the islands.

The Bahamas uses 110-volt electricity, which is identical to the power used in the United States. The islands are on Eastern Standard Time, and Daylight Saving Time is observed between April and October.

# A Bit of Bahamas History

The Bahamas were settled back in the ninth century by the Lucayan Indians, who traveled to these islands from northern parts of the Caribbean. They inhabited the islands for close to 600 years. In 1492, Christopher Columbus "discovered" the islands. The Conquistadors later settled on the islands in search of gold. During their occupation, they enslaved and ultimately killed off virtually all of the Lucayans.

In 1647, English settlers in search of religious freedom began living on the Bahamas islands. They named the island of Eleuther, for example, with the Greek word for freedom. The islands of the Bahamas eventually became a British Crown colony. However, during the American Revolution, Spain took temporary possession of the islands until 1783, when Great Britain again took control. In 1834, the British Emancipation Act made the Bahamas a slave-free society.

After almost 250 years of British colonial rule, the Commonwealth of the Bahamas declared its independence on July 10, 1973. The Bahamas now operates under the rule of a parliamentary democracy with a governor-general as head of state. Today, the primary industry in the Bahamas is tourism, which generates about 70 percent of the total gross national product and employs about half of the total workforce.

# The Local Weather

Thanks to the Gulf Stream and prevailing trade winds, visitors can count on a near-perfect year-round temperature in the Bahamas. Temperatures range from 68 to 86 degrees during the day and 62 to 70 degrees at night.

# Getting to the Bahamas

If you are flying to the Bahamas from a major U.S. city, check **TABLE 7-1** for some of the airlines that offer nonstop or connecting service.

**TABLE 7-1**
**AIRLINES SERVING THE BAHAMAS**

| Airline | Phone Number | Web Site | Destination in the Bahamas |
|---|---|---|---|
| American Eagle | 800-433-7300 | www.aa.com | Abaco and Exuma |
| Bahamasair | 800-222-4262 | www.bahamasair.com | Abaco |
| Chalks | 800-424-2557 | www.chalksoceanairways.com | Bimini and Paradise Island |
| Continental Airlines | 800-525-0280 | www.continental.com | Abaco and Eleuthera |
| Delta Airlines | 800-221-1212 | www.delta.com | Abaco, Eleuthera |
| Lynx Air | 888-596-9247 | www.lynxair.com | Abaco, Cat Island, Exuma |
| Twin Air | 954-359-8266 | www.flytwinair.com | Abaco and Eleuthera |
| US Airways | 800-428-4322 | www.usairways.com | Abaco and Eleuthera |

From South Florida, several smaller airlines offer charter service to Nassau, including those listed in **TABLE 7-2**.

**TABLE 7-2**
**AIRLINE SERVICE BETWEEN FLORIDA AND BAHAMAS**

| Airline | Phone Number | Web Site |
|---|---|---|
| Air Flight | 011-954-359-0320 | www.airflightcharters.com |
| Florida Coastal Airlines | 772-468-2255 | www.floridacoastalairlines.com |
| Island Air Charters | 800-444-9904 | www.islandaircharters.com |
| National Air Transport | 561-483-5070 | www.charterservices.net |
| Sky Limo | 866-SKY-LIMO | www.skylimoaircharter.com |

If you're already in Florida and don't want to fly to the Bahamas, high-speed ferry service is available between Florida and Grand

Bahama Island from Discovery Cruise Line (☏800-937-4477), Bahamas Florida Express (☏866-313-3779), and Cloud X (☏866-GO-FERRY).

Upon arriving at the Bahama airport, visitors pass through immigration and customs. Your airline will provide you with an immigration form that must be completed. Half of this form will be submitted upon your arrival to the Bahamas, while another portion of the form will be submitted as you leave. A valid U.S. passport is required for entry. Also acceptable is a government-issued photo ID along with an original birth certificate (with a raised seal). Contact the Bahamas Immigration Department (☏011-242-322-7530) for details.

## ≡FAST FACT

When you're ready to leave the Bahamas by air, be prepared to pay a $15 per-person departure tax, which is typically not included in the price of your airline ticket.

Over a dozen popular cruise lines, including Holland America, Princess Cruise Lines, Carnival Cruise Lines, Disney Cruise Lines, Celebrity Cruise Lines, Royal Caribbean Cruise Lines, and Norwegian Cruise Lines have at least one Bahamian port of call, usually Nassau.

## Getting Around the Bahamas

When it's time to make your way around individual islands, you'll find that taxis, buses (called jitneys), and mopeds are all popular forms of transportation in the Bahamas. To go island-hopping, several smaller airlines offer flights to nearby islands, plus regular ferry service is also available.

### Taking Taxis

Taxis are widely available on the main islands of the Bahamas. Tourists can flag down taxis on the street or pick one up at the many taxi stands located at hotels, resorts, and popular tourist destinations. The taxis operate based on metered rates, which vary by island. Drivers of taxis with the Bahamahost logo on their vehicle have completed specialized training as tour guides from the Bahamas Ministry of Tourism.

From the airport to popular hotel/resort areas, taxi fare can run anywhere from $12 to $25. While rates vary by island, plan on spending about $2 for the first quarter mile and $.30 for each additional quarter mile.

### Ride the Jitneys: Local Bus Service

In the Bahamas, buses are known by the traditional English name of jitney. Jitneys are available on the major islands, including New Providence Island (Nassau), neighboring Paradise Island, and Grand Bahamas Island. Buses run from early morning until about 7:00 P.M. Exact change ($.75 per adult and $.50 per child) is required to board the jitneys, which follow designated routes. This is a convenient and inexpensive way to get around the popular islands.

### Renting a Car

A wide range of rental-car companies provide tourists with rental cars on the popular islands in the Bahamas. Cars can be picked up at the airport, from the downtown Nassau, or on Grand Bahamas Island. A valid U.S. driver's license and major credit card is required.

### Bike and Moped Rentals

Traditional bicycles and motorized mopeds or scooters can be rented at many locations throughout the Bahamas. Rates for a motorized moped or scooter run from about $28 to $32 per day. The scooters and mopeds carry one or two passengers. This is a fun and convenient way for teens and adults alike to get around the island. Whether traveling by bike or moped, keep in mind that cars drive on the *left* side of the street, and you're expected to follow local driving laws. For information about moped or scooter rentals, call Peace & Plenty ✆800-525-2210, ✐*www.peaceandplenty.com.*

# Taking Ferries Between Islands

Regularly scheduled ferry service is available from Nassau to several Bahamian islands, including Spanish Wells and Harbor Islands via Bahamas Ferries (*www.bahamasferries.com*). This ferry service also offers transportation from Nassau to Andros, Exuma, North Eleuthera, and the Abacos. Contact your hotel's concierge or tour desk for information about other ferry services. Independent water taxis are also readily available. Before departing, negotiate the rate with the boat's captain.

# Island-Hopping by Air

To travel among islands via seaplane, contact Chalks Ocean Airways (*www.chalksoceanairways.com*). For information on traditional flights among islands, contact Bahamasair (800-222-4262, *www.bahamasair.com*). This air service flies from Nassau to and from Andros, Long Island, Grand Bahama, Exuma, Eleuthera, the Abacos, Cat Island, Mayaguana, Inagua, and Acklins.

Chapter plane service is available from the airlines listed in **TABLE 7-3**.

**TABLE 7-3**

**AIRLINES SERVICE BETWEEN THE ISLANDS OF THE BAHAMAS**

| Airline | Phone Number | Web Site (if avail.) | Destination(s) from Nassau |
|---|---|---|---|
| Sky Unlimited | 242-377-8993 | www.bahamasair.com | Abaco, Andros, Bimini, Cat Island, Eleuthera, Exuma and Long Island |
| Southern Air | 242-377-2014 | | Abaco, Cat Island, and Eleuthera |
| Western Air | 242-377-2222 | www.westernairbahamas.com | Andros and Bimini |
| Cat Island Air | 242-377-3318 | | Cat Island |
| BH Charters | 242-377-0017 | | Long Island |
| Flamingo Air | 242-377-0354 | www.flamingoair.com | Exuma |

# Where to Stay: Understanding Your Options

When it comes to hotel or resort accommodations in the Bahamas, your choices are plentiful. There are over 15,000 hotel rooms on the islands. Most vacationers who visit the Bahamas stay at a full-service resort or a traditional hotel. A full-service resort offers a wide range of dining options and activities right on the property, which reduces the need for a rental car in order to travel around the islands.

Many of the resorts in the Bahamas offer supervised activity programs and menus for kids and teens. The following sections describe some of the resorts in Nassau, as well as on Paradise Island and Grand Bahama Island, where you'll find these programs.

### The Radisson Cable Beach Resort

✆800-777-7800

✍*www.radisson.com*

Activities for kids aged four to eleven are available at no additional cost.

### The Atlantis Resort

✆800-321-3000

✍*www.atlantisresort.com*

This resort offers the Discovery Channel Camp for kids between the ages of five and twelve. In-room baby-sitting services are also available for a fee.

### Nassau Marriott Resort

✆800-222-7466

✍*www.marriotthotels.com*

The Marriott has a Kids' Club, which caters to kids aged two to twelve. Many supervised indoor and outdoor activities are available throughout the day and evening.

### The Royal Oasis Crown Plaza Golf Resort and Casino

☏800-2-CROWNE (U.S.), ☏011-242-350-7000

✎*www.theroyaloasis.com*

This resort's Garfield-themed kids program offers a wide range of supervised activities, plus a special restaurant just for kids.

### The Viva Wyndham Fortuna Beach Resort

☏877-999-3223

✎*www.wyndham.com*

Here, you'll find the Kids' Club program, which is part of the resort's all-inclusive vacation package. Activities ranging from Ping-Pong to face painting and windsurfing are offered.

# Calling Home and Surfing the Web

The Bahamas is a country with a modern phone system, so making direct-dial calls to the United States is quick and easy, although potentially expensive. The cheapest way to make calls home, without incurring surcharges imposed by your hotel or resort, is to use an international calling card from a public pay phone. Prepaid calling cards can be purchased at stores throughout the island. Shop around for prepaid calling cards offering the best per-minute international rates that ideally have no additional per-call fees.

BaTelCo (✎*www.batelco.com*), which is the premier cell phone service provider throughout the Bahamas, has international roaming agreements with many service providers in the United States. While your cell phone will mostly likely work there, expect to pay international roaming rates of $3 per day, plus at least $1 per minute to make and receive calls using your existing cell phone. If your cell phone from home has international roaming, in order for others to reach you they must first dial ☏242-359-7626 as an access number. Upon hearing the special tone, callers must then dial your regular cell phone number.

If you own an unlocked GSM cell phone, you can purchase a local prepaid SIM chip for $75, which will grant you service while on Grand Bahama Island. The per-minute rate is $.40 during the day and $.20 at night. You can purchase an unlocked GSM phone in the United States for about $199, which includes $45 worth of airtime minutes. Cell phones can also be rented by the day or week.

From many hotels and resorts, as well as Internet cafés, high-speed Internet service is available for a daily or per-minute fee. Some U.S.-based Internet service providers have local access numbers in the Bahamas, so dial-up Internet access is also readily available using a laptop computer equipped with a modem.

## What to See and Do

In the Bahamas, fishing, boating, golfing, and bird-watching are some of the most popular activities that attract tourists from around the world. Bird-watchers of all ages will be pleased to find that the Bahamas is home to the largest nesting colony of West Indian flamingos, as well as more than 200 species of native Caribbean birds. Wildlife sanctuaries and mangrove swamps are the ideal places to go bird-watching in the Bahamas. Guided bird-watching tours are also available, although this is an activity that serious bird-watchers often choose to embark on themselves, with only a guidebook and binoculars in hand. To learn more about bird-watching activities in the Bahamas, contact the Bahamas National Trust (✆809-393-1317, *www.thebahamasnationaltrust.org*).

Other popular water sports available throughout the Bahamas include sailing, windsurfing, parasailing, Jet Skiing, and waterskiing. Equipment rentals and instruction are readily available, usually right on the popular beaches (with no advance reservations required).

## Must-See Activities and Attractions

In addition to virtually all of the activities you read about in Chapter 5, the Bahamas offers visitors several unique activities, attractions, and tourist destinations. Some of those are featured in the following sections, which highlight the top ten must-see attractions and family-friendly activities in the Bahamas.

## Visit Ardastra Gardens

This five-acre park is the home to dozens of pink flamingos, iguanas, monkeys, snakes, exotic birds and other animals. Ardastra Gardens (✐*www.ardastra.com*) is a lovely zoological park, where visitors can view and in many cases interact with the more than 300 resident animals.

The park is open from 9:00 A.M. to 5:00 P.M. daily. Every day at 10:30 A.M., 2:00 P.M., and 4:00 P.M., the zoo hosts its popular flamingo marching show, which kids and teens will enjoy. Young kids will love the petting zoo area. Ardastra Gardens is a great place to spend a few hours in the morning or afternoon.

The admission fee of $20 includes a welcome drink (nonalcoholic), souvenir T-shirt, admission to the park, and bus transportation from your resort. Tickets can be purchased online or by calling ✆011-242-323-5806.

**ARDASTRA GARDENS**

| Ages up to 5 | Ages 6–15 | Ages 16–20 | Adult | Senior Citizens |
|:---:|:---:|:---:|:---:|:---:|
| ★★ | ★★★ | ★★ | ★★ | ★★ |

## Swim with Dolphins at the Dolphin Encounter

On the coast of Paradise Island, the Dolphin Encounter (✐*www.dolphinswims.com*) at Blue Lagoon is the home to the world-famous dolphin star of *Flipper*. It's here that visitors can interact and swim with dolphins. Three different dolphin-encounter packages are offered daily. The $165 per-person Dolphin Encounter program allows you to swim with and interact with bottlenose dolphins for about thirty minutes. A less involved program, called Close Encounter ($85 per person), allows you to stand in shallow water and pet dolphins. Participants must be over the age of six. Children (under age twelve) must be accompanied by a paying adult. At all times, participants wear life jackets and are supervised by dolphin trainers.

For details, call ☎011-242-363-6734. Advance reservations are required. This is one of several places within the Bahamas where visitors can swim or interact with dolphins in an enclosed environment.

**THE DOLPHIN ENCOUNTER**

| Ages up to 5 | Ages 6–15 | Ages 16–20 | Adult | Senior Citizens |
|---|---|---|---|---|
| N.S. | ★★★ | ★★★ | ★★ | ★★ |

## Participate in the Unique "People-to-People" Program

There are many ways to learn about the places you visit while on vacation. You can read books and travel guides, take guided tours, explore on your own, and/or get to know the place directly from the people who live there. Established by the Ministry of Tourism, the People-to-People program enables tourists to learn about the Bahamas directly from the local Bahamians themselves.

This program matches up visitors (in many cases entire families) with more one of more than 1,500 Bahamian volunteers of similar ages and interests. You can spend a day or evening with a volunteer, who will enthusiastically act as your personal tour guide and accompany you on any number of activities.

The People-to-People program is unique to the Bahamas and has been in existence for almost two decades. This program is ideal for solo travelers, couples, and even families. In many cases, the Bahamian volunteers encourage their own kids and teens to participate, allowing families to experience a one-of-a-kind vacation experience. Since many of the volunteers have day jobs or attend school, the local participants prefer to meet up in the evening or on weekends. Visitors and Bahamian volunteers are matched up after the tourist completes a short questionnaire. Matches are made based on shared interests, hobbies, and age. This is not a dating service. What it does offer is a unique opportunity to experience the local culture of the Bahamas and a chance to learn from someone who lives there.

Especially if you're traveling with kids and teens, reservations must be made at least two weeks in advance through the Ministry of Tourism (☎011-242-356-0425, ✐www.bahamas.com). Arrangements can be made for American kids, for example, to visit local schools in the Bahamas in order to meet and interact with local kids their own age.

**THE PEOPLE-TO-PEOPLE PROGRAM**

| Ages up to 5 | Ages 6–15 | Ages 16–20 | Adult | Senior Citizens |
|---|---|---|---|---|
| N.S. | ★★★ | ★★★ | ★★★ | ★★★ |

## Visit the Pirates Museum

According to the Pirates Museum's Web site (✐www.pirates-of-nassau.com), "The Golden Age of Piracy lasted for thirty years, from 1690 to 1720, and Nassau was at its heart." This unique museum, located in downtown Nassau, offers visitors a historically accurate look at the pirates who once sailed the Caribbean and ruled the seas.

Kids and teenagers will especially appreciate the exhibits here because many of them use interactive, multimedia displays or are hands-on exhibits. As guests learn about famous pirates, like Blackbeard and Mary Read, they can explore a detailed, three-quarter-scale pirate ship. Hours of operation are 9:00 A.M. to 6:00 P.M. Monday through Saturday and 9:00 A.M. to noon on Sunday. Adult admission is priced at $12 per person. Kids under the age of twelve enter free. For more information, call ☎011-242-356-3759.

While at this museum, be sure to drop into the Pirates Pub for a themed lunch or snack. You can also check out the gift shop, which sells pirate-themed merchandise and souvenirs.

**THE PIRATES MUSEUM**

| Ages up to 5 | Ages 6–15 | Ages 16–20 | Adult | Senior Citizens |
|---|---|---|---|---|
| N.S. | ★★★ | ★★★ | ★★ | ★ |

## Visit Roxanne the Dolphin or UNEXSO

Roxanne, a famous movie-star dolphin, currently lives in the waters of Grand Bahama Island. Young people in particular will enjoy visiting this large lagoon area, where they can watch dolphins swim around and at times pet them. Also available are boat tours on which you'll see wild dolphins in their natural habitat. Call the Dolphin Experience at ✆888-365-3483.

UNEXSO is a popular dolphin sanctuary on Grand Bahama Island. Here, guests can interact and swim with dolphins, scuba dive, snorkel, and experience a wide range of other water-based activities in a fun-filled atmosphere that's family friendly. Several different admission packages are available, depending on the activities you want to experience. The Dolphin Close Encounter program, for example, is priced at $75 per adult and $37.50 per child. The Swimming with Dolphins program is priced at $169 per person and lasts twenty-five minutes. The Open Ocean Dolphin Experience is priced at $199 per person. All programs offered through UNEXSO are fully supervised. Certified dive masters oversee all scuba-diving programs, including the shallow water dives which are ideal for novice divers over the age of sixteen.

For details, visit the UNEXSO Web site at ✐www.unexso.com, or call ✆242-373-1244 from the Bahamas or ✆800-992-DIVE from the United States.

**MEET ROXANNE THE DOLPHIN OR VISIT UNEXSO**

| Ages up to 5 | Ages 6–15 | Ages 16–20 | Adult | Senior Citizens |
|:---:|:---:|:---:|:---:|:---:|
| N.S. | ★★★ | ★★★ | ★★ | ★★ |

## Take a Kayak Tour

One way to experience the natural beauty of the Bahamas is to take a guided kayak tour along the coastline or through the mangroves. Some tours incorporate snorkeling, and most cater to families. This activity requires participants to be physically fit, since paddling is required.

Kayak tours and kayak rentals are available throughout the Bahamas. Grand Bahama Nature Tours (☏866-440-4542, ✑*www. grandbahamanaturetours.com*) is just one company that offers family-friendly tours incorporating kayaking with biking, swimming, and/or snorkeling. This type of tour is a must for nature-lovers and eco-tourists of all ages. Free transportation is available from your resort. The Lucayan National Park Kayak Nature & Cave Tour ($79 per person), for example, includes a ninety-minute guided kayak tour, lunch on a private beach, swimming, and nature walks. The entire experience lasts about six hours.

**KAYAK TOUR**

| Ages up to 5 | Ages 6–15 | Ages 16–20 | Adult | Senior Citizens |
|:---:|:---:|:---:|:---:|:---:|
| N.S. | ★ | ★★ | ★★★ | ★★★ |

## Visit the Garden of the Groves

This popular tourist attraction is a petting zoo that's most suitable for kids. In addition to being able to interact with and feed animals, visitors are invited to take guided nature walks.

The Garden of the Groves (☏011-242-373-5668, ✑*www. gardenofthegroves.com*) is open daily from 9:00 A.M. to 4:00 P.M. Admission is $9.95 per adult and $6.95 per child. Guided tours cost extra. Discount coupons, however, can be printed from the zoo's Web site. Plan on spending between one and three hours there. At the time of this writing, this attraction was closed for renovations with no opening date announced. It's expected to open again in late 2005 or sometime in 2006. Visit the Garden of the Groves' Web site for details.

**GARDEN OF THE GROVES**

| Ages up to 5 | Ages 6–15 | Ages 16–20 | Adult | Senior Citizens |
|:---:|:---:|:---:|:---:|:---:|
| N.S. | ★★★ | ★ | N.S. | N.S. |

## Go Horseback Riding at Pinetree Stables

For people over the age of eight, horseback-riding tours can be a fun-filled and exciting way to see parts of the Bahamas. Guided tours are available, and no previous riding experience is necessary.

Pinetree Stables (☎011-242-359-4304, *www.pinetree-stables. com*) offers horseback-riding adventures suitable for kids, teens, and adults alike. The two-hour guided trail ride is priced at $75 per person and will take riders through orange groves, along the beach, and through some wetlands. The operators suggest participants wear long pants and comfortable shoes or sneakers. Tours begin daily at 9:00 A.M. and 11:30 A.M., except on Mondays.

**HORSEBACK RIDING**

| Ages up to 5 | Ages 6–15 | Ages 16–20 | Adult | Senior Citizens |
|:---:|:---:|:---:|:---:|:---:|
| N.S. | ★★★ | ★★★ | ★★ | ★ |

## Adventure Tours with East End Adventures

Looking for tours with thrills and nonstop excitement? Well, plan on spending at least one full day with East End Adventures as you embark on an exciting four-wheel-drive ride through several of the eco-zones on Grand Bahama Island.

Once you've checked out the territory by land, East End Adventures will take you on a high-speed boating tour that includes a stop for snorkeling. Special rates for kids are available. A shuttle bus will transport you from your hotel. For details, contact East End Adventures (☎011-242-373-6662, *www.bahamasecotours.com*).

**ADVENTURE TOUR**

| Ages up to 5 | Ages 6–15 | Ages 16–20 | Adult | Senior Citizens |
|:---:|:---:|:---:|:---:|:---:|
| N.S. | ★★ | ★★★ | ★★★ | ★ |

# Discover Atlantis

There are a handful of full-service resorts in the Bahamas, but none is as famous as the Atlantis Resort. Complete with luxury accommodations, a private beach, swimming pools, multiple restaurants, plenty of indoor and outdoor activities, a large casino, a lovely indoor mall, and the world's largest aquarium, the Atlantis Resort is the ideal place to stay or just visit.

Many passengers from cruise ships choose to spend their afternoon here shopping, gaming, visiting the beach, enjoying the lavish day spa, or dining. From the ship, you can take a taxi or water taxi directly to this lovely and incredibly large resort.

The Atlantis Resort is where the rich and famous come to play when visiting the Caribbean. Staying here isn't cheap, but the accommodations are top-notch. Depending on the season, a basic guestroom is priced between $300 and $900 per night. One- or two-bedroom suites can cost $2,200 per night or more.

 **TRAVEL TIP**

> Kids and teens will love swimming at the Atlantis Resort. The swimming pools are huge, with water slides and rides. There's also a lovely private beach where visitors can swim, sunbathe, or rent Jet Skis, for example.

For reservations and information, call ℒ888-528-7155 from the U.S. or ℒ011-242-363-3000 from within the Bahamas.

Guests staying at the Atlantis Resort should definitely take advantage of one of the available meal plans. They will save you a lot of money and will also allow you to enjoy lavish meals within the resort's many fine-dining restaurants for a flat fee.

# Explore "The Dig" At Atlantis

Part of the gigantic Atlantis Resort, "The Dig" is a re-creation of the Lost City of Atlantis. It's the largest outdoor aquarium in the world. Kids, teens, and adults alike will enjoy observing all of the exotic fish and sea creatures on display here.

The admission fee for nonresort guests is $25 per adult and $19 per child, which is a bit expensive for this attraction; however, the exhibits are very impressive. Plan on spending between one and three hours exploring the aquarium and walking under the aquarium through the glass tunnels.

For information, call ✆800-321-3000 or visit the Atlantis Resort's Web site (✍*www.atlantisresort.com*).

**"THE DIG" AT ATLANTIS**

| Ages up to 5 | Ages 6–15 | Ages 16–20 | Adult | Senior Citizens |
|:---:|:---:|:---:|:---:|:---:|
| ★ | ★★★ | ★★★ | ★★ | ★★ |

# Scuba Diving in the Bahamas

Throughout the Bahamas, the average temperature of the emerald-green and turquoise-blue waters is 80 degrees. Underwater visibility often extends up to 200 feet. This is the perfect environment for scuba divers who want to experience stunning underwater coral reefs, shipwrecks, sharks, dolphins, stingrays, and a wide range of colorful tropical fish. Thanks to perfect diving conditions, vacationers will find no fewer than twenty-five different diving destinations. There are more than 1,000 unique dive locations and expeditions available for people of all skill levels within the waters surrounding the Bahamas. Snorkeling tours are also readily available.

## ≡FAST FACT

In the waters off the island of Andros, scuba divers can see the third-largest barrier reef in the world. This is an extremely popular dive spot.

The following is a list of scuba-diving tour operators in Nassau. Many of these companies offer introductory dives and instruction by certified dive masters. Additional companies are available on all of the popular islands throughout the Bahamas. Contact your hotel's concierge or tour desk for details.

- **Bahama Divers, Ltd.** ☏011-242-393-5644
- **Nassau Undersea Adventures** ☏011-242-362-4171
- **Nassau Scuba Centre** ☏011-242-362-1964
- **Divers Haven** ☏011-242-393-0869
- **Dive Dive Dive** ☏011-242-362-1143
- **Sun Divers** ☏011-242-352-8927
- **Sunskiff Divers, Ltd.** ☏011-242-361-4075

# Making the Bahamas Your Vacation Destination

Beyond the city of Nassau and Grand Bahama Island, some of the less-visited islands offer family-friendly activities and attractions. For information about these islands, called the Out Islands, contact the Bahama Out Islands Promotion Board at ☏800-688-4752 (✎*www.bahama-out-islands.com*). The following sections provide a brief description of what you'll find on some of the more popular Out Islands.

### The Abacos

This island offers a wide selection of boating, fishing, and scuba-diving activities. The Abacos is famous for its 20,500-acre parrot reserve, which is a wildlife sanctuary for the endangered Bahamian parrot. If you'll be staying on this island, consider the Green Turtle Club Resort, which offers private, multibedroom villa rentals equipped with kitchenettes.

### Andros

The beaches on this island are typically extremely calm, making them the perfect place for kids to swim and snorkel. A wide range of water-based activities can be found at Small Hope Bay Resort, for example. This island is also home to the Androsia Batik Works, where locally handcrafted, colorful fabrics are produced and made into clothing and other items.

### Bimini

The island of Bimini is famed for Ponce de Leon's 1513 discovery there of what he believed to be the fountain of youth. Legend also states that the lost city of Atlantis could be located somewhere off the shores of this island, which is a popular destination for sport fishing. It's common to see bottlenose dolphins swimming in the ocean just off Bimini's lovely coastline.

### Eleuthera

This island is unique in that the color of the beach sand is pink. Here, people of all ages will enjoy exploring the Hatchet Bay Caves, a network of caves where it's believed that pirates once buried their vast treasures. If you love surfing (or want to learn), Surfer's Beach is one of the best places in the Bahamas to participate in this sport.

### Exuma

One of the popular destinations on the island of Exuma is Thunderball Cave, where guests are invited to take a swim. If this area looks familiar, it's because two James Bond movies were filmed here (*Thunderball* and *Never Say Never Again*). Kayaking, bird watching, boating, scuba diving, and camping are popular activities on this island.

### Cat Island

Step into the Hermitage, which is located at the top of Mount Alvernia, at 207 feet above sea level the highest point in the Bahamas. This island is known for its secluded beaches and lovely beachfront accommodations. Smaller inns and rentable villas, as opposed to traditional hotels, are common here.

### San Salvador

This is the island where Christopher Columbus first set foot in the Bahamas. Several monuments can be found on the island commemorating this event. Another famous landmark here is the Dixon Hill Lighthouse, one of the world's last manually operated lighthouses.

### Long Island

Not to be confused with Long Island, New York, this island in the Bahamas offers some of the best scuba diving and snorkeling locations in the Caribbean. Many of the dive spots are for more experienced divers, since a variety of different species of sharks can often be found in these waters.

### Inagua

This island's main inhabitants aren't people. What you'll find here are more than 60,000 pink flamingos living in their protected natural habitat in Inagua National Park. On this island, you can also enjoy a tour of the Morton Salt Company's facilities, which manufactures and exports over a million pounds of salt per year from the island.

# Gathering Additional Information

The Bahamas Ministry of Tourism (☎011-242-322-7500) operates an informative Web site (✎*www.bahamas.com*) that's useful for planning a family getaway to any of the popular islands in the Bahamas. For additional assistance in finding hotel or resort accommodations, contact the Bahamas Hotel Association (☎242-322-8381, ✎*www. bhahotels.com*).

While it's easy to book your own airfare and hotel accommodations, many tour operators offer complete travel packages to the Bahamas with stops at Nassau, along with Paradise Island, Grand Bahama Island, and other popular destinations in the Bahamas.

In addition to the vacation package departments at Delta Airlines (✆800-233-7260, ✐*www.delta-air.deltavacations.com*) and US Airways Vacations (✆800-455-0123, ✐*www.usairwaysvacations. com*), independent tour operations include the following:

- **Flyaway Vacations** (✆800-832-8383)
- **GoGo Worldwide Vacations** (✆800-821-3731, ✐*www.gogowwv.com*)
- **Paradise Island Vacations** (✆800-722-7466)
- **Apple Vacations** (✆800-727-3550, ✆800-365-2775)
- **Friendly Holidays** (✆800-221-9740)
- **Fun Jet Vacations** (✆800-559-3060)

Working with a tour operator allows you to book a complete travel package, including round-trip airfare, hotel or resort accommodations (at a property of your choice), ground transportation, and sometimes a meal plan.

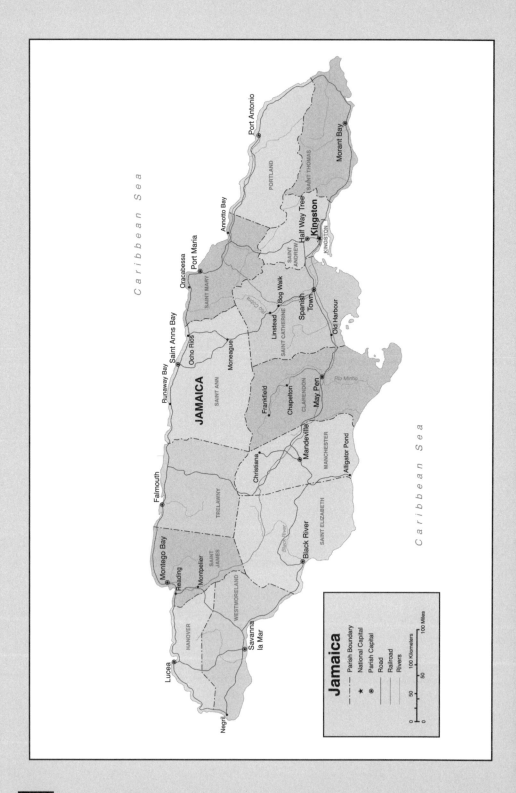

Jamaica

Caribbean Sea

Caribbean Sea

Port Antonio

Morant Bay

PORTLAND

SAINT THOMAS

Annotto Bay

Half Way Tree

Kingston

KINGSTON

SAINT ANDREW

Oracabessa

Port Maria

SAINT MARY

Bog Walk

Linstead

SAINT CATHERINE

Spanish Town

Old Harbour

Saint Anns Bay

Old Cobre

Ocho Rios

Moneague

Runaway Bay

SAINT ANN

JAMAICA

Frankfield

Chapelton

CLARENDON

May Pen

Rio Minho

Falmouth

Christiana

Mandeville

MANCHESTER

Alligator Pond

TRELAWNY

Montego Bay

Reading

Montpelier

SAINT JAMES

Black River

Black River

SAINT ELIZABETH

Lucea

HANOVER

WESTMORELAND

Savanna la Mar

Negril

### Jamaica

- – · – Parish Boundary
- ★ National Capital
- ◉ Parish Capital
  Road
  Railroad
  Rivers

0 50 100 Kilometers
0 50 100 Miles

# CHAPTER 8

# Exploring Jamaica

JAMAICA IS DIVIDED INTO six main areas: Negril, Montego Bay, Ocho Rios, the South Coast, Port Antonio, and Kingston, although the two main tourist areas are Montego Bay (where many of the upscale resorts are located) and Ocho Rios (where one of Jamaica's popular cruise-ship ports is located). Both areas offer tourist attractions, shopping, and plenty of hotels and resorts to choose from. The island itself offers more than 200 miles of beaches.

## By Air or by Sea, Jamaica Is the Place to Be

About a dozen different cruise-ship companies currently use Jamaica as a port of call, including Carnival Cruise Lines, Celebrity Cruises, Holland America, Norwegian Cruise Lines, and Royal Caribbean Cruise Lines. If you're traveling on a cruise line that visits Jamaica, you can typically plan on spending anywhere from several hours to a full day on land enjoying the shopping and nearby tourist attractions.

If you'll be flying to Jamaica, plan to stay at an upscale, all-inclusive resort that's located right on the beach and to leave your resort's property only when embarking on an organized tour with an established tour operator. (It's not a good idea to go off exploring on your own, especially after dark.)

While it continues to be a popular tourist destination, especially among those traveling by cruise ship, Jamaica isn't necessarily an ideal family-oriented vacation spot unless you choose your accommodations wisely. The hotels and resorts in Jamaica vary dramatically in terms of price and quality, yet there isn't always a direct relationship between what you pay and what you get. Thus, while you can't go wrong at a place like the Ritz-Carlton or Half Moon resort, what you can expect from a two- or three-star resort varies greatly in terms of amenities, service, cleanliness, and overall value. This holds true for the restaurants as well.

By staying at an all-inclusive resort, you can stay on the property for the majority of your vacation. You can enjoy the activities and amenities of the resort, dine at the resort's restaurants, and venture out on half-day or full-day tourist or shopping excursions that are planned and coordinated by the resort. This is definitely the easiest and safest way to enjoy Jamaica, especially if you're traveling with kids or teens.

When it comes to vacationing in Jamaica, how much fun you have and how much extra money you spend will be directly related to the place you stay. Instead of relying on travel brochures and ads, it's important to seek out reliable referrals for accommodations, since you'll quickly discover you can't always rely on travel brochures for accurate information. When referring to a resort's offering, terms like "all inclusive" are used very loosely here. If you'll be staying at an all-inclusive resort in Jamaica, plan on upgrading each person you're traveling with to the resort's premium or add-on package for activities and meals.

## ═══FAST FACT

Jamaica was where the concept of all-inclusive resorts was born. These packages typically include guestroom accommodations, all the food you can eat, beverages (sometimes including alcohol), and unlimited participation in certain activities on the resort's property.

By paying up front for the offered upgrade or premium package, you will usually enjoy much better food in a larger variety of restaurants or dining rooms. These upgrades are not always mentioned in brochures or Web sites, so be sure to ask about them when you check in. Premium packages will also save you money on activities, since you'll probably discover that some activities at the all-inclusive resort aren't actually included in the base price for your vacation package. The add-on cost can be anywhere from $10 to $50 per person, per day, but at many all-inclusive resorts in Jamaica the upgrade is a must if you want to get the most out of your vacation experience.

##  TRAVEL TIP

If you want to travel relatively easily and quickly between Kingston, Montego Bay, and Ocho Rios, Air Jamaica Express (✆800-523-5585) offers regularly scheduled air service among these cities.

Jamaica is definitely a more adult-oriented vacation destination, with resorts like Hedonism III being popular destinations for more open-minded adults. In Jamaica, you'll find a handful of very upscale resorts suitable for families, as well as much lower-end family-oriented all-inclusive resorts. These include SuperClub's StarFish Resort, where you can expect to pay for a wide range of extras during your stay.

The shopping in Jamaica includes an abundance of duty-free shops offering everything from jewelry and perfume to designer watches. There are also several popular outdoor markets, such as Craft Park in Ocho Rios, where locally made crafts are sold by hundreds of exhibitors in a flea-market–style atmosphere. Here, negotiating is definitely the way to buy.

# The Scoop on Jamaica

The island of Jamaica encompasses 4,244 square miles and is located about 200 miles from the Florida coastline. It is a vacation destination that requires some common sense in order to thoroughly enjoy. In other words, as long as you stay around the populated tourist areas, and stick with your reliable tour guide, chances are you will have a safe and pleasant stay.

Unfortunately, the sale and use of drugs is rather prevalent on Jamaica. If you're traveling with teens, don't be surprised if people approach them trying to sell them marijuana, even on the beach at your resort.

The U.S. dollar is widely accepted in Jamaica; the local currency is the Jamaican dollar. ATM machines and full-service banks can be found throughout the island, but be prepared to pay a hefty surcharge to withdraw money from independent ATMs not affiliated with a major bank. The US$ Cool Cash ATMs (✆888-266-5227), for example, dispense U.S. dollars, but they also charge a $6 per transaction fee. Major credit cards are widely accepted in stores, hotels, resorts, tourist attractions, and restaurants.

Throughout the country, standard 110-volt electricity is available (the same as that used in the United States). However, some older resorts still use 220-volt electricity, which means you'll need to use special power adapters to plug in any personal electronics you bring from home (camcorder, laptop computer, electric shaver, and so on). Be sure to check with your resort in advance if you'll need to plug in personal electronics.

Rental cars are readily available in Jamaica, but the roads aren't always easy to navigate. Cars drive on the left side of the road, and road signs aren't plentiful. In some areas, road conditions are downright awful, although a major highway improvement project is underway throughout the island. You're definitely better off relying on tour buses and taxis to get around. While Jamaica does not observe Daylight Saving Time, it does go by Eastern Standard Time.

As a popular tourist destination, Jamaica boasts over 25,000 hotel rooms, many of which are found within upscale resorts, all-inclusive resorts, traditional hotels, private villas, and smaller inns.

# Five Tips for Traveling with Kids in Jamaica

Young kids tend to have special needs while on vacation. The better prepared you are to deal with these, the better your vacation will be for the whole family. Here are a few tips:

1. When packing for your kids, keep in mind that much of their time will probably be spent at the beach. Pack light. Include multiple bathing suits, but also pack items to protect your child from the sun. Sunblock, a hat, and sunglasses are an absolute must! A light jacket will also come in handy in Jamaica.

2. Always have at least one change of clothes (or a dry bathing suit) available for your child, especially if you'll be visiting a beach that's not within walking distance of your hotel room. It's also a great strategy to bring at least one or two dry towels with you. Many of the activities you may choose to experience in Jamaica involve getting wet and/or swimming.

3. Pack at least two pairs of comfortable walking/activity shoes, such as sneakers for each child. If they own a pair of rubber-soled beach shoes or water shoes, these will come in handy, not just at the beach but when participating in activities like climbing the Dunn's River Falls.

4. Pack games, books, and activities for your children to entertain themselves during downtime. A handheld video game system as well as beach toys (such as shovels and buckets) are definitely things you should bring along. You might also want to bring along the travel version of one or two popular board games. One of the most popular games among Jamaican children is dominoes.

5. Finding familiar snack foods in Jamaica can be a challenge. If your child has a favorite packaged snack food, consider bringing an ample supply with you.

# A Bit of Jamaica History

When Christopher Columbus landed at Jamaica in 1494, the island was then called Xaymaca, which means "an island of wood and water." Back then, the island was home to local Indians, known as the Tainos.

The Tainos opened their island to Spanish explorers and settlers, but this proved to be disastrous for the locals, who soon found themselves annihilated. Columbus himself spent some of his later life in Jamaica, which was ultimately passed to his son, Diego, upon his death.

In 1655, the British took control. By 1739, the island won itself some autonomy, which it's held ever since. The island received its official independence from the United Kingdom in August of 1962 and is now governed by a constitutional parliamentary democracy. Today, Jamaica is inhabited by over 2.6 million people who come from a wide range of cultural backgrounds, including Africa, Europe, East India, China, and the Middle East.

The majority of Jamaicans speak fluent English, but the local dialect (or patois) is more common. While the island is a popular tourist destination, it's also famous for its reggae music, thanks in large part to the popularity of Bob Marley. The island is also known for its sugarcane, bananas, coffee, cocoa, citrus, poultry, sugar, rum, and alumina (the main ingredient in aluminum).

# The Local Weather

Throughout the year, the average temperature in Jamaica is a lovely 82 degrees. Inland, you'll find Jamaica offers a tropical climate, while temperatures can drop to about 50 degrees up in the mountains.

# Getting to Jamaica

Many cruise-ship passengers have an opportunity to visit Jamaica for a day or so on one of their ports of call. This is probably the best way to get a taste of Jamaica, although even if you arrive by cruise ship, it's important to plan your time here carefully and hire only established tour operators.

If you travel to Jamaica by air, you will land at one of two international airports. The Norman Manley International Airport is located fifteen miles from Kingston, and the more popular Sangster International Airport is three miles from Montego Bay (and sixty-seven miles from Ocho Rios). Some of the major airlines that service these airports include Air Canada, Air Jamaica, American Airlines, British Airways, Continental Airlines, Delta Air Lines, Northwest Airlines, and US Airways.

Both international airports in Jamaica are large, relatively modern, and well equipped, offering all of the services you'd expect from a major U.S. airport. When arriving in Jamaica, be prepared to present your valid passport along with your return airline ticket and the appropriate, fully completed customs declaration form and immigration form, which will be provided by your airline. Your luggage will need to pass through customs.

Upon leaving Jamaica by air, each passenger will be required to pay a departure tax of about $28. This fee isn't always included in airfares or travel packages.

 **TRAVEL TIP**

For up-to-date flight information for flights in and out of the Norman Manley International Airport, go online to ✐www. manley-airport.com.jm.

# Getting Around Jamaica

Jamaica is the third-largest island in the Caribbean, but you won't have any trouble finding several modes of transportation, including buses, taxis, bikes, and other for-hire services. In Kingston, the capital, buses are large and air-conditioned, but outer areas tend to be serviced by smaller, more crowded buses. Families visiting Jamaica would probably be best served by taking a taxi to their destination.

### Taking Taxis

All taxi fares are predetermined by the local government and are based upon distance traveled. Before you get in a taxi, agree on a fare in advance based on the distance you'll be traveling. Make sure the driver plans to adhere to the predetermined and published rates. As with virtually everything in Jamaica, be prepared to negotiate a bit, and don't be surprised if the car driver requests a larger tip. Also be sure you have a destination in mind before getting in a cab. Don't allow the cab driver to recommend destinations, since the drivers are often paid by businesses to lure customers.

## ≡FAST FACT

The only taxis you should take in Jamaica are marked with a red "PP" license plate (for "public passenger" vehicle). These are licensed taxis. Unlicensed taxis are plentiful and may be cheaper, but these drivers are usually not insured.

### Renting a Car in Jamaica

In Jamaica, you'll find Hertz (✆www.hertz.com), Dollar Rent-A-Car (✆www.dollar.com), Avis (✆www.avis.com), and Thrifty (✆www. thrifty.com) along with a handful of other well-known and locally operated car-rental agencies. As you've already read, however, renting a car in Jamaica is not recommended if you're not extremely familiar with the territory.

The roads there are bad and difficult to navigate. Cars drive on the left side of the road, and drivers don't always pay attention to speed limits. Beyond those shortcomings, there are few road signs to help you navigate. You'll also find daily rental fees to be expensive. They start at $60 per day, plus gas and daily insurance.

##  TRAVEL TIP

When evaluating the fee for a rental car, determine if the cost of the required daily insurance is included in the quoted price. Also make sure unlimited mileage is included with the rental agreement. Finally, don't forget to calculate in the cost of gas.

An alternative to renting a car in order to go sightseeing is to hire a taxi for an entire day. This will cost anywhere from $100 to $200, depending on where you travel. Be sure to agree in advance on a half-day or full-day rate.

It does make sense to rent a car if you want to explore the territory between Montego Bay and Ocho Rios (an almost three-hour drive) or any two or three of Jamaica's other cities, which are relatively far apart. In addition to daily rental fees and insurance, the per-gallon price of gas in Jamaica is high. Flying between cities may be a more suitable option for your family. If you do decide to drive, however, here are the estimated driving times between several cities:

- **Montego Bay to Kingston**: 3.5 to 4 hours (119 miles)
- **Montego Bay to Negril**: 1 hour (52 miles)
- **Montego Bay to Ocho Rios**: 1½ to 2 hours (67 miles)
- **Ocho Rios to Negril**: 3 hours (117 miles)
- **Kingston to Ocho Rios**: 1½ to 2 hours (54 miles)
- **Kingston to Negril**: 4 hours (153 miles)

# Where to Stay: Understanding Your Options

If you'll be staying in Jamaica, your two primary options are to find a traditional hotel, where you pay a per-night fee for accommodations plus extra for meals and activities, or an all-inclusive resort.

As you read in Chapter 3, all-inclusive resorts offer an excellent option for families. The trick is to choose a resort that's well equipped. In Jamaica, you typically get what you pay for. The good thing about all-inclusive resorts is that even tips are included. One thing you'll find in Jamaica is that people who assist or serve you, including taxi drivers, waiters, doormen, salespeople, and tour guides, are not at all shy about asking for tips or asking for larger tips when a tip is offered. This can be disconcerting for some tourists. Tipping, however, is never allowed at all-inclusive resorts.

## ⩵FAST FACT

The majority of resorts, including virtually all of the all-inclusive resorts, offer baby-sitting services at a per-child, per-hour rate (typically under $10 per hour, per child). Most of the resorts also offer supervised, organized programs for kids and teens.

### SuperClubs Resorts in Jamaica

SuperClubs (✆800-859-SUPER, ✍*www.superclubs.com*) has the most all-inclusive resorts in Jamaica, operated under the StarFish, Breezes, Grand Lido, and Hedonism brands.

The StarFish Resorts are considered family oriented, but they are also the least expensive and offer the lowest level of amenities and service. Unless you're looking for a no-frills vacation experience, consider upgrading to one of the nicer all-inclusive resorts.

The Breezes Resorts offer mid-priced accommodations and improved service, a larger selection of amenities, more activities, and vastly more comfortable guestrooms. The Breezes Resorts are a nice option for families and are reasonably priced.

The Grand Lido Resorts offer first-class accommodations at a premium price. Here, you can expect to find an upscale day spa, golf course, spacious guestrooms, finer dining facilities, and additional services, like twenty-four-hour in-room dining and an abundance of available water sports.

Finally, the Hedonism III resort in Jamaica, which is also operated by SuperClubs, is definitely for adults only. Don't even consider visiting this resort with kids or teens.

Sandals' Beaches resort (☎888-SANDALS, *www.sandals. com*) is another highly respected, all-inclusive resort which is family friendly. As with all of the popular resorts, be sure to shop around for discounted packages. These are often available online, from travel agents, and directly from the resort companies.

## 🧳 TRAVEL TIP

The benefit to staying at an all-inclusive resort is that usually, everything is readily available right on the resort's property. The drawback is that you're not necessarily encouraged to leave the property. If you want to explore, you need to rent a car or pay extra to participate in an organized tour.

If you're looking for the ultimate in top-of-the-line luxury accommodations, the Ritz-Carlton Resort (☎800-241-3333, *www. ritzcarlton.com*) or the Half Moon Resort (☎800-626-0592, *www. halfmoon.com.jm*) in Montego Bay are your best options in Jamaica.

# Calling Home and Surfing the Web

No matter where you travel in the Caribbean, including Jamaica, be prepared to pay a hefty per-minute premium to call the United States from your hotel or resort. Prices can start at $3 to $5 per minute and go up from there. There are even surcharges if you call collect or use a prepaid calling card (which is strongly recommended).

If you know you'll be making a lot of international calls from Jamaica, especially if you're staying at an all-inclusive resort where public pay phones aren't readily available, consider renting a cell phone. You can also find out ahead of time if your existing cell phone offers international roaming (most do).

Purchasing a prepaid SIM card for your unlocked GSM cell phone is a very cost-effective option for making calls to America. Rates for calls to the United States can be as low as $.30 per minute. DigiCel (✆888-DIGICEL), for example, offers a prepaid SIM card called DigiFlex. For details, go online to ✐*www.digiceljamaica.com* or ✐*www.cellularabroad.com.*

Virtually all hotels and resorts offer high-speed Internet access, usually from a kiosk or computer workstation located in the main lobby. For this, you'll either pay a flat per-minute rate or be required to prepay for fifteen or thirty minutes of surfing time. E-mail is a cost-effective way to communicate with friends and relatives in America while you're traveling in Jamaica.

# Must-See Activities and Attractions

As you'd expect from any tropical getaway, Jamaica offers a wide range of water sports, beach-based activities, and plenty to see and do on land. The trick is choosing how to best spend your time. If you're staying at an all-inclusive resort, be sure to consult with the tour desk to determine what tours, activities, and excursions are available. There is typically a flat, per-person fee for each tour that you take off the resort property.

At your resort, chances are you can participate in a wide range of activities, such as snorkeling, scuba diving, parasailing, windsurfing, boating, surfing, boogie boarding, body surfing, swimming, golf, or a treatment at a day spa. Many of the more upscale resorts, including some operated by SuperClubs, now offer eighteen-hole golf courses. Once you've experienced what your resort has to offer, get ready to explore the rest of the island. You'll probably discover that it will be these half-day or full-day activities outside of your resort that generate the most exciting vacation memories.

##  TRAVEL TIP

When choosing optional tours or excursions (at an extra charge), be sure to talk to other tourists staying at your resort to find out what their experiences were like. Seek out recommendations and referrals, and don't rely only on suggestions from the tour desk operator or hotel concierge.

The following sections provide information about the top ten must-see activities and attractions you'll enjoy most, especially if you're traveling with kids or teens.

### Swim with Dolphins at Dolphin Cove

This activity is mainly of interest to teenagers and adults, although for kids (ages six to 12), the Jungle Trail offers a chance to interact with exotic animals. Dolphin Cove, which is located in Ocho Rios, offers a chance to swim with dolphins in a closed-in, supervised environment. While somewhat costly, this is a fun and highly memorable experience. Dolphin Cove allows participants to actually interact with dolphins, rather than simply pet or observe them.

Dolphin Cove is located within a two-minute drive from the ever-popular Dunn's River Falls. When swimming and interacting with the dolphins, it's important to leave any and all jewelry behind. It's best to leave these valuables within a safe at your hotel.

Also, photo opportunities using your own equipment are limited, so be prepared to pay a bit extra for souvenir photos.

Reservations for the Dolphin Cove program are strongly recommended. Programs begin daily at 9:30 A.M., 11:30 A.M., 1:30 P.M., and 3:30 P.M. Food is available on the premises. After the initial orientation program, the actual swim with the dolphins lasts about thirty memorable minutes. A life jacket and fins are provided to all participants. Included in the price is admission to Dolphin Cove's Jungle Trail, where you'll get an up-close view of a wide range of exotic birds, iguanas, and other creatures.

Three different dolphin swim and interaction programs are available at different price points. Plan on spending at least $50 per person for the swimming-with-dolphins experience. For more information, call ✆011-876-974-5335 or visit ✐*www.dolphincovejamaica.com*. For a full day of excitement, combine a trip to Dolphin Cove with a visit to Dunn's River Falls.

**DOLPHIN COVE**

| Ages up to 5 | Ages 6–15 | Ages 16–20 | Adult | Senior Citizens |
|:---:|:---:|:---:|:---:|:---:|
| ★ | ★★ | ★★★ | ★★★ | ★ |

## Climb Dunn's River Falls

One of the least expensive, yet most memorable experiences you'll have in Jamaica is climbing the famous Dunn's River Falls. Located within a park, a tour guide will help you climb up more than 600 feet of cascading waterfalls surrounded by a lush tropical setting. This activity is suitable for kids over the age of ten, and is only recommended for people who are physically fit. Be sure to bring a bathing suit and a change of clothes, or at least a dry towel—you're going to get soaked on the trek up the waterfall!

It's necessary to wear rubber-soled beach shoes or sneakers for this adventure, as many of the rocks are very slippery. Shoe rentals are available for an additional fee. Admission to Dunn's River Falls is only $10 per adult and $8 per child.

Food offerings are limited at this park, so eat something before you leave your hotel. As you exit the park, you'll walk through a marketplace area where dozens of local crafters will try to lure you over to purchase a souvenir. These vendors can be a bit pushy and will make statements like, "I recognize you from your resort, come see what I have to offer." They'll know where you're staying from your tour guide or resort ID bracelet, so don't be tricked.

If you plan on bringing a camera on this adventure, either allow your tour guide to hold it and take photos for you (yes, you'll need to tip the guide), or purchase a one-time-use waterproof camera. It's very easy to slip and drop your camera equipment into the water as you climb the falls.

Dunn's River Falls and Park is an exciting adventure that takes about ninety minutes to enjoy. The park itself is open from 8:30 A.M. to 5:00 P.M. daily. On Wednesdays, Thursdays, and Fridays, the park opens at 7:00 A.M. (when cruise ships are in port). No reservations are needed, but it's best to coordinate your visit through your hotel or cruise ship to ensure you get a reputable guide.

For more information, call ☎011-876-974-2857 or go online to ✍*www.dunnsriverja.com*. When you visit Dunn's River Falls and Park, consider combining your trip with a visit to Dolphin Cove. You might also choose to spend a few hours shopping at the relatively new and modern outdoor mall, called Island Village (located less than a three-minute drive from the falls). Island Village offers a movie theater, food, several upscale duty-free shops, a handful of local stores and boutiques, plus an Internet café and the Reggae XPlosion museum.

## DUNN'S RIVER FALLS

| Ages up to 5 | Ages 6–15 | Ages 16–20 | Adult | Senior Citizens |
|:---:|:---:|:---:|:---:|:---:|
| N.S. | ★★ | ★★★ | ★★★ | ★ |

## Explore the River Walk

If you want to be an outdoor explorer and adventurer for a day and hike around extremely lush and tropical settings, cross suspended bamboo bridges, and dive into small lakes with refreshing and beautiful waterfalls, you'll definitely want to visit the River Walk.

Trained and knowledgeable tour guides are available. Special tour packages provide for a full day's worth of sightseeing, hiking, exploring, and eating. Round-trip transportation from your resort can be arranged and included in the admission package.

For details, call ✆888-957-5555 (U.S.) or ✆011-876-957-3444 (Jamaica), or visit the park's Web site at ✍*www.theriverwalk. netfirms.com.* The River Walk is most convenient if you're staying in or near Negril or Montego Bay. Visiting the River Walk involves a lot of somewhat strenuous physical activity. It's definitely recommended for physically fit people over the age of twelve.

**THE RIVER WALK**

| Ages up to 5 | Ages 6–15 | Ages 16–20 | Adult | Senior Citizens |
|---|---|---|---|---|
| N.S. | ★ | ★★★ | ★★★ | ★ |

## Visit Green Grotto Caves

Green Grotto Caves offers a unique opportunity to explore a network of limestone caves, some of which descend to more than 100 feet underground. Guests will encounter underground lakes filled with crystal-clear water and be able to explore many connected chambers and passageways, all with a tour guide. Be sure to wear comfortable shoes or hiking boots.

Admission is $20 for adults and $10 for children. The caves are open daily, from 9:00 A.M. to 4:00 P.M. For details, call ✆011-876-973-2841 or go online to ✍*www.greengrottocaves.com.*

Kids and teens in particular will enjoy this activity, but it also offers a beautiful and unusual place for adults to explore. Be sure to bring a camera! The Green Grotto Caves are located in Discovery Bay, which is conveniently located between Montego Bay and Ocho Rios.

## THE GREEN GROTTO CAVES

| Ages up to 5 | Ages 6–15 | Ages 16–20 | Adult | Senior Citizens |
|:---:|:---:|:---:|:---:|:---:|
| ★ | ★★★ | ★★★ | ★★ | ★★ |

## Experience Chukka Cove Adventure Tours

This all-in-one, outdoor adventure complex is a fun place for an entire family to spend a full day. With locations in Falmouth, Runaway Bay, Ocho Rios, and Boscobel, Chukka Cove facilities offer horseback riding, Jeep safari tours, bike-riding tours, river tubing, and other activities all in one place. You can pick and choose which activities and tours you want to experience. For example, the horseback-riding tours last about three hours. No previous riding experience is required. Children, in particular, will enjoy the river-tubing adventure.

For older guests, an underwater SeaTrek (✑*www.sea-trek.com*) experience is available. You can experience an undersea adventure without any scuba diving or swimming experience. SeaTrek allows you to put on a special helmet and explore underwater while breathing normally. It's called a "helmet diving" experience, and the only skills you'll need are the ability to breath normally and walk. This unique adventure lasts about three hours and is suitable for anyone over the age of eight.

For more information, call ✆011-876-972-2506 or visit the Chukka Cove Adventure Tours Web site (✑*www.chukkacove.com*).

## CHUKKA COVE ADVENTURE TOURS

| Ages up to 5 | Ages 6–15 | Ages 16–20 | Adult | Senior Citizens |
|:---:|:---:|:---:|:---:|:---:|
| N.S. | ★★ | ★★★ | ★★★ | ★ |

## Horseback Riding

Throughout Jamaica, there are many equestrian centers and stables offering experienced and novice riders alike a chance to explore the beaches and landscaping of Jamaica by horseback. These are guided tours. Be sure to dress accordingly and to wear a hat and sunblock. To determine what horseback riding tours are available near where you're staying, contact your hotel's tour desk or concierge. One-, two- or three- hour rides, along with half-day and full-day tours are typically available.

**HORSEBACK RIDING**

| Ages up to 5 | Ages 6–15 | Ages 16–20 | Adult | Senior Citizens |
|:---:|:---:|:---:|:---:|:---:|
| N.S. | ★★ | ★★★ | ★★★ | ★ |

## Duty-Free Shopping

Like many Caribbean destinations, Jamaica is a haven for duty-free shoppers looking for bargains on jewelry, liquor, perfume, cigarettes, cigars, and designer watches. The trick to finding the best bargains is to decide, in advance, what specific things you're looking for and to price those items in the United States (including sales taxes).

It's important to research specific models numbers and styles, when appropriate. Next, when you get to Jamaica, start shopping around and negotiate. No matter what duty-free shop you peruse, the prices are always negotiable. Also, you'll find that many of the shops have similar inventories, which makes your bargaining position that much stronger.

Before making your purchase, visit at least a handful of stores. You'll often receive bigger discounts if you pay by cash or traveler's check. However, all duty-free shops accept credit cards. Keep in mind that the salespeople can be a bit pushy, so stand your ground and purchase only what you're in the market to buy.

When purchasing a designer watch, for example, be sure that all of the watch's original packaging, certificate of authenticity, and warranty card are included with your purchase. By shopping around and negotiating, you can typically save between 20 and 50 percent from suggested retail prices in America on name-brand designer merchandise, from companies like Gucci, Montblanc, Movado, Rolex, Cartier, Versace, and TAG Heuer, as well as on diamonds, gold, silver, platinum, and other gemstones or jewelry.

Stores are typically open Monday through Friday, between 8:30 A.M. and 4:30 P.M. On Saturdays, stores tend to be open from 8:00 A.M. until 1:00 P.M. They're closed on Sundays. (Hours vary greatly depending on whether you're visiting a major tourist area during a peak travel season or whether there are cruise ships in port.)

**DUTY-FREE SHOPPING IN JAMAICA**

| Ages up to 5 | Ages 6–15 | Ages 16–20 | Adult | Senior Citizens |
|---|---|---|---|---|
| N.S. | ★ | ★ | ★★ | ★★ |

## Shopping for Locally Made Crafts

No matter where you travel in Jamaica, chances are good you will encounter local residents trying to sell you a wide range of hand-crafted items. You'll be approached at the beach, near all tourist attractions, and in all of the craft marketplaces throughout the island. Artwork, wooden sculptures, and jewelry are among the common offerings. In fact, you'll find very little variety as you explore the various outdoor craft marketplaces.

Prices for handcrafted goods tend to be extremely reasonable and negotiable. The people selling the goods, however, are often pushy and often don't like to take no for an answer from tourists.

As you shop around for souvenirs, keep in mind that you are not allowed to take any living creatures, fruits, or vegetables back home to the United States. Similarly, be sure you don't purchase any products made from protected or endangered wildlife. Even if your conscience won't bother you, customs officials will. Also, depending on how you'll be traveling, think about how you'll safely get your purchases home safely (especially if they're fragile).

**SHOPPING FOR CRAFTS IN JAMAICA**

| Ages up to 5 | Ages 6–15 | Ages 16–20 | Adult | Senior Citizens |
|---|---|---|---|---|
| N.S. | ★★ | ★★ | ★★ | ★★ |

 **TRAVEL TIP**

Hair-weaving, braiding, and hair wrapping are all art forms commonly practiced in Jamaica. Female tourists (especially kids and teens) love having their hair braided or wrapped with colorful threads and beads. As with most services, the cost varies dramatically, so be sure to agree on a price *before* you get started.

### Visit the Reggae XPlosion (Reggae Hall of Fame)

Located within the Island Village shopping area (a modern outdoor mall), you'll find a movie theater, Internet café, restaurants, shops, and the Reggae XPlosion, the Reggae Hall of Fame (☎011-876-675-8895, ✎*www.islandjamaica.com*). For fans of reggae music, this is a self-paced, indoor museum that features videos, music, photos, and plenty of memorabilia. The nearby gift shop sells a large selection of reggae CDs. (Despite his worldwide popularity, Bob Marley is not the biggest reggae star in Jamaica, where scores of talented musicians can be found.)

Explore the history of reggae and its impact on the world as you walk through this ever-changing museum. Plan on spending about an hour in the museum itself. This stop will mainly be of interest to teens and adults, not kids. You can easily spend three or more hours exploring Island Village, which is the nicest shopping area on the island.

**REGGAE XPLOSION (REGGAE HALL OF FAME)**

| Ages up to 5 | Ages 6–15 | Ages 16–20 | Adult | Senior Citizens |
|---|---|---|---|---|
| N.S. | ★ | ★★ | ★★ | ★★ |

### Explore Montego Bay's "Hip Strip"

The "Hip Strip" (Gloucester Avenue) in Montego Bay offers a collection of stores, restaurants, bars, and outdoor activities (right on the beach) that are designed for tourists. This area is best visited in the afternoon or evening. It'll mainly appeal to older teens and adults. Also in Montego Bay, you'll find an abundance of duty-free shopping.

**MONTEGO BAY'S "HIP STRIP"**

| Ages up to 5 | Ages 6–15 | Ages 16–20 | Adult | Senior Citizens |
|:---:|:---:|:---:|:---:|:---:|
| N.S. | ★ | ★★ | ★★★ | ★★ |

# Scuba Diving in Jamaica

Throughout the Caribbean, including the waters surrounding Jamaica, you'll find many popular dive sites for novice and certified scuba divers alike. For a list of dive shops, check out ✍*www.jamaicans. com.* You can also contact your resort's tour desk or concierge for referrals. Equipment is provided by the dive operator. For additional information about scuba-diving opportunities in and around Jamaica, go online to ✍*www.resortdiver.com.*

# Making Jamaica Your Vacation Destination

If you plan accordingly and use some caution, you'll find Jamaica a fun-filled and very beautiful place to visit. There's plenty to do both on land and in the water.

Be aware that crime is an issue, especially after dark in cities like Kingston. As you explore, plan on staying in popular tourist areas, and when possible, stick with your local tour guide. The hotels and resorts are generally very safe. In case of an emergency, dial 119 (not 911) to reach the police from any public phone.

One trick for having a well-planned and safe vacation in Jamaica is to take organized tours from respectable tour operators when you plan to go exploring. Your hotel or resort's tour desk or concierge can offer advice and help you make arrangements.

Also, if you're staying at an all-inclusive resort, where your package includes all food, drinks, accommodations, and activities, understand exactly what you're getting for your flat fee. Determine in advance what extras you'll have to pay once you actually check into the resort itself in case you decide you want to enjoy the better restaurants or participate in all of the activities offered.

## ═══FAST FACT

No matter how much you're paying for an all-inclusive resort experience, package prices rarely include treatments at the resort's day spa, tours, scuba diving, or activities outside the resort's property. To participate in these popular activities, you will almost always have to pay extra.

Contact the Jamaica Tourist Board to learn more about Jamaica, to obtain more detailed hotel or resort recommendations, or to obtain information about many of the other tourist attractions this popular vacation destination offers (℡800-223-4582, ℡212-856-9727, ✐*www.jamaicatravel.com*). On the island of Jamaica itself, the tourist board has several offices you can visit. They're located in Kingston (℡011-876-929-9200), Montego Bay (℡011-876-952-4425), Negril (℡011-876-957-4243) and Ocho Rios (℡011-876-974-2570).

Other useful Web sites include Go Jamaica (✐*www.go-jamaica.com*), Jamaicans (✐*www.jamaicans.com*) and the SuperClubs Web site (✐*www.superclubs.com*).

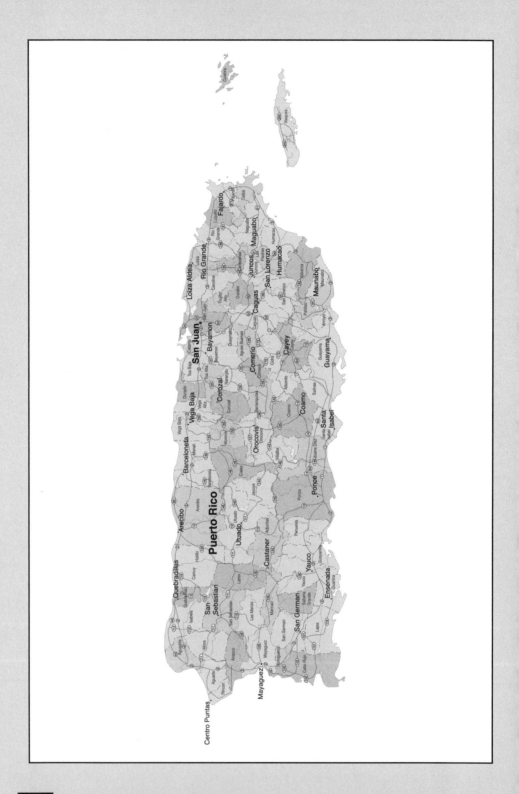

# CHAPTER 9

# *Puerto Rico*

PUERTO RICO IS THE fourth-largest island in the Caribbean. It measures 100 miles long and thirty-five miles wide, covering more than 3,500 square miles, . While most people are familiar with San Juan, which is the most popular tourist destination on the island, vacationers can also find plenty of resorts, hotels, and tourist attractions all over the island.

One thing you'll notice immediately upon arriving in Puerto Rico is that this island nicely combines old and new. The resort accommodations, for example, tend to be ultramodern, while in many areas, you'll be surrounded by historic sights, natural (undeveloped) landscapes, lovely beaches, lush forests, or even mountains.

## San Juan: The Hub of the Caribbean

Because of its location, San Juan has become a hub for the entire Caribbean. Thus, if you're traveling to many other Caribbean islands by air, there's a good chance you'll have a stopover in San Juan. If you have time, the trip from the airport to Old San Juan (the historic, tourist, dining and shopping area of San Juan) is a quick one, so you can easily enjoy the city for a few hours or more if your travel plans allow.

Also, many popular cruises either originate from San Juan or feature San Juan as a port of call. Either way, many people who choose to explore the Caribbean via cruise ship get a chance to experience this island. If your ship departs from San Juan, consider arriving a day to two early to enjoy this thriving metropolis and popular tourist destination before starting your cruise.

## When to Visit

Mid-December through mid-April is the peak tourist season in Puerto Rico. It's during this time that hotel rates and airfare will be at their highest and crowds at their largest. If you're planning to travel during this peak time, it's an excellent strategy to make your travel reservations at least two or three months in advance. During the time from Christmas to New Year's, it's also recommended that you make advance dining reservations (up to two months early), at least for meals at the nicer and better known restaurants.

## The Scoop on Puerto Rico

Puerto Rico is an ideal vacation destination for eco-tourists (people who enjoy vacationing in nature and participating in outdoor activities). Among the island's most popular tourist attractions are the Caribbean National Forest (El Yunque), the Rio Camuy Cave Park (one of the largest underground cave networks in the world), and the island's bioluminescent bays, where the water literally lights up, thanks to the bioluminescent organisms living near the water's surface.

Puerto Rico offers plenty of water sports and more than 300 pristine, white sandy beaches. In fact, you'll find over 270 miles of sandy beaches surrounding the island. Scuba diving, parasailing, snorkeling, Jet Skiing, sailing, windsurfing, surfing, and a wide range of other sports are readily available at or near many of Puerto Rico's resorts.

For golfers, Puerto Rico also offers more than two dozen eighteen-hole championship golf courses, some of which offer spectacular ocean views, while others are situated within lush tropical landscaping. Greens fees start at about $35 per round and go up considerably from there.

For adults who just want to relax, many of the higher-end resorts features world-class day spas that offer a wide range of massages, facials, and body treatments for both men and women. You'll find these upscale spas at resorts, such as the Caribe Hilton, Wyndham El Conquistador, Condado Plaza Hotel & Casino, El San Juan Hotel & Casino, Hyatt Regency Cerromar Beach, Doral Resort at Palmas del Mar in Humacao, and Ritz-Carlton.

For the kids, many of the popular resorts offer evening movies or organized activities, but these tend to end at around 10:00 P.M. Plan on going to sleep early and waking up early every morning to hit the beach or participate in activities.

##  JUST FOR PARENTS

The majority of activities offered in San Juan happen during the day. At night, plan on enjoying lengthy dinners, visiting the casinos, or participating in the few nighttime activities at your resort. For adults, Puerto Rico offers a wide range of nightclubs and bars, some of which feature live music and dancing nightly. In-room baby-sitting services are available (for a fee) at many resorts and hotels.

Three other popular activities for tourists visiting Puerto Rico include shopping, visiting the tourist attractions (historical sights and museums, for example), and casino gambling.

Because it's part of the United States, Puerto Rico is *not* a duty-free island. However, you don't have to pay any sales tax or customs duties. In addition to souvenirs, Puerto Rico offers an excellent selection of locally made art and jewelry. Some of the more upscale shopping areas and malls feature designer fashions, boutiques, and galleries as well.

## 📼 TRAVEL TIP

In addition to cash and all major credit cards, traveler's checks are widely accepted. Most U.S. banks offer traveler's checks for a small fee. American Express (✆800-221-7782) offers traveler's check in denominations of $20, $50, $100, $500, and $1,000, which can be ordered by phone, obtained at some banks, or purchased from American Express Travel Services offices worldwide. The benefit to traveler's checks is that they're easily replaceable if they get lost or stolen.

Stores are typically open Monday through Saturday, between 9:00 A.M. and 6:00 P.M., and on Sundays between 11:00 A.M. and 5:00 P.M., with extended hours during peak holiday seasons. All major U.S. credit cards and traveler's checks are accepted virtually everywhere. Local currency is the U.S. dollar.

Puerto Rico uses standard, 110-volt electrical power, the same as in the rest of the United States. Virtually all of the driving laws are also the same, so Americans will have little trouble finding their way around, even though the majority of the traffic signs are displayed in Spanish.

Puerto Rico goes by Atlantic Standard Time, which is one hour ahead of Eastern Standard Time. Puerto Rico does not observe Daylight Saving Time.

## A Bit of Puerto Rico History

San Juan, Puerto Rico, is the second-oldest city in the Western Hemisphere and the oldest under the American Flag. The city itself was founded back in 1508 after Christopher Columbus's "discovery" of the island in 1493, during his second voyage to the New World. The first settlement was created by Juan Ponce de León, who arrived from Hispaniola in 1508.

Puerto Rico quickly became a popular port for ships crossing the Atlantic in the 1500s. In 1521, Spain had the city of San Juan completely fortified with a series of walls and forts, some of which can still be seen today. Puerto Rico was under Spanish rule for about 400 years.

In 1917, under President Woodrow Wilson, Puerto Rico became a territory of the United States. The United States granted residents of Puerto Rico U.S. statutory citizenship, and English was declared the official language of the island. In 1940, all native Puerto Ricans were granted full U.S. citizenship. Later, in 1993, Spanish was added to English as the island's official language.

##  RAINY DAY FUN

Today, the Castillo de San Felipe del Morro and El Morro Fortress in Old San Juan are popular tourist destinations. They are especial favorites among kids and teens, who enjoy exploring the 400-year-old fortress. It's open daily from 9:00 A.M. to 5:00 P.M. Admission is $2 for adults and $1 for children. The fortress features underground tunnels to explore, as well as dungeons, barracks, and gun turrets.

## The Local Weather

Throughout the year, the temperature in Puerto Rico ranges from 75 to 85 degrees, with the temperature maxing out in August, during the rainy season. Particularly during the rainy season, expect frequent but short rainfalls, typically in the afternoon. As in much of the Caribbean, the worst period of local weather usually occurs during hurricane season, which lasts from June 1 to November 30. However, most tourists have no trouble enjoying their vacations, even during this period.

If a hurricane is in the forecast, ample precautions can be taken. If you're traveling during hurricane season, purchasing optional travel insurance is definitely a good idea. This will ensure that you are reimbursed if your trip is cut short or cancelled due to bad weather.

## 📋 TRAVEL TIP

For an up-to-date report on the weather in Puerto Rico, call ☎787-766-7777 or visit one of the popular weather or news Web sites, such as the Weather Channel (✎*www.weather.com*).

# Getting to Puerto Rico

Virtually all of the major airlines offer direct or connecting daily flights to San Juan from most major U.S. cities. American Airlines (☎800-433-7300, ✎*www.aa.com*), for example, offers nonstop daily flights from Baltimore, Boston, Chicago, Dallas-Fort Worth, Hartford, Los Angeles, Miami, Newark, New York (JFK), Orlando, Philadelphia, Tampa, Fort Lauderdale, and Washington (Dulles).

Delta Airlines (☎800-221-1212, ✎*www.delta.com*), Song (☎800-FLY-SONG, ✎*www.flysong.com*), Northwest Airlines/KLM (☎800-225-2525, ✎*www.nwa.com*), Continental Airlines (☎800-523-3273, ✎*www.continental.com*), US Airways (☎800-428-4322, ✎*www.usairways.com*), JetBlue (☎800-538-2583, ✎*www.jetblue.com*), Spirit Air (☎800-772-7117, ✎*www.spiritair.com*) and Cape Air (☎800-352-0714, ✎*www.flycapeair.com*) also offer nonstop and connecting flights from a wide range of U.S. cities.

Many of the airlines that service Puerto Rico offer discounted package deals that include airfare and hotel accommodations. A rental car can also be added to the package. Be sure to contact the various airlines' vacation-planning department for details. Contact: American Airlines Vacations (☎800-321-2121, ✎*www.aavacations.com*), Delta Vacations (☎800-221-6666, ✎*www.deltavacations.com*), US Airways Vacations (☎800-455-0123, ✎*www.usairwaysvacations.com*), Continental Airlines Vacations (☎800-301-3800, ✎*www.coolvacations.com*) or United Vacations (☎888-854-3899, ✎*www.unitedvacations.com*).

Cruise lines whose Caribbean cruises originate from Puerto Rico (usually San Juan) or that offer San Juan as a port of call include

Carnival Cruise Lines, Celebrity Cruises, Princess Cruises, Radisson Seven Seas Cruises, and Royal Caribbean Cruises. See Chapter 4 for details on planning a money-saving Caribbean cruise for your family.

## Airport Security and Inspections

While U.S. residents do not have to go through customs or immigration when entering or exiting Puerto Rico (a huge time-saver), airport security continues to be tight. Upon leaving Puerto Rico, all luggage must first be inspected by the U.S. Agriculture Department *before* you check in with your airline. This involves passing each of your bags through a special X-ray machine that's located near the airport's main terminal's entrances. It is illegal to transport fruits and vegetables back to the mainland.

Plan on arriving at to the airport at least two hours prior to your scheduled departure time to allow ample time to get through airport security and check in with your airline. During peak travel times, it is a good idea to allow an extra thirty minutes, especially if your airline makes seat assignments upon check-in.

## The San Juan Luis Munoz Marin International Airport

The San Juan Luis Munoz Marin International Airport (☎787-791-3840, *http://lmm.150m.com*) is a modern, full-service airport located about ten miles east of Old San Juan. The largest airport in the Caribbean, it is used as a hub or stop-over for close to half of all American flights to other islands within the Caribbean.

Passengers arriving from the mainland will find themselves in one of the airport's two main terminals. As you make your way to baggage claim, you'll discover the airport offers plenty of amenities, including shops, restaurants, bars, and banks. There's also a barber shop and beauty salon, medical service center, and a chapel.

Near the Baggage Claim area, you'll find a tourist information desk that's operated by the Puerto Rico Tourism Company (☎800-866-7827, *www.gotopuertorico.com*). It's open daily, between 9:00 A.M.

and 5:30 P.M. Here, you can obtain information and assistance with reservations for hotels, resorts, rental cars, and tourist attractions.

From this tourist information desk, be sure to pick up a free copy of *Go to Puerto Rico Travel Planner.* This full-color publication is a useful resource for vacationers visiting Puerto Rico for the first time.

##  TRAVEL TIP

If you miss your connecting flight on your way to another Caribbean destination and find yourself stuck at Luis Munoz Marin International Airport, the Puerto Rico Tourism Company's information desk is a useful resource for helping you find last-minute, inexpensive overnight accommodations. For convenience, there's a Best Western hotel (☎787-791-1700) right on the airport's property. However, within a five-minute taxi ride, you'll find nicer, less expensive accommodations.

## Taking Taxis

Throughout Puerto Rico, the fares for taxis are typically quoted on a flat-rate basis, based on time and distance. You should be quoted, in advance, the exact fare for your trip. Taxis Turisticos (white taxicabs that display a sentry box logo) are endorsed by the Puerto Rico Tourism Company and offer reliable service. These taxis all offer flat rates. Some taxis that are privately owned and operated, however, rely on meters to calculate fares.

If you're staying at a resort and want to tour the island or visit a specific tourist attraction at your own pace, an alternative to renting a car is to hire a taxi for a half or full day. Rates for this can be negotiated with a cab driver directly or arranged through your resort. This will be more expensive than renting a car, but you'll benefit from having a private tour guide, plus someone who will do the driving for you and who won't get lost.

# Renting a Car in Puerto Rico

All of the popular international rental car companies, including Avis (*www.avis.com*), Budget (*www.budget.com*), Dollar (*www. dollar.com*), Hertz (*www.hertz.com*) and National (*www. nationalcar.com*) operate in Puerto Rico. You'll also find literally dozens of local rental car agencies through your resort's concierge.

If you're renting from one of the well-known rental car agencies, call the company's toll-free number before you leave home to reserve your vehicle. This is definitely recommended if you want a rental car for part or all of your vacation, especially if you're visiting during a peak tourist season. Between Christmas and New Year's especially, it's common for the rental agencies to have trouble meeting the demand for cars.

It's often cheaper to reserve your rental car in advance and then pick up your vehicle at the airport when you land. Another option, which can sometimes be more expensive, is to rent a car from a branch office for a rental car company located at your resort (or one nearby). The cheapest option is almost always to visit one of the travel-related Web sites (such as Priceline.com, Hotwire.com, Travelocity.com, and Orbitz.com) to reserve your rental car.

## ≡FAST FACT

A metropolitan mass transit train system, the Tren Urbano, is currently being built to link various cities and regions within Puerto Rico. Upon its completion, this will offer an excellent way for tourists to get around the island quickly and inexpensively.

To rent a car in Puerto Rico, drivers must be at least twenty-five years old and have a valid U.S. driver's license. While the roads are in excellent shape and navigating around Puerto Rico is relatively easy, keep in mind that virtually all of the road and traffic signs are in

Spanish. Speed limit signs are also displayed in kilometers rather than miles per hour. Gasoline is also sold by the liter, not by the gallon.

If you're planning to rent a car in order to tour the island (a popular alternative to hiring a taxi or taking an organized bus tour), you'll discover that the roads are less congested in the middle of the week. (The exception is during morning and late-afternoon rush hours, as the local population heads to and from work or school.)

## Where to Stay: Understanding Your Options

It's important when choosing accommodations to focus first on location. Do you want to be near the popular tourist attractions, so taxi rides to reach them will be relatively inexpensive? Some of the resorts are located an hour or more from the popular tourist attractions. While these resorts offer all of the dining options and many of the activities you'd want right on the property, sightseeing can get expensive if you need to rent a car or take taxis.

## ═FAST FACT

If you're spending at least a week in Puerto Rico, a money-saving option is to rent a fully-equipped townhouse or villa for your family, as opposed to staying in multiple guestrooms at a resort. There are many real estate rental agencies, such as Casa Verde Vacation Rentals (☎787-823-3271, ✎www.enrincon.com), that manage rental properties throughout Puerto Rico. Using any Internet search engine, use the search phrase "Puerto Rico Villa Rental" to find additional resources.

If staying in or near the beach is important to you, keep in mind that some resorts—such as those located near Old San Juan, for example— offer swimming pools as opposed to beach access. Some of the nicest beaches are located in the Condado, Ocean Park, and Isla Verde areas.

As you choose your accommodations in Puerto Rico, consider the following:

- Location
- Access to the beach
- Distance from popular tourist attractions
- Water- and land-based activities offered on the property (and their cost)
- Configuration of the guestroom accommodations available
- Dining options available at the resort/hotel and what type of meal plans are offered
- Whether you'll have a rental car to get around

An alternative to staying at a luxurious, full-service resort is to stay at a smaller hotel or even a guesthouse. Puerto Rico offers literally hundreds of traditional high-rise hotels. In addition, you'll find many full-service resorts and smaller hotels, as well as villas and townhouses which can be rented. There are also a handful of time-share properties throughout Puerto Rico.

While you'll find several all-inclusive resorts in Puerto Rico, the majority of the resorts offer luxurious guest-room accommodations for a per-night fee, plus a wide array of land- and water-based activities (available at an extra cost). Some of the resorts offer meal plans (two or three meals per day), while others offer several different on-property restaurants, but all meals can be paid for separately or billed to your room.

Each of these accommodation options will provide you and your family with a very different vacation experience. So, before booking your accommodations, determine how you're interested in spending your time, what services and amenities are important to you, and what type of accommodations are best suited to meet your needs. You can then contact the Puerto Rico Tourism Company, a travel agent, or one of the popular travel-related Web sites to help you find and reserve the ideal accommodations at a price you can afford.

The advantage of staying at a full-service resort is that these properties tend to be located on or near a beach. They offer a wide range of on-property activities, and they have several dining options located on the property, so it's not necessary to constantly leave the resort to enjoy a fun-filled or relaxing vacation.

# Calling Home and Surfing The Web

If you have an existing cellular phone with a nationwide service plan (with no roaming charges), chances are good that your cell phone will work flawlessly throughout your vacation in Puerto Rico. If no roaming fees are part of your service plan, you will incur no international roaming charges when using your phone anywhere on the island to make or receive calls.

All of the hotels and resorts charge a premium for making long-distance calls using the phone in your guest room. You can easily purchase a prepaid phone card to make calls back to the United States from a pay phone instead. This is a much cheaper option. Prepaid phone cards are sold in stores, convenience stores, and gas stations throughout Puerto Rico.

The telephones in Puerto Rico works exactly as they do in America. To make a long distance call, simply dial 1 plus the area code and phone number. (If calling from your hotel room, you may need to dial 9 first to get an outside line.) Toll-free numbers also work flawlessly.

If you need access to the Internet, the majority of hotels offer in-room high-speed Internet service (for a daily fee), plus computer workstations in their lobbies or business centers (where you'll pay for access by the minute).

There are also many Internet cafés located throughout Puerto Rico. Dial-up Internet services based in America, including America Online, typically offer local dial-up numbers in Puerto Rico. If your hotel charges a per-minute premium for making even local calls from your room, it'll probably be cheaper to use any high-speed Internet services offered.

# Must-See Activities and Attractions

If you're staying at a full-service resort, you will find plenty of activities for you and your family to experience right on the property without ever needing to leave your resort in order to fully enjoy your vacation. If, however, you want to take some time to see Puerto Rico, experience the culture, and explore the famous historical sights and attractions, it's worthwhile to think ahead and plan your itinerary.

Puerto Rico is the ideal vacation destinations for those who enjoy the outdoors. Many of the island's most exciting attractions and activities are based outside and involve swimming, hiking, or exploring the island's exotic and beautiful landscapes.

The following sections describe the top ten must-see activities and attractions you'll probably enjoy the most in Puerto Rico if you're traveling with kids or teens. As you're planning your daily itinerary, consider the travel times between destinations. Don't try to fit too much into each day.

## Shop and Explore Old San Juan

When most people think of Puerto Rico, they think of San Juan, the oldest and most populated city on the island. Old San Juan offers a look into the past, and the area makes for a wonderful day's worth of sightseeing, shopping, and dining. At night, visitors can enjoy fine restaurants and nightclubs, with many offering live music and dancing.

Old San Juan is a truly historic area, with narrow cobblestone streets, beautiful architecture, and a handful of museums, galleries, shops, restaurants, and cafés. Exploration of Old San Juan will require some walking, so wear comfortable shoes.

Older tourists should consider taking a historical walking tour of the area. If you're with kids or teens, however, self-paced exploration will allow you to see the sights without getting too caught up in learning about the city's rich history.

While you're visiting Old San Juan, be sure you drop into La Casita. Here, you'll find the Puerto Rico Tourism Company's office (☎787-722-1709), which is staffed by friendly and knowledgeable people who can help you get the most out of your vacation. Located around this historical building is a popular outdoor crafts market. It's usually open on weekends and whenever there's a cruise ship in port. The La Casita building overlooks San Juan Bay, the busiest port in the Caribbean. This is where cruise ships visiting Puerto Rico dock.

If you have a car, you'll definitely want to combine your tour of this area with a visit to Fort San Felipe Del Morro. This can easily all be done in one day. If you get an early start, you can begin your day with a visit to the Rio Camuy Cave Park (located about fifty miles away), then make your way to Old San Juan for lunch and an afternoon of exploration and shopping.

### SHOP AND EXPLORE IN OLD SAN JUAN

| Ages up to 5 | Ages 6–15 | Ages 16–20 | Adult | Senior Citizens |
|:---:|:---:|:---:|:---:|:---:|
| ★ | ★★★ | ★★★ | ★★★ | ★★★ |

## Hike in the Caribbean National Forest (El Yunque)

This large national park is a beautiful rainforest with extensive hiking trails, places to picnic, and several large waterfalls and lagoons where swimming is permitted. Plan on spending at least three to five hours (or even a full day) visiting this park, hiking and swimming in the streams and under the waterfalls.

El Yunque is the only rainforest in the U.S. National Forest System. You'll find over 240 different species of tress, countless types of plants, plus many different species of wildlife, including exotic birds. There are some great photo opportunities there.

The visitor's center contains a gift shop and regularly shows an introductory movie, suitable even for youngsters, about the park. You'll also be given a free map of the hiking trails. Guests are encouraged to explore the many trails on their own, although guided tours are available.

Due to the sometimes rugged and slippery terrain, be sure to wear comfortable sneakers or hiking boots, and bring along a bathing suit and dry towel for each person. The hiking is not suitable for older people or those with any type of physical disability. A hat and light jacket are also useful to block the sun or for protection if it starts to rain for a few minutes. (After all, this is a rain forest.) There are many places to take some amazing photos, so don't forget your camera.

The Caribbean National Forest is an absolutely beautiful place to explore and experience nature. The availability of food and drinks is somewhat limited, so come prepared with your own bottled water and snacks. The park is open daily. One way to really get the most out of your visit here is to hire a park ranger as your private tour guide. For additional information, call ☎787-887-2875.

A visit to the Caribbean National Forest is a wildlife adventure that kids, teens and adults alike will find both visually beautiful and exciting.

### THE CARIBBEAN NATIONAL FOREST (EL YUNQUE)

| Ages up to 5 | Ages 6–15 | Ages 16–20 | Adult | Senior Citizens |
|:---:|:---:|:---:|:---:|:---:|
| ★ | ★★★ | ★★★ | ★★★ | ★ |

## Rio Camuy Cave Park

This unique natural attraction is both breathtaking and exciting. Rio Camuy Cave Park comprises one of the world's largest networks of underground caves. A tropical river flows through the caves, enabling guests to go for a swim midway through their exploration. The limestone caves were 160 million years in the making and are something that only nature could create.

Your visit to the caves begins with a narrated trolley ride down a massive sinkhole. Eventually, you'll reach a platform that overlooks the 400-foot-deep Tres Pueblos Sinkhole, which is truly a sight to behold.

The Cathedral Cave, which is part of the underground cave network, features a collection of ancient petroglyphs that were etched into the walls by the Tainos Indians. This is just a sampling of what you'll see during your visit.

The park is open Wednesday through Sunday, from 8:00 A.M. to 4:00 P.M. (with the last tour departing at 3:30 P.M.). The 268-acre park also features a cafeteria, picnic area, gift shop, small theater, and exhibit hall. Part of the underground cave complex is only open to experienced cave explorers, so pay attention to the signs for your own safety.

A visit to Rio Camuy Cave Park is both educational and fun for kids, teens, and adults. Be sure to wear comfortable sneakers or hiking shoes. A lot of walking is required, so guests should be physically fit. The caves are located about fifty miles west of San Juan, but it's definitely worth the trip!

The entrance fee is $10 per person. Only a limited number of people are allowed in the caves at once, so during peak holiday times, you should be prepared to wait or even be shut out if you don't arrive early enough in the day. For more information, call ☎787-898-3100.

**RIO CAMUY CAVE PARK**

| Ages up to 5 | Ages 6–15 | Ages 16–20 | Adult | Senior Citizens |
|:---:|:---:|:---:|:---:|:---:|
| ★ | ★★★ | ★★★ | ★★★ | ★★ |

## Arecibo Radio Telescope & Observatory: The Perfect Side Trip

As part of your sightseeing adventure when you visit Rio Camuy Cave Park, take a short side trip (about three miles) to the Arecibo Radio Telescope & Observatory (☎787-878-2612, *www.naic.edu*).

This attraction features the world's largest single-dish radio telescope: 1,000 feet in diameter and 167 feet deep. The surface of the dish is constructed from more than 40,000 perforated aluminum panels, each measuring about three by six feet. The observatory itself covers about twenty acres. From here, research in radio astronomy, planetary radar, and terrestrial aeronomy is conducted every day, around the clock, by scientists from around the world.

The visitors' center is open to the public, Wednesdays through Fridays (noon to 4:00 P.M.), and on weekends and holidays (9:00 A.M. to 4:00 P.M.). Admission is $4 for adults and $2 for children.

**ARECIBO RADIO TELESCOPE & OBSERVATORY**

| Ages up to 5 | Ages 6–15 | Ages 16–20 | Adult | Senior Citizens |
|---|---|---|---|---|
| N.S. | ★★ | ★★ | ★★ | ★★ |

## The Tanama River-Rafting Adventure

Another exciting and memorable outdoor adventure for physically fit thrill-seekers involves a visit to the beautiful Tanama River, located south of Arecibo. Flowing through a lush forest, the river is the ideal place to go rafting (with an experienced tour guide, of course). Along your journey, you'll pass through beautiful caves and canyons.

For information about rafting tours, contact Acampa (✆787-706-0695, ✎*www.acampapr.com*) or Aventuras Tierra Adentro at (✆787-766-0470, ✎*www.aventuraspr.com*).

The cost of this once-in-a-lifetime adventure runs from $100 to $150 per person. Advance reservations are required. A tour guide and all equipment is provided. Be sure to speak with the tour guide and understand exactly what this adventure entails before embarking on it. It'll be of particular interest to teens and adults.

For people who enjoy camping, the Tanama River area offers a variety of campsites, plus hiking trails and places to picnic.

**THE TANAMA RIVER-RAFTING ADVENTURE**

| Ages up to 5 | Ages 6–15 | Ages 16–20 | Adult | Senior Citizens |
|---|---|---|---|---|
| N.S. | ★ | ★★★ | ★★★ | N.S. |

## Popular Arts-and-Crafts Center

Puerto Rico's Institute of Culture sponsors this popular crafts marketplace, where many local, certified artisans display and sell their crafts and folk art. For details, call ✆787-722-0621 or ✆787-724-0700.

Within Old San Juan, for example, you'll find locally made crafts for sale at Darsenas Plaza (Plaza de la Darsena, located in front of Pier 1), Eugenio Maria de Hostos Plaza, and the Princess Promenade

(Paseo de la Princesa). At the Plaza Las Americas mall (described on page 200), you'll also find local artisans selling their crafts daily.

Artwork, jewelry, hand-carved religious figures (called santos), carnival masks, clothing, woven hammocks, mundillo lace items, and a wide range of other locally crafted items can be purchased as a souvenir of your trip.

### POPULAR ARTS-AND-CRAFTS CENTER

| Ages up to 5 | Ages 6–15 | Ages 16–20 | Adult | Senior Citizens |
|:---:|:---:|:---:|:---:|:---:|
| N.S. | ★ | ★★ | ★★ | ★★★ |

## Bioluminescence Lagoon/Phosphorescent Bays

In certain areas of Puerto Rico, nighttime is the best time for a sail or swim because the waters are inhabited by single-celled bioluminescent organisms that literally glow in the dark. You'll definitely want to experience this phenomenon on a dark night and with a tour guide. These glow-in-the-dark organisms are like tiny fireflies in the air, only they're swimming near the surface of the water.

Puerto Rico is one of only a few places in the world where this type of ocean life can be seen almost nightly within specially protected bays. One such location is La Parguera, located between Mayaguez and Ponce. An even larger bay where you can see the bioluminescent organisms is within Vieques. Local tour operators will take you out on a boat. In some areas, swimming is allowed.

Contact your resort's concierge for details about how to participate in an organized tour departing from your hotel or resort. Kayak tours of these bays are available from several tour operators, including the Kayak Rental in Condado Lagoon (☎787-762-3928).

### BIOLUMINESCENCE LAGOON/PHOSPHORESCENT BAYS

| Ages up to 5 | Ages 6–15 | Ages 16–20 | Adult | Senior Citizens |
|:---:|:---:|:---:|:---:|:---:|
| N.S. | ★ | ★★ | ★★ | ★★ |

## Puerto Rico's Beaches

Puerto Rico is known for having some of the most attractive white-sand beaches in the world. While swimming and sunbathing are extremely popular pastimes for tourists, many of the beaches also offer windsurfing, surfing, snorkeling, Jet Skiing, and many other activities. From January to May, humpback whales and their calves may be seen near the western end of the island.

If your hotel or resort isn't situated right on a beach, consider visiting any of Puerto Rico's most famous beaches, such as these:

- Ballenas
- Caja de Muerto
- Crashboat
- Isla Verde
- Punta Santiago
- Seven Seas
- Sun Bay
- Boquerón
- Caña Gorda
- Flamenco
- Luquillo
- Rincon Bay
- Shacks

**PUERTO RICO'S BEACHES**

| Ages up to 5 | Ages 6–15 | Ages 16–20 | Adult | Senior Citizens |
|---|---|---|---|---|
| ★★ | ★★★ | ★★★ | ★★★ | ★★★ |

## Kite-Flying and Exploring El Morro Fort

Old San Juan's El Morro Fort (built to protect the city in the seventeenth and eighteenth centuries) is a fun and historic place to visit for people of all ages. This fort towers over 140 feet high and is filled with places to explore.

Another popular activity to participate in here is kite-flying. You can purchase kites from small shops and vendors located near the fort. Kids in particular will love exploring the fort, running around outside and flying a kite in this tropical environment. For more information, call ✆787-729-6754.

**KITE-FLYING AND EXPLORING EL MORRO FORT**

| Ages up to 5 | Ages 6–15 | Ages 16–20 | Adult | Senior Citizens |
|---|---|---|---|---|
| ★ | ★★★ | ★★★ | ★★ | ★★ |

## The Children's Museum (Museo del Niño)

After exploring El Morro, consider taking a short walk with your kids (about ten minutes on foot) to Museo del Niño (the Children's Museum). The museum is open Tuesdays through Sundays. As with most museums of this type, this one is totally interactive. Kids can touch anything they see. On weekends, kids can enjoy special events, such as puppet shows. For details, call ✆787-722-3791. This is a fun place for parents and kids to spend two or three hours.

**THE CHILDREN'S MUSEUM (MUSEO DEL NIÑO)**

| Ages up to 5 | Ages 6–15 | Ages 16–20 | Adult | Senior Citizens |
|---|---|---|---|---|
| ★★★ | ★★★ | N.S. | N.S. | N.S. |

## Shop at Plaza Las Americas

For a taste of mainland America, the Plaza Las Americas (✆787-767-5202, ✑*www.plazalasamericas.net*) is a huge indoor mall featuring more than 300 upscale stores, a movie theater with twenty-one screens, and more than thirty restaurants. JC Penny, Macy's, and Sears are among the major department stores in this mall, which all includes many locally owned shops and boutiques, plus a mix of popular chain stores, such as The Gap, and several designer fashion clothing stores.

The mall is located just five miles from the airport and less than a fifteen-minute drive from Old San Juan and the cruise-ship port. Hours of operation are Monday through Saturday, from 9:00 A.M. to 9:00 P.M., and on Sundays from 11:00 A.M. to 5:00 P.M. The restaurants are open nightly until 10:00 P.M.

**PLAZA LAS AMERICAS**

| Ages up to 5 | Ages 6–15 | Ages 16–20 | Adult | Senior Citizens |
|:---:|:---:|:---:|:---:|:---:|
| N.S. | ★★ | ★★ | ★★ | ★★ |

# Scuba Diving in San Juan

Throughout the Caribbean, including the waters surrounding Puerto Rico, you'll find many popular dive sites for novice and certified scuba divers. The following table provides a list of dive operators in Puerto Rico. You can also contact your resort's tour desk or concierge for referrals. The necessary equipment (and some training) will be provided by the dive operator.

**TABLE 9-1**
**SCUBA DIVING TOUR OPERATORS**

| Company Name | Phone Number |
|---|---|
| Mundo Submarino | 787-791-5764 |
| La Casa del Mar | 787-863-1000, ext. 7917 |
| Sea Ventures Pro Dive Center | 787-863-3483, 800-739-3483 |
| Scuba Centro | 787-781-8086 |
| Dive Copamarina | 787-821-0505, ext. 729, 800-468-4553 |
| Parguera Divers | 787-899-4171 |
| Marine Sport & Dive Shop | 787-844-6175 |
| Island Venture Water Excursions | 787-608-3082 |
| Paradise Scuba and Snorkeling Center | 787-899-7611 |
| Aquatic Underwater Adventures | 787-890-6071 |
| Caribbean School of Aquatics | 787-728-6606 |
| Caribe Aquatic Adventures | 787-724-1882 |
| Grand Illusion Charters | 787-796-4645 |

# Golfing in San Juan

Throughout Puerto Rico, you'll find more than two dozen nine- or eighteen-hole championship golf courses, almost all of which are open to the public (with advance reservations). These courses are all located within a two-hour drive from San Juan.

The Puerto Rico Golf Association (✆787-721-7742, ✐*www.prga. org*) is an excellent resource for learning more about any of the golf courses located on the island. You can bring your own clubs and equipment or rent what you need once you arrive.

**TABLE 9-2**
## POPULAR GOLF COURSES IN PUERTO RICO

| Course | Phone Number |
|---|---|
| Punta Borinquen Golf (18 holes) | 787-890-2987 |
| Club Deportivo del Oeste (9 holes) | 787-851-8880 |
| Roosevelt Road Gold Club (9 holes) | 787-865-4851 |
| Coamo Springs Golf & Tennis Club (18 holes) | 787-825-1370 |
| Dorado del Mar Golf Club (18 holes) | 787-790-3070 |
| Hyatt Dorado Beach & Golf Club (two 18-hole courses) | 787-796-8961 |
| Hyatt Regency Cerromar Golf Club (two 18-hole courses) | 787-796-1234 |
| Wyndam El Conquistador Resort (18 holes) | 787-863-6784 |
| Doral Resort (two 18-hole courses) | 787-285-2256 |
| Bahia Beach Public Golf Course (18 holes) | 787-256-5600 |
| Berwind Country Club (18 holes) | 787-876-3056 |
| Westin Rio Mar (two 18-hole courses) | 787-888-6000 |
| Aguirre Golf Club (9 holes) | 787-853-4052 |
| Fort Buchanan Golf Club (9 holes) | 787-707-3852 |
| Inter-Continental Cayo Largo (18 holes) | 787-791-6100 |
| Hampton Inn (18 holes) | 787-791-8777 |
| Paradisus Sol Melia (18 holes) | 787-809-1780 |

## Casino Fun At Night

The casinos in Puerto Rico tend to be found within the upscale resorts, such as the Ritz-Carlton, Wyndham Old San Juan, Intercontinental San Juan Resort & Casino, Radisson Ambassador Plaza, Condado Plaza, Diamond Plaza, San Juan Marriott Resort, Wyndham El San Juan Hotel, and Embassy Suites. Within the casinos, you'll find slot machines plus a wide assortment of table games, with craps, black-jack, poker, and roulette being the most popular.

Some of the casinos are open twenty-four hours a day, but most open in the early afternoon (around noon) and close at around 4:00 A.M., making this more of a nighttime activity for vacationers over the age of eighteen.

## Travel-Related Web Sites for Puerto Rico

The following Web sites offer an abundance of useful information designed to help you plan the perfect family vacation in Puerto Rico:

- **Caribbean-On-Line:** *www.caribbean-on-line.com*
- **CIA FactBook:** *www.cia.gov* (click on The World Factbook link)
- **Puerto Rico Tourism Company:** *www.gotopuertorico.com*
- **Puerto Rico Travel Maps:** *www.travelmaps.com*
- **Puerto Rico WOW!:** *www.puertoricowow.com*
- **Welcome to Puerto Rico:** *http://welcome.topuertorico.org*
- **Yahoo! Travel Guide:** *http://travel.yahoo.com*

# Making San Juan Your Vacation Destination

While Puerto Rico is considered part of the United States, your experience there will make feel as if you're visiting another country, not another U.S. city. Especially if your family enjoys eco-tourism, participating in beach activities, visiting historical sites, and exploring nature, Puerto Rico has a lot to offer.

Before leaving home, you can learn all about the resorts, hotels, restaurants, activities, and attractions this tropical island has to offer by contacting the Puerto Rico Tourism Company (*www. gotopuertorico.com*).

The Puerto Rico Tourism Company has several offices you can visit within the United States. These offices are staffed by travel experts who can help you plan the best possible vacation to Puerto Rico. You'll find the tourism offices in the following places:

666 Fifth Avenue, New York, NY 10013
800-223-6530, 212-586-6262

3575 W. Cahuenga Blvd., Suite #405, Los Angeles, CA 90068
800-874-1230, 213-874-5991

901 Ponce de León Blvd., Suite #101, Coral Gables, FL 33134
800-815-7391, 305-445-9112

From the Puerto Rico Tourism Company, you can request free, full-color vacation-planning brochures and other information. The island offers all of the conveniences of vacationing within the United States, but it's culture and history is unique to the Caribbean.

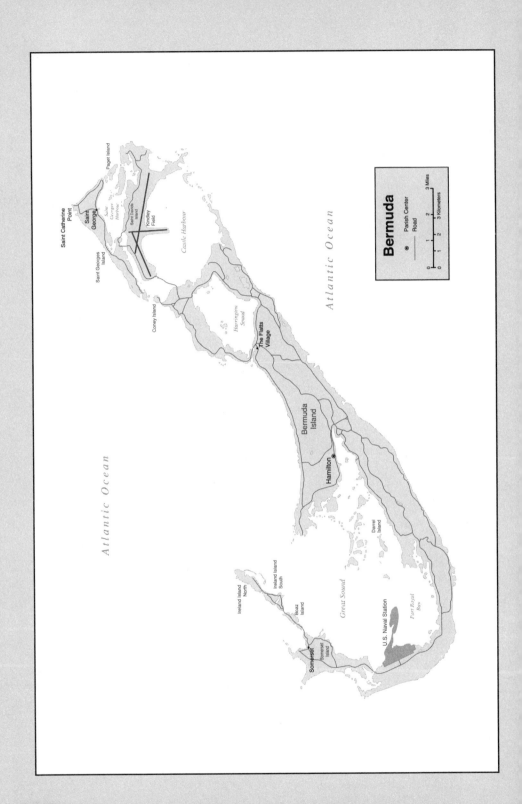

Bermuda

● Parish Center
— Road

0 1 2 3 Miles
0 1 2 3 Kilometers

Atlantic Ocean

Atlantic Ocean

Saint Catherine Point
Saint George
Saint Georges Island
Paget Island
Saint Davids Island
Kindley Field
Saint Georges Harbour
Castle Harbour
Coney Island
Harrington Sound
The Flatts Village
Bermuda Island
Hamilton
Darrel Island
Ireland Island North
Ireland Island South
Boaz Island
Somerset
Somerset Island
Great Sound
U.S. Naval Station
Port Royal Bay

# CHAPTER 10

# *Bermuda*

FOR FAMILIES LOOKING FOR an upscale Caribbean get-away that's easy to reach from the United States, Bermuda is an ideal destination. This island offers many beautiful beaches, countless activities, and a near-perfect climate year-round. For adult travelers, world-class golf courses, racquet clubs, many fine-dining restaurants, and elegant day spas also await.

## The Scoop on Bermuda

Bermuda encompasses twenty-one square miles and is made up of a few relatively small islands. Most are linked together by bridges and roads. Bermuda is conveniently located about 650 miles east of Cape Hatteras, North Carolina.

The official currency in Bermuda is the Bermuda dollar, which is equivalent in value to the U.S. dollar. The U.S. dollar, however, is widely accepted everywhere on the island. In terms of electricity, all of the resorts offer standard 110-volt power, which is identical to the power used in the United States. The island falls in the Standard Time Zone (Greenwich Mean Time minus four hours). Between the first Sunday in April and the last Sunday in October, Daylight Saving Time is observed.

While Bermuda is one of the nicest Caribbean islands for tourists, it's also one of the most expensive to visit. However, if you shop around, money-saving package deals on airfares, hotels/resorts, meals, and activities can be found, especially during off-peak travel times.

In terms of dining, you'll find well over 150 restaurants on the island, offering a wide range of international cuisine. The majority of the restaurants can be found in the popular hotels and resorts. Most independent restaurants are family friendly, although at night, some transform into hot nightspots with full-service bars. As with most places you visit, you'll find restaurants suitable for almost any budget. Keep in mind that prices in Bermuda tend to be a bit higher than you'd find elsewhere in the Caribbean, especially at the finer restaurants.

No matter where you go in Bermuda, the overall atmosphere will be one of dignified informality and "British reserve." Conservative dress in dining rooms and restaurants and within clubs is the norm. Beachwear, for example, is acceptable only at the beach, not in other public areas.

## A Bit of Bermuda History

Bermuda was discovered by the Spanish navigator Juan de Bermudez almost 500 years ago. Sailors referred to this island as "The Isle of Devils" because of the dangers posed by surrounding reefs. Since its discovery, the island has had a rich history, influenced by numerous countries and cultures.

In terms of its population, Bermuda is the third most densely populated region on the planet, with more than 3,372 people populating each square mile of the island. The total population of the island in 2003 was 64,500.

## The Local Weather

Throughout the year, the temperature rarely goes above 85 degrees. Between mid-December and March, the average temperature is in the mid 70s, perfect for enjoying outdoor activities. Between May and October, you can expect the average temperature to be between 75 and 85 degrees. Seldom does Bermuda experience any extreme high or low temperatures. Throughout the year, average rainfall is between 3.5 and 5.8 inches per month. The island doesn't have a rainy season as severe as that on other Caribbean islands, although the island has been known to experience hurricanes, as do other islands in the region.

For an up-to-the-minute forecast of the weather on Bermuda, go online to ✑*www.weather.bm*.

# Getting to Bermuda

Bermuda is one of the easiest Caribbean destinations to reach from the United States, with one of the shortest flight times. Here's what to expect if you're taking a nonstop flight to Bermuda from any of these East Coast cities:

- **Atlanta**: 2.5 hours
- **Boston**: Under 2 hours
- **Chicago**: 3 hours
- **New York**: Under 2 hours
- **Orlando**: 2.5 hours

Multiple U.S. airlines, including American Airlines (✆800-433-7300, ✑*www.aa.com*), Continental Airlines (✆800-231-0856, ✑*www.continental.com*), Delta Airlines (✆800-221-1212, ✑*www.delta.com*), US Airways (✆800-428-4322, ✑*www.usairways.com*), and United Airlines (✆800-241-6522, ✑*www.united.com*) offer nonstop or connecting flights to Bermuda International Airport from most major U.S. cities.

To enter Bermuda, U.S. travelers must pass through immigration and customs and will need to show a return ticket as well as a valid passport. A driver's license alone is not accepted as proof of citizenship. For U.S. travelers without a passport, a birth certificate (with a raised seal or official stamp) *and* government-issued photo ID is usually acceptable if accompanied by a U.S. re-entry permit, U.S. naturalization certificate, and/or a U.S. permanent resident card (as applicable).

If you're entering from a country other than the United States or you don't have a valid U.S. passport, contact the Bermuda Immigration

Authority (✆441-295-5151, ✎*www.bermudatourism.com* or ✎*www.bdatanks.bm/tanks/immigration_regs.pdf*) prior to your arrival to determine what you'll need to be granted entry.

Upon clearing immigration and customs, tourists will find plenty of taxis as well as airport shuttle buses outside of the baggage claim area. Depending on your destination, taxi fare from the airport to your resort will range between $10 and $25. Expect to pay a surcharge of $.25 for each piece of luggage.

## ≡ FAST FACT

Upon leaving Bermuda, air passengers must pay a $25 per-person departure tax. This fee is typically not included in the price of your airline ticket or travel package. Cruise-ship passengers pay a $60 passenger tax, but this fee is collected by the cruise-ship company in advance.

Bermuda is also a popular port of call among cruise ships sailing the Caribbean. Celebrity Cruise Line's *Zenith* and *Horizon* ships, Norwegian Cruise Line's *Majesty* and *Crown*, Radisson Seven Seas Cruises' *Navigator* and Royal Caribbean's *Empress of the Seas* all make regular stops in Bermuda.

# Getting Around Bermuda

Public transportation is the best way to get around the island, since rental cars are not available to tourists. Popular modes of transportation are taxi, bus, ferry, and motor scooter. (No driver's license is required to ride a motor scooter.) Throughout the island, cars drive on the left-hand side of the road.

### Taking Taxis

Taxis are readily available throughout the island. They may be hired by the mile, the hour, or by the day (a six-hour consecutive period). If you'll be paying by the mile, metered rates will be in effect. Most taxis hold a maximum of six passengers.

The following taxi companies operate in Bermuda and can also be hired for private tours:

- **Bermuda Taxi Radio Cabs, Ltd.** ✆441-295-4141
- **B.I.U. Taxi Co-Op Transportation** ✆441-292-4476
- **Bermuda Taxi Operators Company, Ltd.** ✆441-292-4175
- **Bermuda Taxi Services, Ltd.** ✆441-295-8294
- **Trott Travel, Ltd.** ✆441-295-0041

### Renting a Scooter

Rental cars are not available in Bermuda, but rental scooters are, and they're a popular mode of transportation. You must follow all traffic laws while driving a scooter. The speed limit is 35 kilometers (21 miles) per hour, and cars (and scooters) drive on the left-hand side of the road. Gas stations are open only from 7:00 A.M. to 7:00 P.M. daily, so plan accordingly.

Scooter rental locations are available throughout the island, especially in popular tourist areas. Oleander Cycles (✆441-236-5235, ✐www.oleandercycles.bm) has scooter locations in Paget, Hamilton, Southampton, and Dockyard, which are open seven days a week. Wheels Cycles (✆441-292-2245) offers scooter rental locations in Hamilton, Coral Beach, Surfside, Devil's Hole, Flatts Village, and at several resorts and hotels throughout the island. Located at the Bermuda International Airport is Bermuda Fly 'N Ride (✆441-293-6188). This company allows you to pick up your scooter(s) at the airport and arrange to have your luggage delivered to your hotel.

### Ferry Service

Ferry service is available to transport tourists inexpensively to various parts of the island. There are four separate routes (blue, pink, orange, and green) depending on your destination. You can purchase single-trip tickets or money-saving one-, three-, or seven-day passes. Child and student rates are available. Cash is not accepted aboard the ferry, so it is necessary to prepurchase ferry tickets or tokens, which are available at a variety of locations, including many hotels and resorts. All ferry tokens and passes are also valid on the public buses. For information about ferry service, including locations, destinations, and schedules, call ☎441-295-6575 or go online to the Sea Express Web site (✐*www.seaexpress.bm*).

### Getting Around by Bus

Throughout the island, the public bus system offers an inexpensive and relatively easy way to get around. The color-coded system is easy to learn. For example, if a bus has a pole with a pink top, it's headed to Hamilton. A bus with a blue-topped pole is outbound from Hamilton. To ride the bus, exact change (in coins) is required. Tokens and multiple-day bus tickets are also available from many hotels, resorts, visitors' service bureaus, and at the bus terminal in Hamilton.

# Where to Stay: Understanding Your Options

When it comes to finding the perfect accommodations, your options are plentiful in Bermuda. For families, Bermuda offers traditional hotel accommodations, upscale resorts, cottages, and fully equipped multibedroom apartments. Hotels, resorts, inns, and guesthouses offer several standard package options, including the following:

- **American Plan (AP)**: Room accommodations with breakfast, lunch, and dinner included.
- **Bermuda Plan (BP)**: Room accommodations and full breakfast is included.
- **Continental Plan (CP)**: Room accommodations and a light breakfast is included.
- **European Plan (EP)**: Room only, with no meals.
- **Modified American Plan (MAP)**: Room accommodations, breakfast, and dinner included.

Many of the island's dozens of traditional hotels and full-service resorts are located right on the beach, enabling guests to enjoy many water-based activities right on the premises and without any additional hassle. One kind of accommodation that is unique to Bermuda are cottage colonies. In this arrangement, you'll find a central club house area, which typically contains a dining room, lounge, and bar for all guests. The cottages, however, are spread out throughout the property's grounds, offering families comfortable and spacious accommodations, as well as privacy. Many of the cottages offer kitchenettes and are close to a beach or swimming pool. Cottage colonies tend to be more upscale and pricey than stand-alone rental cottages or apartments because of the added amenities and services. One resource for finding the perfect rental property for your family is Bermuda Accommodations (✆416-232-2243, ✐*www.bermudarentals.com*). Additional agencies can be found online using any Internet search engine. Enter the search phrase "Bermuda cottage rentals."

The cottages and apartments that can be rented throughout Bermuda are all fully furnished and offer housekeeping services. These accommodations are far more relaxed and homey than traditional hotel or resort guestrooms. If renting a cottage or apartment doesn't appeal to you, you can choose one of Bermuda's full-service resorts, which is often the best option when traveling with children and teenagers. In addition to the wide range of activities offered right on the property, virtually all of Bermuda's resorts have their own beaches, swimming pools, housekeeping services, shops, restaurants, bars, nightclubs, and fitness centers. Some also have their own golf courses and/or tennis courts, plus organized activities for young people.

# Dining Options

In virtually every hotel and resort on the island, you'll find at least one family-friendly restaurant. There is also a wide range of independent restaurants, serving everything from Bermudian cuisine and seafood to Mexican, French, Italian, or Oriental cuisine. At many of the restaurants, outdoor dining is available. Most restaurants offer a selection of local favorites that somehow incorporate the Bermuda onion. Other local favorites include Bermuda fish chowder and plenty of seafood.

Prices vary dramatically at the various restaurants. You'll find plenty of fast-food options, mid-priced dining (which is most suitable for families), and a multitude of fine-dining options available throughout Bermuda.

For mid-priced dining, expect to pay between $10 and $14 per person for breakfast, $18 to $22 per person for a two-course lunch, and at least $30 per person for a three-course dinner.

The Bermuda.com (✑*www.bermuda.com*) Web site offers a selection of online money-saving coupons that can be printed before your trip. For information about specific restaurants, the BermudaDining. com (✑*www.burmudadining.com*) Web site features reviews, sample menus, and detailed restaurant listings.

For an upscale, fine-dining experience, the Palms Restaurant (✆441-236-7100) is an excellent option for breakfast, lunch, dinner, or afternoon tea. The oceanfront location and outdoor dining area make for a memorable dining experience.

For fine Italian food, visit the Tuscany Restaurant (✆441-296-8546). The Sea Breeze Café (✆441-232-3999) overlooks Elbow Beach and offers al fresco dining for breakfast and lunch. Dinner is also served.

Families that enjoy barbeque will love the Bayside Bar & Grill at the Grotto Bay Hotel (✆441-293-8333). Here, you'll find hamburgers, hot dogs, sandwiches, salads, and a wide range of family-friendly favorites at a reasonable price. Of course, the restaurant also offers an extensive barbeque menu, plus a fresh seafood buffet on Monday and Thursday nights.

Another great casual dinner option for lunch or dinner is Mickey's Beach Bistro (✆441-236-9107), which offers an award-winning menu and a wonderful indoor and outdoor dining area. In the evening, this is also a great place for adults to enjoy cocktails.

# Calling Home and Surfing the Web

Throughout the island, you'll find modern telephone service, high-speed Internet access, and wireless (international roaming) cell-phone services. At many gift shops and stores on the island, you can also purchase prepaid calling cards for making direct-dial pay phone calls back to the United States without having to pay high hotel surcharges.

For information about prepaid GSM wireless cell-phone service and international roaming using your existing cell phone, contact your current wireless service provider. In Bermuda, contact Mobility, Ltd. (✆441-295-4810, ✑*www.mobilityltd.bm*) or Cingular (✆441-500-5000, ✑*www.cingular.bm*).

# What to See and Do

As with all of the islands in the Caribbean, Bermuda offers many different kinds of water-based sports and activities, as well as countless things to see and do on land. The island also offers several popular tourist attractions.

If you're interested in visiting eight of Bermuda's most popular cultural attractions, an all-inclusive ticket, the Heritage Passport, is available for $25 per adult and $15 per child. To purchase this special ticket, call Axiom at ✆441-294-4907. The Heritage Passport allows unlimited admission for seven consecutive days to the following attractions:

- The Bermuda Maritime Museum
- The Bermuda National Gallery
- The Globe Hotel
- The Tucker House Museum
- The Bermuda Underwater Exploration Institute
- The Bermuda Aquarium, Museum & Zoo
- Fort St. Catherine

From your hotel's tour desk, you can schedule a wide range of tours and activities. Many hotels and resorts also offer a wide selection of water-based activities on the property.

# Must-See Activities and Attractions

Although Bermuda offers visitors many activities geared to older travelers without children, it also offers plenty for families to enjoy. When you're ready to venture beyond the grounds of your resort, consider the following top ten must-see attractions in Bermuda. Advance reservations are required for some of these activities and attractions.

For additional information or for assistance in making tour reservations, contact your hotel's concierge or tour desk.

### Bermuda Aquarium, Museum & Zoo (BAMZ)

The Bermuda Aquarium, Museum & Zoo offers an educational experience combined with pure entertainment. The aquarium and zoo aspect of this attraction will definitely appeal more to young people. Here, visitors can see more than 100 species of fish and aquatic wildlife native to Bermuda.

The natural-history museum element of this attraction offers a series of interactive exhibits, while the zoo showcases animals from throughout the Caribbean and the world. This attraction is more family oriented than the Bermuda Maritime Museum, for example, which is more of a cultural attraction that showcases elements of Bermuda's history. The Bermuda Aquarium, Museum & Zoo is open daily, although hours of operation vary. Call ✆441-293-2727 or go online to ✑www.bamz.org.

**BERMUDA AQUARIUM, MUSEUM & ZOO**

| Ages up to 5 | Ages 6–15 | Ages 16–20 | Adult | Senior Citizens |
|:---:|:---:|:---:|:---:|:---:|
| ★★ | ★★★ | ★★★ | ★★ | ★★ |

### Bermuda Underwater Exploration Institute

Located in Hamilton Harbor, the Bermuda Underwater Exploration Institute offers a look at the ocean's depths, while teaching visitors about planet Earth and how the land and the sea are interrelated. Exhibits include a shell collection, a bioluminescence room, and a shipwreck gallery. Souvenirs can be purchased from the gift shop. This attraction will appeal more to teens and adults. For more information, call ✆441-292-7219 or visit the institute on the Web at (🖳www.buei.org).

**BERMUDA UNDERWATER EXPLORATION INSTITUTE**

| Ages up to 5 | Ages 6–15 | Ages 16–20 | Adult | Senior Citizens |
|:---:|:---:|:---:|:---:|:---:|
| ★ | ★★ | ★★ | ★★ | ★★ |

## Stroll Through the Botanical Gardens

Here, an abundance of tropical plants, trees and flowers are used to create breathtaking landscapes that nicely showcase the natural beauty of Bermuda. This thirty-six-acre park has several unique areas and is a delightful place to enjoy an afternoon walk. Within this park is the official residence of Bermuda's premier. The house itself is open for guided tours; however, visitors can stroll the gardens at their own pace. For more information, call ✆441-236-4201.

**BOTANICAL GARDENS**

| Ages up to 5 | Ages 6–15 | Ages 16–20 | Adult | Senior Citizens |
|:---:|:---:|:---:|:---:|:---:|
| ★ | ★ | ★★ | ★★★ | ★★★ |

## Explore the Crystal Caves

Although visitors to Bermuda can snorkel, scuba dive, take a glass-bottomed boat ride, or visit the Ocean Discovery Center to get an exciting look at the mysterious world under the seas, the Crystal Caves offer an equally fascinating and exciting look underground. Here, visitors travel eighty feet underground to explore the island's most famous networks of underground caverns.

Older visitors will enjoy the natural beauty of this attraction, while kids will find the cave exploration exciting. One highlight is crossing the pontoon bridge, which sprawls across the Cahow Lake (an underground, crystal-clear body of water). Kids are invited to participate in special activities here, like panning for hidden gems at

Captain Jack's Treasure Trove. The Crystal Caves also has a charming gift shop and a snack bar on the premises.

**CRYSTAL CAVES**

| Ages up to 5 | Ages 6–15 | Ages 16–20 | Adult | Senior Citizens |
|:---:|:---:|:---:|:---:|:---:|
| N.S. | ★★★ | ★★★ | ★★ | ★ |

## Swim with Dolphins: The Dolphin Quest Program

Dolphins are mysterious creatures that share a unique bond with humans. Most people, however, never get a chance to interact with these creatures. Those who do find the experience to be extremely memorable. In Bermuda, the Dolphin Quest Program allows people of all ages to interact and swim with dolphins in a supervised and secure lagoon environment. Four different Dolphin Quest programs are offered throughout the day, ranging in price from $195 to $275 per person. The different programs offer different levels of interaction with the dolphins. Advance reservations are definitely recommended.

The Dolphin Quest program is located at the Bermuda Maritime Museum at the Royal Navy Dockyard. For information and reservations, call ✆441-234-4464 (Bermuda) or ✆800-248-3316 (U.S.) or go online to ✑*www.dolphinquest.org*. Hours of operation are 8:30 A.M. to 4:30 P.M. daily.

**THE DOLPHIN QUEST PROGRAM**

| Ages up to 5 | Ages 6–15 | Ages 16–20 | Adult | Senior Citizens |
|:---:|:---:|:---:|:---:|:---:|
| N.S. | ★★★ | ★★★ | ★★ | ★★ |

## Tour Bermuda's Forts and Historical Sites

History and architecture buffs will enjoy exploring Bermuda's many historical buildings, which include a series of seventeenth- and eighteenth-century forts. Fort Hamilton, for example, was originally built to protect Hamilton Harbor. Visitors have a chance to see picture-perfect panoramic views from atop the fort, plus explore a garden moat, dungeons and 18-ton artillery pieces.

The Royal Naval Dockyard is another historical site which was originally built by slave laborers as a strategic outpost for the Royal Navy. Now, many of the historic buildings have been transformed into lovely shops, restaurants and art galleries.

The Tucker House Museum is another historical building that has been opened to the public. Built in the 1750s, this mansion was the home to the Tucker family, Bermuda's most famous residents. Many of the Tuckers' original belongings are on display within the house, which offers a look back at what life was like in the late 1700s and early 1800s.

Some of Bermuda's historical sites, like the forts, will be of interest to people of all ages. Others, however, are more like museums and will appeal mainly to adults interested in Bermuda's history. While tourists are welcome to explore each of these sites at their own pace, organized half-day and full-day tours are also available. Contact your hotel's concierge or the Bermuda Department of Tourism (✆441-292-0023, ✆800-BERMUDA, ✍*www.bermudatourism.com*).

**BERMUDA'S HISTORICAL SITES**

| Ages up to 5 | Ages 6–15 | Ages 16–20 | Adult | Senior Citizens |
|---|---|---|---|---|
| N.S. | ★ | ★★ | ★★★ | ★★★ |

## Pamper Yourself with a Day At the Spa

In addition to all of the high-energy activities Bermuda offers, the island is also a perfect vacation getaway for relaxing. To maximize your relaxation potential, consider hiring a baby-sitter for your kids (or getting them involved in the organized activities offered at your resort), while you and your spouse visit one of the world-class day spas on the island. Many types of massages, body treatments, facials, manicures, pedicures, and hydrotherapy treatments are offered at these upscale day spas.

Sure, you can sign up for a basic sixty- or ninety-minute massage, but to truly get the most out of your day-spa visit, consider experiencing one of the spa's unique signature treatments. Many of the treatments offered at the spas are suitable for both men and women, and you can often purchase the products used during your treatments.

A few of the world-class day spas in Bermuda include the following:

- **Cedars Spa**: ☎441-238-8122, ext. 3218
- **Coolwaters Spa & Salon**: ☎441-297-1528
- **Coral Beach Spa**: ☎441-239-7222
- **Face and Body Day Spa**: ☎441-292-8081
- **Hideaways at Surf Side**: ☎441-238-5738, ✑*www.surfside.bm*
- **Inner Sanctum Urban Spa**: ☎441-296-9009
- **Ocean Spa at Cambridge Beaches**: ☎441-234-3636
- **Serenity Message & Body Treatment**: ☎441-234-0222, ext. 218
- **Spa at Ariel Sands**: ☎441-235-5300, ✑*www.arielsands.com*
- **Spa at Elbow Beach**: ☎441-239-8900
- **Strands Day Spa**: ☎441-295-0353, ✑*www.strands.com*
- **Total Fitness Center**: ☎441-295-0087
- **Willow Stream Spa**: ☎441-239-6924

**DAY-SPA VISIT**

| Ages up to 5 | Ages 6–15 | Ages 16–20 | Adult | Senior Citizens |
|:---:|:---:|:---:|:---:|:---:|
| N.S. | N.S. | ★★ | ★★★ | ★★★ |

## Visit Bermuda's Pink Beaches

One thing that sets Bermuda apart from other islands in the Caribbean is its beaches. Thanks to the small shell particles, calcium carbonate deposits, and tiny bits of coral mixed with the sand, the beaches along Bermuda's coastline have a slightly pink hue. This adds to the beauty and serenity of this tropical getaway and helps create the picture-perfect beach settings Bermuda is famous for.

There are over twenty popular beaches on this island, plus countless other beaches located near resorts and hotels. If you're looking for a remote beach that's seldom crowded, check out Astood Cove. For a great picnicking spot (during low tide), visit Black Bay Beach on Ireland Island. To see a wonderful array of underwater life while snorkeling, Church Bay is the place to spend the day. This beach has calm waters, making it great for snorkeling and swimming. Another beach that offers very calm waters (ideal for young swimmers) is Parson's Bay, found in the Ireland Island area.

Three other great beaches for swimming can be found in Clarence Cove, Elbow Beach (in Paget Parish), and at Daniel's Head Beach Park. The water at these beaches tends to be very calm, with many shallow areas that are great for snorkeling. Mangrove Bay is a favorite beach among fishermen, sailors, and swimmers alike.

If you happen to be visiting Bermuda in April, be sure to visit West Whale Bay (in Southampton Parish). This lovely beach got its name from the large number of whales that migrate north toward their summer feeding grounds each year, a spectacle that visitors to the beach are likely to witness.

**BERMUDA'S BEACHES**

| Ages up to 5 | Ages 6–15 | Ages 16–20 | Adult | Senior Citizens |
|:---:|:---:|:---:|:---:|:---:|
| ★★ | ★★★ | ★★★ | ★★★ | ★★★ |

## Go Jet Skiing, Scuba Diving, Snorkeling, or Boating

Snorkeling and scuba diving are extremely popular activities in Bermuda. If your resort or hotel doesn't offer these and other water-based activities, there are dozens of independent tour operators you can contact. For novice and certified scuba divers, the following companies offer dive tours operated by certified dive masters. All necessary equipment is provided. For novice divers, introductory scuba dive programs are also offered. Many of these tour operators also offer snorkeling tours. Rates vary, based on the length of the tour, location, and experience level.

When booking your scuba diving or snorkeling reservations, ask the tour operator if underwater camera rentals are available. If not, be sure to purchase a disposable waterproof camera. You can purchase one for between $10 and $20 wherever film and photography equipment is sold.

For more information about scuba-diving tours and available snorkeling adventures, contact one of these dive tour operators:

- **Bermuda Bell Diving**: ☎441-295-4434
- **Greg Hartley's Under Sea Adventure**: ☎441-234-2861, ✐*www.hartleybermuda.com*
- **Peppercorn Diving**: ☎441-297-1459
- **Blue Water Divers & Watersports**: ☎441-234-1034, ✐*www.divebermuda.com*
- **Deep Blue Dive Training Centre**: ☎441-292-0080
- **Fantasea Bermuda, Ltd.**: ☎441-238-1833, ✐*www.fantasea.bm*
- **Nautilus Diving, Ltd.**: ☎441-295-9485
- **Scuba Look Bermuda**: ☎441-293-7319

Blue Water Divers & Watersports (☎441-232-2911, ✐*www.divebermuda.com*) offers an exciting twist to traditional snorkeling tours. Your adventure begins with a one-hour guided Jet Ski tour, which takes you racing along the island's shoreline. Before heading back, your tour will make a stop at a beach or reef area, where you'll enjoy a fun-filled snorkeling adventure. The Jet Skis carry between one and three passengers each. The tour is ideal for teens and adults alike. Prices start at $105 per person, $130 for two people riding one Jet Ski, or $140 for three people on one Jet Ski.

Two other companies that offer guided Jet Ski tours are :

- **Fantasea Bermuda, Ltd.** (☎441-238-1833, ✐*www.fantasea.bm*) and
- **Windjammer Watersports** (☎441-234-0250)

You can rent a boat from any of the following operators:

- **Blue Hole Water Sports**: ☎441-293-2915

- **Blue Water Divers & Watersports**: ✆441-232-2911, ✐*www.divebermuda.com*)
- **Fantasea Bermuda, Ltd.**: ✆441-238-1833, ✐*www.fantasea.bm*
- **Pompano Beach Club Watersports Center**: ✆441-234-0222, ✐*www.pompano.bm*)
- **Rance's Boatyard**: ✆441-292-1843
- **Windjammer Watersports**: ✆441-234-0250

Rentals are usually offered by the hour, although two-, three-, four-, or eight-hour rentals are also available, depending on the type of boat. Thirteen-foot Boston Whalers, sunfish sailboats, kayaks, pedal boats, windsurfers, glass-bottomed boats, personal aqua scooters, and even a seventeen-foot power catamaran are among the types of boats that can be rented.

## ≡ FAST FACT

Deep Blue Dive Training Centre (✆441-292-0080) operates scuba-diving classes just for kids over the age of eight. These classes are held in a swimming pool by a certified dive master.

Guided kayak tours are popular in Bermuda. All equipment is provided. The tour guides not only ensure your safety, they also offer detailed information about the places you paddle. Kayak tours last between one and three hours and are more suitable for teens and adults who are physically fit (since a lot of paddling is required). No previous experience is necessary.

Prices for kayaking tours average about $50 per person.

### SCUBA DIVING

| Ages up to 5 | Ages 6–15 | Ages 16–20 | Adult | Senior Citizens |
|:---:|:---:|:---:|:---:|:---:|
| N.S. | N.S. | ★★★ | ★★★ | ★ |

**SNORKELING**

| Ages up to 5 | Ages 6–15 | Ages 16–20 | Adult | Senior Citizens |
|:---:|:---:|:---:|:---:|:---:|
| N.S. | ★★★ | ★★★ | ★★★ | ★★ |

**JET SKIING**

| Ages up to 5 | Ages 6–15 | Ages 16–20 | Adult | Senior Citizens |
|:---:|:---:|:---:|:---:|:---:|
| N.S. | N.S. | ★★★ | ★★★ | ★ |

## Play Golf on a Championship Course

Bermuda offers more than eight independent golf clubs featuring eighteen-hole championship golf courses, plus several golf ranges. In addition, several of the resorts on the islands have their own courses. Most offer club, cart, and shoe rentals. Private instruction is also available for an additional fee. Greens fees vary, based on the course, day of the week, and season; in general, they range from $35 to $280 per person.

The Bermuda Golf Association (☎441-295-9972, ✐*www. bermudagolf.org*) can help golfers choose the best courses to experience, as well as assist vacationers in booking the ultimate golf getaways.

## ══FAST FACT

Most courses have strict dress codes. "Proper attire" at the golf clubs and courses means a shirt with collar and sleeves with golf slacks or shorts. No jeans, gym shorts, or cut-offs are permitted.

Be sure to book tee times well in advance, especially during peak travel seasons. The independent golf clubs in Bermuda include the following:

- **Belmont Hills Golf Club (Warwick)**: ✆441-236-0694, ✐*www. belmonthills.com*
- **Bermuda Golf Academy (Southampton)**: ✆441-238-8800
- **Fairmont Southampton Golf Club (Southampton)**: ✆441-239-6952, ✐*www.fairmont.com*
- **Mid Ocean Club (Tucker's Town)**: ✆441-293-0330, ✐*www. themidoceanclubbermuda.com* (Note: An introduction by a club member or the concierge at one of the major hotels is required.)
- **Ocean View Golf Course (Devonshire)**: ✆441-295-9093
- **Port Royal Golf Course (Southampton)**: ✆441-234-0974
- **Riddell's Bay Golf Course & Country Club (Warwick)**: ✆441-239-1060, ✐*www.riddellsbay.com* (Note: An introduction by a club member or the concierge at one of the major hotels is required.)
- **St. George's Golf Course (St. George's)**: ✆441-297-8353
- **Tucker's Point Golf Course (Tucker's Town)**: ✆441-298-6970, ✐*www.tuckerspoint.com* (Note: An introduction by a member or the concierge at one of the major hotels is required.)

**GOLF**

| Ages up to 5 | Ages 6–15 | Ages 16–20 | Adult | Senior Citizens |
|:---:|:---:|:---:|:---:|:---:|
| N.S. | ★ | ★★ | ★★★ | ★★★ |

# The Bermuda Triangle: Fact or Fiction?

Throughout the world, stories, legends, and even some facts have circulated concerning the mysteries surrounding the Bermuda Triangle. This area is a triangle-shaped region of the ocean that connects Bermuda, Fort Lauderdale, and San Juan.

Reports of strange happenings in this region date back to the days of Christopher Columbus, who is reported to have experienced problems with his compasses while seeing strange lights in the sky as he sailed through this area. Since then, boats and airplanes have mysteriously vanished, adding to the legends and folklore surrounding this area. Some of these so-called mysteries have been solved with scientific explanations, while others have not.

## Making Bermuda Your Vacation Destination

Adults traveling to Bermuda without kids should definitely consider staying at one of the many bed-and-breakfasts or smaller inns that offer luxurious accommodations and travel packages. For families, a cottage, villa, or a more mainstream hotel or resort offers a multitude of accommodation options that will allow everyone to enjoy Bermuda.

To find just about any business, service, or tour operator you need, you can contact your hotel's concierge or visit the Bermuda Yellow Pages Web site (*www.bermudayp.com*). From this Web site, you can also access the Bermuda Menu Pages, which displays menus and prices from some of the island's most popular restaurants. The Bermuda Hotel Pages listing provides comprehensive information for all the hotels, inns, and resorts on the island. This Web site also provides up-to-date listings for special events taking place on the island, as well as local movie listings.

### 📋 TRAVEL TIP

The Bermuda Yellows Pages (*www.bermudayp.com*) Web site features money-saving online coupons for many restaurants, tourist attractions, and activities. Before leaving home, be sure to print out some of these coupons.

The Bermuda Online Web site (*www.bermuda-online.org*) is an comprehensive online resource covering everything having to do with this Caribbean island. This Web site seamlessly links over 120 other Web sites relating to this popular vacation destination, which makes finding the information you need online quick and easy.

The Bermuda Department of Tourism has its main office in Hamilton, Bermuda (☎441-292-0023), with offices also in New York City (☎800-223-6106), Atlanta (☎404-524-1541) and Boston (☎617-422-5892). Travel information, accommodation recommendations, and other information for families planning a trip to Bermuda can be obtained by calling (☎800-BERMUDA or visiting the Bermuda Department of Tourism's Web site (✎*www.bermudatourism.com*).

**Anegada**
(U.K.)

# British
# Virgin Islands

Great
Camanoe

Guana Island

**Virgin Gorda**
(U.K.)

Jost
Van Dyke

Beef Island
Airport

**Road
Town**

• Spanish Town

*Sir Francis Drake Channel*

**Tortola**
(U.K.)

Ginger Island

Coral •
Harbor

Cruz
• Bay

Cooper Island

Peter Island

*Sound*

Norman Island

*Anegada Passage*

*C a r i b b e a n    S e a*

# CHAPTER 11

# *The British Virgin Islands (BVI)*

NOT TO BE CONFUSED with the U.S. Virgin Islands, the British Virgin Islands (BVI) offer the ultimate vacation experience for anyone who wants to surround themselves with the incredible beauty of the Caribbean, without exposing themselves to the blatant commercialism found throughout many popular Caribbean tourist destinations.

## Get Ready for a Low-Key Vacation

The BVI offers natural beauty and seclusion, white-sand beaches, a wide range of water-based activities, and absolutely no franchises. To your dismay or your delight, you won't find a McDonald's, Starbucks, The Gap, or even a Hilton or Sheraton hotel anywhere in the BVI. As you'll discover in this chapter, the BVI offers a vacation opportunity that's affordable and ideal for families looking for beach, boating, or other water-oriented activities.

If you'll be spending several days or more, the BVI is best experienced by renting a villa near the beach along with a rental car. A villa near the beach will allow you to enjoy plenty of water-based activities, plus have plenty of living space for your entire family. It'll also give you access to a fully equipped kitchen so you can conveniently prepare your own meals and snacks—of course, this won't be a plus for any parent whose idea of a vacation doesn't include cooking! A rental car will give you the freedom to get around and explore without being dependent on taxis, which can get expensive.

## The Scoop on the BVI

The BVI is unlike other Caribbean destinations. It features a handful of islands, each of which offers a different vacation experience, although island-hopping is relatively simple by boat. Tortola is the main island, where you'll find shopping, hotels, resorts, restaurants, and plenty of beaches. Other islands in the BVI, like Virgin Gorda, focus more on resorts that offer restaurants, beaches, and activities all on the property. Out of all the places in the Caribbean, the BVI is one of the least commercial, so don't expect to find The Gap in the shopping area or a McDonald's near every tourist attraction.

One of the most exciting and popular ways to experience the BVI is to charter a boat for several days and then sail around the various islands, making stops at various marinas to enjoy local dining, land-based activities, and beaches. Depending on your budget and skill level when it comes to sailing, boats are available in many sizes and configurations. It's also possible to hire a captain and crew, even a private chef, if you choose.

Tortola, which is the largest island in the BVI, is located about fifty miles east of San Juan, Puerto Rico, and a mere fifty miles from the U.S. Virgin Islands. A few things you need to know about the BVI is that only U.S. currency is accepted (along with major credit cards). The BVI does not support the Euro.

All electrical power throughout the islands is standard 110-volt, which is identical to the power used in the United States. Also, virtually everyone speaks English, although many of the locals have a thick West Indies accent that is sometimes difficult for Americans to understand. The BVI goes by Atlantic Standard Time.

If you choose to rent a car, you should know that the steering wheel is located on the left side of the car (just like in the United States); however, the cars drive on the left of the road (as they do in Great Britain). Many of the roads throughout the BVI are very narrow, have extremely steep hills, and are poorly paved. In addition, road signs are limited, so it'll take most tourists some time to get accustomed to driving in this terrain. Most driving trips, however, are short.

 **TRAVEL TIP**

> Upon arriving in the BVI, be sure to pick up a free copy of *Welcome* magazine. It's available at all hotels, resorts, and at many tourist attractions. This is an information-packed, full-color magazine offering timely details about everything happening in the BVI during your visit. Information about hotels, resorts, activities, restaurants, shopping, and special events are all featured. Boat and ferry schedules are also included, which makes island-hopping easier.

When it comes to banking, shopping, and dining, Road Town in Tortola is the main tourist and commerce area. Outside of Road Town, conveniences like ATM machines are scarce, and those that work are often not compatible with U.S. banks. Thus, if you need cash or need to conduct any form of banking, you'll most likely need to visit a bank in the Road Town area. Many hotels and resorts, however, will cash checks or offer cash advances from credit cards for guests.

One of the unique things you'll discover when you visit the BVI is the abundance of natural wildlife and farm animals that roam freely. For example, instead of the pigeons you would see in many U.S. cities, you'll see wild roosters and chickens walking about freely along the roads, in fields, and almost everywhere you travel. Cows, goats, mules, pigs, and other animals are also commonplace as you explore the islands. Although these animals present great photo opportunities, it's typically not a good idea to feed or pet these animals. Luckily, there are few dangerous land-based wild animals in the BVI that tourists need to concern themselves with.

 **TRAVEL TIP**

> Because there are no franchises or popular chain restaurants located in the BVI, when it comes to dining, you'll be experiencing restaurants owned and operated by hotels, resorts, and individual restaurateurs. For dining suggestions, be sure to pick up a free copy of *The BVI Restaurant and Food Guide*. It's available at virtually all hotels, resorts, and tourist destinations. This guide describes many of the popular restaurants you'll find on the islands, with price ranges and menu highlights.

## A Bit of BVI History

In 1493, Christopher Columbus "discovered" the BVI and U.S. Virgin Islands, although the first inhabitants of the islands were the Ciboney, Arawak, and Carib Indians. It was, however, pirates like Bluebeard and Captain Kidd who were the first foreigners to inhabit the islands.

In the seventeenth century, the British took control over the region by establishing a permanent plantation colony on Tortola and several other islands.

For almost 150 years, the sugar industry was popular until slavery was abolished in the mid-1800s. These days, tourism is the main industry throughout the BVI. The islands are governed by a British-appointed leader, although with so much American influence, little British culture can actually be found on the island.

## The Local Weather

Throughout the year, you can expect the weather to be in the 80- to 90-degree range. Sunny weather with warm tropical breezes is the norm virtually year-around. During certain times of the year, it does rain. Most storms, however, are short-lived and will be replaced by sunshine quickly.

Be sure to pack plenty of sunscreen, sunglasses, a hat, and light-weight clothing that can protect you from the sun, which much of the time is intense. Comfortable shoes are also a must. It's a good idea to bring along waterproof beach shoes for exploring the beaches. Teva (*www.teva.com*), for example, offers a complete line of waterproof footwear for adults and kids. These popular shoes are ideal for walking around on land, boating, and playing at the beach. You can find similar, less expensive footwear at many department stores, such as Target.

# Getting to the BVI

The Tortola International Airport (actually located on Beef Island, which is connected to Tortola) is small and can't accommodate full-size airplanes. Thus, to reach the BVI, you'll most likely need to fly from your home city to San Juan, Puerto Rico, then take a connecting flight on a smaller aircraft to Tortola. American Airlines, US Airways, and a few other major carriers offer service to Tortola. Several island-hopper airlines, such as Cape Air (800-352-0714 (U.S.), 011-284-495-2100 (BVI), *www.flycapeair.com*), CaribbeanStar Airlines (800-744-STAR, *www.flycaribbeanstar.com*) and Air Sunshine (800-327-8900 (U.S.), 011-284-495-8900 (BVI), *www.airsunshine.com*) also fly to Tortola from San Juan and nearby Caribbean Islands, including St. Thomas. If you're not staying on Tortola, upon flying into the Tortola International Airport, you'll need to take a boat or ferry to your final destination.

The BVI can be reached from other Caribbean Islands, either by small airplane, cruise ship, or ferry. Several popular cruise-ship lines, including Holland American, Princess Cruises, and Carnival Cruise Lines stop in the BVI as a port of call during their respective Caribbean cruises. There are also several boats and ferries offering regular service between St. Thomas (U.S. Virgin Islands) and Tortola, all of which arrive and depart from the Road Town area.

### Entering the BVI

If you arrive at the BVI by air, you'll exit your airplane at the Tortola International Airport and walk a few hundred yards to the main terminal. (The flight between San Juan and Tortola takes approximately thirty minutes.)

Once in the Tortola airport, you'll pass through immigration and present your passport. You'll then collect your luggage from the small baggage-claim area and proceed through customs. You'll be required to present a few completed forms, including the HM Customs BVI Declaration Form, which will be given to you on the airplane during your flight to the BVI. Be sure to fill out these forms completely. If you have any questions, ask your flight attendant.

 **TRAVEL TIP**

When leaving the BVI, be sure to arrive at the Tortola International Airport at least ninety minutes before your flight. Checking in with the airline and passing through security can be a time-consuming process. You're required to check in for your flight a minimum of thirty to forty-five minutes before the scheduled departure time.

U.S. citizens are required to present either a current U.S. passport *or* a valid U.S. driver's license and an original birth certificate (with raised seal) in order to enter and exit the BVI. Upon leaving the BVI, each passenger will be required to pay a $5 security tax plus a $15 airport departure tax. These fees must be paid, in cash, after checking in at the airline ticket counter, before passing through airport security to board your airplane.

Once you've gotten through customs with your luggage, which will be a relatively quick process, you can take a taxi, rent a car, or take a boat to your final BVI destination. Located less than a quarter of a mile from the airport (a three- to five-minute walk) is a dock where you can catch a boat to several nearby BVI islands. Van service to this dock area is available if you have a lot of luggage. Near the docks, you'll also find a small convenience store, bar/restaurant, coffee shop, and Internet café.

## Getting Around the BVI

The BVI is comprised of many small islands. The most economical way to travel between islands is by boat or ferry. Helicopter or charter airplane service, however, can also be arranged. Once on the island you'll be visiting, rental cars or taxi service is available.

If you're not familiar with the area or accustomed to driving in the BVI, it's a good idea to take a taxi initially, since there are few road signs and navigating along the poorly paved roads can be tricky. The average speed limit as you drive throughout the BVI is 20 miles per hour.

### Renting a Car

Many of the popular U.S.-based rental car companies have a presence on Tortola, so you can reserve a car using your preferred rental car company's toll-free number or Web site before leaving home. You will also find a handful of local car rental companies. Plan on spending between $35 to $50 per day to rent a car in the BVI.

One of the familiar car rental agencies you'll find on Tortola is Avis, which has offices in Road Town, the Tortola International Airport and in the West End (*www.avis.com*). Hertz (*www.hertz.com*), Dollar (*www.dollar.com*), and National Car Rental (*www.nationalcar.com*) are also available in the BVI.

In Virgin Gorda, L&S Jeep Rental (011-284-495-5297) offers four- to eight-passenger Jeeps and SUVs for rental by the day or week. Rates range from $45 to $80 per day. In Tortola, iTHO Car Rental (011-284-494-5150) also offers several types of four-wheel-drive vehicles for daily or weekly rentals.

### Taking a Taxi

Finding a taxi on many of the BVI islands is as easy as picking up the telephone. If you're in Tortola, there are also several taxi stands located throughout the island, such as in Road Town. Many of these companies also offer sightseeing tours. The following are phone numbers for taxi services in the BVI:

- **Andy's Taxi & Jeep Rental (Virgin Gorda)**: ☎011-284-495-5511
- **Beef Island Taxi Association (Tortola, near airport)**: ☎011-284-495-1982
- **BVI Taxi Association (Tortola)**: ☎011-284-494-3942
- **Mahogany Taxi Service (Virgin Gorda)**: ☎011-284-495-5469
- **Nanny Cay Taxi Association (Tortola)**: ☎011-284-494-0539
- **Quality Taxi Association (Tortola)**: ☎011-284-494-8397
- **Waterfront Taxi Stand (Tortola)**: ☎011-284-494-3456
- **West End Taxi Association (Tortola)**: ☎011-284-495-4934

Before taking a taxi, be sure to agree upon the fare in advance. Taxis in the BVI do not have fare meters. Your hotel's front-desk attendant or concierge will be able to advise you on appropriate taxi fares.

 **TRAVEL TIP**

Unless your destination is extremely close, walking is not typically a viable form of transportation for getting around in the BVI. The terrain typically offers many extremely steep hills, poorly paved roads, and no sidewalks.

### Island Hopping

One of the most popular ways to island hop throughout the BVI is by water taxi, boat, or ferry. Speedy's (☎011-284-495-5240, ✉*www.speedysbvi.com*), Water Taxi (☎011-340-775-6501, ✉*www.watertaxi-vi.com*) and the Road Town Fast Ferry (☎011-284-494-2323, ✉*www.tortolafastferry.com*) are among the companies that offer easy and inexpensive ways to reach several of the BVI islands from Tortola, where many of the water taxis, boats, and ferries depart from a dock located in the Road Town area or from near the Tortola International Airport. You'll find regular ferry service between the following ports:

- Jost Van Dyke and West End Tortola, via New Horizon Ferry Service: ☎011-284-495-9278
- Marina Cay and Beef Island, Tortola: ☎011-284-494-2174
- Peter Island and Road Town, Tortola, via the Peter Island Ferry: ☎011-284-495-2000
- Virgin Gorda and Tortola: via Speedy's Ferry: ☎011-284-495-5240; Smith's Ferry Service, ☎011-284-495-4495; or North Sound Express, ☎011-284-495-2138
- North Sound Islands and Gun Creek, Virgin Gorda via Bitter End Ferry, ☎011-284-494-2746); or Saba Rock Resort Ferry Service, ☎011-284-495-7711

# Where to Stay: Understanding Your Options

Unlike many places in the Caribbean, the BVI does not offer traditional chain hotels, like Hiltons or Sheratons. While there are plenty of hotels located throughout the BVI, many tourists opt to either stay in guesthouses or to rent villas, as opposed to staying at a more traditional hotel.

Affluent vacationers who enjoy boating might choose to stay at one of the many upscale yacht clubs, such as the Bitter End Yacht Club & Resort (☎800-872-2392) or The Moorings (☎800-368-9444, ✎*www.moorings.com*).

Another popular way of exploring the BVI is to charter a yacht and go island-hopping. This gives you the option to sleep on the boat or dock at a marina and obtain nightly accommodations on the various islands you visit. There are dozens of yacht charter companies in the BVI. Depending on your needs and skill level, you can hire a captain and crew, or you can choose to captain the chartered boat yourself.

Yet another common practice in the BVI is for families to rent a villa. This is a fully equipped home or cottage, often located on or near a beach, which is affiliated with a resort. Thus, while you'll have the amenities of a resort available (such as organized water-based activities and restaurants), as well as the convenience, living space, and comfort of staying in a multibedroom home or cottage. Prices for villas vary dramatically, based on their location, size, amenities available, and the time of year. During peak travel seasons (such as between Thanksgiving and New Year's), many villas require a five-, seven-, or ten-night stay.

### Strategies for Choosing the Best Accommodations

Chapter 3 outlined some of the things that you should consider when choosing the best resort or hotel accommodations for your family when traveling to the Caribbean. Instead of an onslaught of commercial hotel chains lining the beaches, what you'll find in the BVI is a wide range of smaller hotels, resorts, guesthouses, yacht clubs, and villa rental opportunities.

 **TRAVEL TIP**

Be sure to pack at least one small flashlight for everyone you're traveling with. Power failures are somewhat common on the BVI, and if you'll be walking at night, many of the streets don't have lighting. Plenty of bug repellent is also an absolute must! Mosquitoes tend to come out at night.

Once you've decided to visit the BVI, you'll need to decide on which island you'd like to stay, what type of vacation experience you're looking for, and how close to the beach you'd like to be. Throughout the BVI, you can choose from a diverse range of accommodations, from those literally a few feet from the beach to those are located on a mountain, offering a spectacular view but requiring a short walk or drive to the beach.

After you've reviewed Chapter 3, some additional things to consider when selecting accommodations within the BVI include the following:

- How close the resort, villa, or hotel is to the beach and water-based activities?
- How close the resort, villa, or hotel is to the nearest town where restaurants are located?
- Is a full-service restaurant offered on the property?
- Are any activities available on the property?
- Do accommodations include an in-room telephone?
- Is there an in-room television with cable/satellite programming?
- Is a kitchen or kitchenette offered within the room, so you can prepare some of your own meals or snacks?
- Does the resort have its own backup generator to provide electricity if power on the island fails (a somewhat common occurrence)?
- Are the accommodations air-conditioned, or is only a ceiling fan offered?

## Resort Recommendations

In the BVI, there are only a handful of truly luxurious, full-service resorts that are upscale and family friendly and that offer a wide range of land- and water-based activities suitable for the entire family.

## ≡FAST FACT

For additional information about planning a vacation in the BVI, go online to ✑*www.bviwelcome.com*. You can also call the BVI Tourist Board at ✆800-835-8530.

In addition to offering water-based activities, such as boating, these resorts also offer luxurious and spacious accommodations (by BVI standards), modern amenities (most offer telephones and televisions in each room, as well as high-speed Internet access), plus tennis courts, swimming pools, day spas, supervised child activity centers, multiple restaurants, and shops, all on the resort's property.

While the BVI offers accommodations to meet virtually any travel budget, two of the nicest, most popular, most luxurious resorts are the Bitter End Yacht Club & Resort and Little Dix Resort. Reservations for these properties should be made well in advance. Especially during peak travel seasons, you'll find these resorts at capacity. Both report a tremendous amount of repeat business from guests, many of whom make an annual trip to the resort and have been doing so for many years. It's common to see a family that's been visiting one of these resorts annually for two or three generations.

### The Bitter End Yacht Club & Resort

✆011-284-494-2746

✆800-872-2392

Located on a small, virtually private island, the Bitter End Yacht Club & Resort, which recently celebrated its thirtieth anniversary, is the ultimate vacation destination for families that enjoy boating. In addition to a wide range of traditional resort amenities, the Bitter End offers a fleet of over 100 boats (including windsurfers and kayaks) that are available to guests. The overall atmosphere of this resort is that of an upscale yacht club.

There's also a world-renowned sailing school (operated by John Kantor, the foremost leader in sailing education and founder of the Longshore Sailing School in Westport, Connecticut) and an onsite dive shop, plus snorkeling and kiteboarding. Fishing trips for guest are offered daily.

Three on-property beaches, hiking trails, a swimming pool, several restaurants, three bars (featuring live music almost nightly), and spacious accommodations have made this resort a popular vacation destination for three generations. The resort is also kid friendly, with its own supervised child activity center and nightly movies shown in the open-air theater. The sailing school and other water-based programs also offer highly skilled instructors and supervised activities for kids and teens.

In terms of accommodations, seventy-seven beachfront villas and various types of deluxe suites are available.

##  TRAVEL TIP

Several live-aboard yachts are available for charter. Each room or suite sleeps two people, although rooms can be connected via a lockable door on the outside deck.

All rooms and suites overlook the water and are fully air conditioned. While telephones are located in each room, the open-air theater located near the main dining room and in the bars are where you'll find the only television sets. Thus, if you're traveling with kids, be sure to bring along activities they can enjoy in their rooms at night.

For guests, the Bitter End Yacht Club & Resort is pretty much all-inclusive in terms of meals and activities. While many guests arrive by airplane, then take a ferry from the Tortola airport to the resort's island, many sailors who are exploring the BVI dock at the resort's private marina for one or more nights and enjoy the amenities as guests. The resort offers a private heliport for the rich and famous who want to arrive in style.

Because of its somewhat remote location—you need to take a ferry to the closest town or island, such as Tortola or Virgin Gorda—the Bitter End Yacht Club & Resort offers a truly relaxing and enjoyable vacation experience for those looking to lose themselves in a tropical paradise. The resort is located on a small island near Virgin Gorda, about twelve miles from Tortola, seventy-five miles from Puerto Rico, and thirty miles from St. Thomas.

During the peak holiday season, the resort has a seven-night minimum stay. Throughout the rest of the year, nightly, seven-night, and nine-night all-inclusive packages are available. Additional nights can be added to the packages. Based on double occupancy, a seven-night stay at The Bitter End Yacht Club & Resort during the high season (January 7 through April 30) will range between $4,200 and $12,600. Rates are slightly lower during off-peak travel seasons.

### Little Dix Bay
☎011-284-495-5555
☎888-ROSEWOOD
✍*www.littledixbay.com*

Just as famous as the Bitter End Yacht Club & Resort, the Little Dix Bay Resort is located on Virgin Gorda. It has a more traditional atmosphere, featuring luxurious accommodations ranging from a one-room hotel suite to a three-bedroom villa.

In addition to offering a wide range of water-based activities (water-skiing, snorkeling, sailboats, kayaks, and swimming, for example), Little Dix Bay Resort also offers tennis courts, a fitness center, one of the most luxurious day spas in the BVI, baby-sitting services, a child activity center, and multiple restaurants and bars.

##  TRAVEL TIP

While visiting the BVI, if your resort doesn't offer organized and supervised activities for your kids, private baby-sitting service is available from Tropical Nannies (☎011-284-495-6493, ✍*www.tropicalnannies.com*). Rates are $10 per hour for one child or $15 per hour for two children. There is a $2-per-hour surcharge from midnight to 6:00 A.M. Charges for incidentals and travel are extra. You can also contact your hotel for additional recommendations for local baby-sitting or child-care services.

The Little Dix Bay Resort offers a beautiful, family-friendly environment. Most guests arrive by air, flying into Tortola International Airport, then take the resort's private ferry service directly to the resort on Virgin Gorda (a twenty-minute trip). While this is not an all-inclusive resort, several package deals are available that can include two or three meals per day, plus a wide range of activities.

In terms of accommodations, the majority of the guest rooms, suites, and villas are spacious enough to add cots for one or two children, although multiple-bedroom suites and connecting rooms are available and definitely more comfortable. The resort is located right on the beach and offers a stunning atmosphere overlooking the water as well as immaculate landscaping.

# Calling Home and Surfing the Web

From virtually any public telephone in the BVI, you can use a major credit card to call the United States by first dialing ☎1-800-CALL-USA and following the instructions. Collect calls can also be made using this phone number. Depending on where you're calling from (a public phone versus a hotel phone, for example), rates for calling the United States can be anywhere from $.50 to $3 per minute or more.

Another alternative is to purchase a prepaid calling card from Cable & Wireless. These cards come in $10 and $20 denominations and work with public telephones owned and operated by Cable & Wireless, the BVI's main phone company. Many privately owned pay phones (such as those in hotels) don't support any prepaid calling cards and charge a premium for making international calls.

Cellular phone service in the BVI is still extremely limited. No international roaming is available. Cellular phones can be rented for a daily fee, although calls to the United States from these phones average about $4 per minute and service is not available throughout all of the BVI islands. For details about cellular phone service in the BVI, call CCT Boatphone ☎011-284-494-3825 in Tortola or ☎011-284-495-5639 in Virgin Gorda (✍*www.bvicellular.com*).

Many hotels and resorts offer high-speed Internet access from a computer located in the main lobby. Few resorts or hotels currently offer in-room Internet access, although a few offer wireless hotspots. There are also a handful of cyber cafés located throughout the BVI. Plan on spending anywhere from $.50 to $2 per minute to surf the Web or access your e-mail. While high-speed Internet access is available, the service isn't always reliable and periodically goes down.

 **TRAVEL TIP**

To make a call to the United States or Canada from the BVI using a public telephone, simply dial 1 followed by the area code and phone number. Follow the dialing instructions either printed on the phone or that you hear after dialing. You can pay for calls using a prepaid calling card, credit card, or U.S. coins.

# Dining Options

If you're renting a villa, it's cheaper to prepare the majority of your own meals in the villa's kitchen. Food markets are readily available on each of the islands. Tortola offers several large supermarkets. However, few parents include cooking and cleanup on their list of fun things to do on vacation in the Caribbean. If you feel like eating out, you have several options in the BVI.

Many of the restaurants in the BVI are found in the major hotels and resorts. These restaurants offer varied menus and a wide range of dining experiences. Depending on where you're staying, dining outside of your hotel or resort might not be practical unless you have a rental car. Check with your concierge for dining recommendations and accessibility.

Independent restaurants can typically be found on each island that comprises the BVI. Because the BVI isn't at all commercial, virtually none of the restaurants are affiliated with popular chains. While you'll find some restaurants offering American-influenced menus, most feature "Continental dare," a cuisine that's infused with plenty of local Caribbean flavor. Chicken and seafood are particularly popular. In Tortola, across from the seaport (in the heart of the shopping area), one of the best, family-friendly restaurants around is Pussar's Road Town (℡011-284-494-2467). This is a mid-priced, casual dining eatery offering a wide range of American dishes. There's also a full-service bar. Along the water, you'll also find a handful of cafés and restaurants that are ideal for a casual lunch.

Myett's Garden & Grille (☎011-284-495-9649, ✉*www.myettent. com*), located on Cane Garden Bay, is an excellent, affordable, family-oriented place to have lunch, with a choice of chicken dishes, sandwiches, and wraps. Plan on spending between $7 and $15 per person for breakfast, lunch, or dinner. At night, this open-air restaurant transforms into a tropical nightclub that's primarily for adults. Here you'll find some of the best live entertainment on the island.

Also for adults, and for the ultimate in beach parties, if you're lucky enough to be visiting Tortola during a full moon, you can experience a legendary full-moon party at Bomba's Shack. Located along the beach in Apple Bay (Tortola), this literal shack is where some of the most outrageous beach parties in the BVI are held. These parties attract hundreds of locals and tourists alike. With live entertainment, plenty of alcohol, and partying that goes until the wee hours of the morning, a college frat party seems tame in comparison to this beach party experience. For details, call ☎011-284-495-4148.

Located right on the water within the Village Cay Marina is another excellent restaurant, the Village Cay Marina Seaside Grille (☎011-284-494-2771). Here, lunch and dinner are served daily in an open-air environment that overlooks the marina. This is located a short walk from the Road Town area. American-style sandwiches, salads, soups, and a wide range of other entrees are served. A full bar is also available. Plan on spending between $9 and $14 per person for lunch or dinner.

# Must-See Activities and Attractions

For families who enjoy the beach and water-based activities, such as swimming, snorkeling, scuba diving, fishing, and boating, the BVI offers the ultimate vacation opportunity thanks to its pristine white-sand beaches and beautiful landscapes. This is the place to visit if you truly want to get away.

As for land-based activities, the options are a bit more limited. Several extremely scenic hiking trails are available throughout the island. The top ten must-see attractions and family-friendly activities in the BVI are described in the following sections.

### Beaches

Whether you're looking for virtually total seclusion or a busy beach that's jam-packed with activities like tanning, surfing, snorkeling, parasailing, windsurfing, or Jet Skiing, the main reason to visit the BVI is to experience the beaches. While wearing sunblock is an absolute must, most vacationers can spend virtually their entire vacation enjoying the various beaches.

Aside from visiting the bars, there's not a whole lot to do after dark in the BVI, so most people hit the beaches early for a full day of fun in the sun. All of the beaches in the BVI are public, yet some are dominated by guests of particular resorts and others are visited primarily by the locals.

##  RAINY DAY FUN

At the time this book was written, the only movie theater in Tortola was under construction. When completed sometime in 2005, it'll offer five theaters and a bowling alley. It'll be the ideal place for families to enjoy rainy days or their evenings after dinner.

Cane Garden Bay, for example, is a lovely beach on Tortola that offers several beachside cafés, restaurants, bars, and water-sport activity rentals (such as jet skis, windsurfing boards, snorkeling gear) It's probably the most popular beach in the BVI. On the west side of Tortola, Smuggler's Cove is another popular beach spot. Apple Bay and Carrot Bay also offer pristine beaches.

During the winter months, the beaches along the north shore of Tortola are popular destinations for surfers. Sun bathing, snorkeling, windsurfing, parasailing, Jet Skiing, kayaking, surfing, and scuba diving are among the most popular water-based activities offered at the more popular beaches in the BVI. Of course, beach chairs can also be rented. Many of the beaches have snack bars and full-service bars that can whip together a wonderful assortment of tropical alcoholic and nonalcoholic beverages and smoothies.

##  TRAVEL TIP

Be sure to bring your own towels to the beach. You can borrow beach towels from your hotel or resort. You'll also want to bring plenty of sunscreen, a hat, beach shoes, and bottled water to drink.

**BVI'S BEACHES**

| Ages up to 5 | Ages 6–15 | Ages 16–20 | Adult | Senior Citizens |
|:---:|:---:|:---:|:---:|:---:|
| ★★ | ★★★ | ★★★ | ★★★ | ★★★ |

### Scuba Diving

You don't have to be a certified scuba diver to experience a beginner's dive with a certified dive master. All the equipment you need is provided, and many companies in the BVI offer introductory scuba diving courses and dives. For noncertified divers, these introductory programs are suitable for teens and adults who are physically fit.

We Be Divin' (☎011-284-499-2835) at Cane Garden Bay, for example, is within walking distance from Road Town. This company offers a four- to five-hour introductory scuba-diving experience that takes novice divers through a training program. You'll then experience a memorable forty-minute dive off the coast of Peter Island, accompanied at all times by a dive master/instructor. Introductory courses and dives are priced under $100 per person. Advance reservations are required.

**TRAVEL TIP**

If you're going scuba diving, be sure to purchase a disposable waterproof camera, so you can take underwater photos of your adventure. Kodak Water & Sport disposable cameras cost under $10 in the United States, but they're about $20 in the BVI. Available wherever film, souvenirs, and camera supplies are sold, these cameras take twenty-seven photos.

Many other companies in the BVI also offer scuba diving, equipment rentals, and training. There's Dive BVI (☏011-284-495-5513), AquaVenture (☏011-284-494-4320, ✍www.aquaventurebvi.com), Dive Tortola (☏011-284-494-9200, ✍www.divetortola.com), Banana Wind (☏011-284-499-2558), Blue Water Divers (☏011-284-494-2847), and UBS Dive Center (☏011-284-494-0024, ✍www.scubabvi.com).

**SCUBA DIVING IN THE BVI**

| Ages up to 5 | Ages 6–15 | Ages 16–20 | Adult | Senior Citizens |
|---|---|---|---|---|
| N.S. | N.S. | ★★★ | ★★★ | ★ |

### Swim with Dolphins

Kids and teens especially will enjoy this unique opportunity to swim and snorkel with six dolphins. Groups are limited to ten people, and all participants wear a safety vest. The actual experience takes place in an enclosed area along the beach and lasts about ninety minutes. Photos and videos of the experience can be purchased. Dolphin Discovery is part of the Prospect Reef Resort (☏284-494-7675, ✍www.dolphindiscovery.com). Prices range from $79 to $129 per person.

**DOLPHIN DISCOVERY**

| Ages up to 5 | Ages 6–15 | Ages 16–20 | Adult | Senior Citizens |
|---|---|---|---|---|
| N.S. | ★★★ | ★★★ | ★★ | ★ |

### BVI Helicopter Tour

One of the most spectacular ways to see the BVI is by air. Experience a privately chartered helicopter tour of Tortola and/or other popular islands from Island Helicopters International (☎011-284-495-2538, ✎*www.helicoptersbvi.com*). You can choose from a variety of different tours and sightseeing excursions, ranging from thirty- to forty-five-minute flights to full-day trips.

**BVI HELICOPTER TOURS**

| Ages up to 5 | Ages 6–15 | Ages 16–20 | Adult | Senior Citizens |
|--------------|-----------|------------|-------|-----------------|
| N.S. | ★★ | ★★★ | ★★★ | ★★ |

### Hike at Sage Mountain National Park

Sage Mountain National Park covers ninety-two acres. Established in 1964, it features Sage Mountain, at 1,716 feet above sea level the highest point in the BVI. Because the park is located on a mountain, it offers several scenic hiking trails for novice and advanced hikers. Be sure to experience this attraction during the daylight hours and pick up a free trail map before exploring. Many of the trails are labeled. Bring along extremely comfortable shoes, a hat, bug repellent, and water.

There's a parking lot located at the edge of the park. Beyond this lot, only foot traffic is allowed. For additional information and hiking opportunities, call ☎809-494-3904.

Either before or after your trek, consider stopping for lunch or dinner at the nearby SkyWorld restaurant. Located near the mountaintop, the view is stunning.

**SAGE MOUNTAIN NATIONAL PARK (HIKING)**

| Ages up to 5 | Ages 6–15 | Ages 16–20 | Adult | Senior Citizens |
|--------------|-----------|------------|-------|-----------------|
| N.S. | ★ | ★★ | ★★ | ★ |

### Visit a Day Spa

A growing number of upscale spas are opening in the BVI. On Tortola, for example, the Oasis Salon & Spa (☎011-284-494-8891, ✎www.oasissalon.com) offers a wide range of massages and full-body treatments. There's also the BVI Spa (☎011-284-495-7375, ✎www.thebvispa.com) and the Wellness Spa & Salon at Long Bay Beach Resort (☎011-284-494-0138).

Perhaps the nicest and most exclusive day spa in the BVI, however, is the Spa at Little Dix Bay Resort (☎284-495-5555). Located on Virgin Gorda, this spa offers private-treatment bungalows that feature spectacular ocean views. Visitors can experience several types of massages, skincare services, body wraps, and a wide range of other luxuries in a beautiful and peaceful setting. Multiple spa packages are available, such as the Spa Sampler ($205), which includes a twenty-five- or fifty-minute massage and a twenty-five-minute cleansing facial. More elaborate three- and five-hour packages are also available, as are a wide range of individual treatments. If you need to leave your kids while pampering yourself at the spa, Little Dix Bay Resort offers a full-service child-care and activity center for an hourly fee.

The day spas located in the BVI are for adults only. Appointments for treatments should be booked in advance.

**DAY SPA VISIT**

| Ages up to 5 | Ages 6–15 | Ages 16–20 | Adult | Senior Citizens |
|:---:|:---:|:---:|:---:|:---:|
| N.S. | N.S. | N.S. | ★★★ | ★★★ |

### Rent/Charter a Sailboat or Power Boat

Whether you rent a sailboat or motor boat and explore the BVI by water for an hour, a half day, a whole day, or an entire week, you will see why boating is so popular throughout this region. Several yacht clubs, including the Bitter End Yacht Club & Resort, offer dozens of different types of boats to rent or charter, as well as sailing courses and other programs for novice and experienced boaters alike.

In Tortola, The Moorings Yacht Club & Resort (☎011-282-494-2332, ✎*www.moorings.com*) is just one place you can charter a thirty-two- to sixty-two-foot yacht for a day, several days, or a week.

**BOAT RENTALS**

| Ages up to 5 | Ages 6–15 | Ages 16–20 | Adult | Senior Citizens |
|:---:|:---:|:---:|:---:|:---:|
| N.S. | ★ | ★★★ | ★★★ | ★★ |

### Explore the Virgin Gorda Baths

Located on Virgin Gorda, this national park area features an incredibly beautiful beach, hiking trails, and a series of stone caves and grottos that can be climbed and explored. This is particularly exciting for kids and teens. Be sure to wear waterproof shoes when exploring the caves, as you'll be going through shallow water, climbing on rocks, and walking along unpaved trails. This is also a great place to snorkel or swim. You'll find a few gift shops and restaurants here, all of which are family friendly. Plan on spending at least several hours at the park.

**VIRGIN GORDA BATHS**

| Ages up to 5 | Ages 6–15 | Ages 16–20 | Adult | Senior Citizens |
|:---:|:---:|:---:|:---:|:---:|
| N.S. | ★★★ | ★★★ | ★★ | ★ |

### Visit the Callwood Rum Distillery (Cane Garden Bay, Tortola)

Early in the BVI's history, sugar cane and rum production were two of the region's primary industries. The Callwood Rum Distillery is one of the oldest rum distilleries on the island, and it's one of the few that's still fully functional. See firsthand how rum is created as you tour this working distillery. Some of the equipment that's used is over 200 years old and has been passed down within the Callwood family for generations. This is an interesting place for adults to visit. At the end of your tour, you can sample the eighty-proof rum that's made here.

## CALLWOOD RUM DISTILLERY TOUR

| Ages up to 5 | Ages 6–15 | Ages 16–20 | Adult | Senior Citizens |
|:---:|:---:|:---:|:---:|:---:|
| N.S. | N.S. | ★ | ★★ | ★★ |

### Shop in Road Town (Tortola)

Like any tourist destination, Tortola offers a shopping district, which can be found within the Road Town area. Here, you'll find a small selection of shops, boutiques, restaurants, and bars, along with an outdoor crafts market created specifically for tourists. Plan on spending two to four hours wandering through this commercial area of the BVI.

Colombian Emeralds International (☎011-284-494-7477) is a lovely jewelry shop that offers a large selection of jewelry and gifts. Located on Main Street (Road Town's main road, where many shops are located) is Sunny Caribbee Spice Company (☎011-284-494-2178, *www.sunnycaribbee.com*), a unique store that sells a wide selection of exotic teas, Caribbean spices, fragrances, locally made fine art, and other exclusive merchandise. A few doors down, you'll find the Courtyard Coffee Shop (located at 145 Main Street). While there are no Starbucks coffee shops in the BVI, this shop may be even better, offering a wide selection of gourmet coffees and teas, plus baked goods.

 **JUST FOR PARENTS**

Cigar aficionados will appreciate the fact that genuine Cuban cigars are available for sale throughout the BVI. While you can't take these cigars back to the U.S., they are relatively inexpensive and can be enjoyed during your stay in the BVI.

Part of your exploration of this shopping area should definitely include lunch or dinner at Pusser's Road Town (☎011-284-494-3897), which offers a restaurant, bar, and clothing shop. Pusser's offers its own line of rum, although the restaurant is family friendly, serving a wide range of inexpensive American and Caribbean-style dishes for lunch and dinner. Hamburgers, sandwiches, steaks, and pizza are among the menu options.

**SHOPPING IN ROAD TOWN**

| Ages up to 5 | Ages 6–15 | Ages 16–20 | Adult | Senior Citizens |
|:---:|:---:|:---:|:---:|:---:|
| ★ | ★ | ★★ | ★★ | ★★★ |

# Making the BVI Your Vacation Destination

With its unrivaled beauty and lack of commercialism, the BVI is truly unlike other Caribbean destinations. No matter where you travel throughout the BVI, you will find that the people are extremely friendly and the atmosphere is relaxed. People who enjoy spending countless hours at the beach or enjoying various water-based sports or activities will appreciate what the BVI has to offer.

With the exception of the bar scene, the activities offered through-out the BVI take place mainly during daylight hours. If you're traveling with kids or teens, be sure to bring along ample activities to occupy them during downtime, especially at night. After all, not all of the hotel or resort accommodations offer in-room televisions. Those that do, however, feature satellite programming from the United States.

 **JUST FOR PARENTS**

The nightlife in the BVI happens at the many outdoor or open-air bars located along the beaches. In Tortola, for example, Bomba's Shack is a famous outdoor nightspot for adults only. It's open Sunday and Wednesday nights. Many of the bars offer live enter-tainment or disc jockeys.

Throughout the BVI, you'll find plenty of inexpensive as well as moderately priced dining options. Most restaurants offer a wide range of American-style chicken, steak, seafood, and even vegetarian dishes, along with local Caribbean favorites. Thus, even if your kids are finicky about what they eat, you'll easily be able to find entrées and snacks they'll enjoy.

The best way to plan your stay within the BVI is to find a travel agent who specializes in this region. You can also contact the BVI Tourist Board (✆800-835-8530, ✐*www.bvitouristboard.com*) at one of these locations:

- **New York City:** ✆212-696-0400
- **Los Angeles:** ✆212-736-8931
- **Atlanta:** ✆404-567-4741
- **Tortola:** ✆011-284-494-3134
- **Virgin Gorda:** ✆011-284-495-5181

To research hotel or resort accommodations and other information about the BVI, go to any of these three excellent Web sites:

- **The BVI Tourist Board:** ✐*www.bvitouristboard.com*
- **Welcome Online:** ✐*www.bviwelcome.com*
- **BritishVirginIslands.com:** ✐*www.britishvirginislands.com*

The BVI Tourist Board also maintains visitor information centers in Road Town (Tortola) and at the Tortola International Airport.

Unless you're specifically looking for seclusion, the location of your resort or hotel, along with the amenities it offers, is important. Where you stay will also determine whether you need a rental car to get around the island.

Aside from Tortola and Virgin Gorda, which are the two most popular BVI islands, there are dozens of other less populated islands that can be reached by boat or ferry transport. Virtually all popular activities and attractions, however, can be found on these two islands.

This is definitely a destination to consider if boating or spending the majority of your time at the beach is how you'd describe your ideal vacation. In addition to the more popular beaches, which tend to attract tourists, it's easy to find secluded beaches, especially during off-peak travel times.

# CHAPTER 12

# *Cancun*

LOCATED AT THE NORTHEAST point of the Yucatan Peninsula in the Caribbean Sea, Cancun is unique because it's a part of Mexico that was created specifically for tourism. Thus, you'll find a wide range of modern and fully equipped resorts here, all located along a fourteen-mile stretch of pristine white-sand beaches. Combine this with the near-perfect weather Cancun is known for, and you have all the makings of a fun-filled tropical vacation.

## The Ultimate Spring Break Destination

Cancun is a famous spring break destination among college students for several reasons. First, it's relatively easy and inexpensive to reach from the United States. Second, in addition to offering plenty of inexpensive and mid-priced resorts, Cancun is world famous for its nightlife, thanks to the abundance of popular bars and clubs.

If you're staying at one of the more upscale resorts, such as the Ritz-Carlton, Hyatt Cancun Caribe Villas & Resort, or Hyatt Regency Cancun, it doesn't matter when you visit Cancun with your family. However, if you'll be traveling during a period when college students are typically on break and you're planning to stay at one of the less expensive (economy) resorts with your kids or teens, beware! The wild college parties tend to go round-the-clock, throughout the resorts and in all of the nightclubs and bars.

# The Scoop on Cancun

Mexico offers a wide range of vacation opportunities. Perhaps the most notable and definitely the most popular vacation destination in Mexico is Cancun. This island offers a wide range of luxurious beachfront hotels, resorts, and all-inclusive resorts, operated by companies like Club Med, Iberostar, Hyatt, Radisson, Omni, Sheraton, Westin, Ritz-Carlton, and Hilton.

Throughout Cancun, you'll find a great selection of water- and land-based activities (often offered at the various hotels and resorts), plenty of shopping, and an exciting nightlife (for adults). When it comes to dining and nightlife, for example, Cancun offers over 350 restaurants and clubs. No matter what your taste or budget, there's a memorable vacation waiting to be had in Cancun.

It's no wonder that Cancun attracts over 3 million visitors per year. Aside from its beauty, one of Cancun's most appealing aspects is its accessibility to the American tourist. Most people in Cancun speak English, the U.S. dollar is widely accepted (although the local currency is the Mexican peso), and the majority of the hotels and resorts offer the modern amenities and conveniences you'd want. All of the resorts use standard 110-volt electricity (which is identical to that found in the United States).

 **TRAVEL TIP**

If you're not fluent in Spanish, before leaving home, pick up a Spanish/English dictionary to help you communicate more easily with the locals.

Virtually all of the hotels and resorts in Cancun are conveniently located in one area along the beach, known as the hotel zone. Since there's only one main road—Kukulcan Boulevard, which runs along the hotel zone—it is relatively easy to get around by foot, taxi, or bicycle.

Kukulcan Boulevard also leads to an area commonly known as the party zone, which is where you'll find many popular nightclubs, bars, and restaurants, along with shopping malls. The nearby downtown area of Cancun offers a more traditional Mexican atmosphere, with more shopping and dining options.

First and foremost, Cancun is a beach community for tourists. The majority of activities you'll find in Cancun somehow involve the Caribbean Sea. There are, however, various day trips and sightseeing tours, which you'll read about later in this chapter. In the downtown Plaza de Toros, for example, you can witness a traditional bullfight every Wednesday afternoon.

 **TRAVEL TIP**

While in Cancun or anywhere in Mexico, drink only distilled or bottled water. Refrain from eating raw fruits and vegetables or any foods prepared with water that hasn't been properly treated. As a precaution, be sure to pack a bottle of Pepto-Bismol, as well as antacids like Tums.

## A Bit of Cancun History

Just over thirty years ago, Cancun was little more than a barrier island. It has since evolved into a vacation destination that was created for one purpose: to attract tourism. Cancun is a fourteen-mile long island that connects to the mainland of Mexico via two bridges. Along this strip of land, vacationers will find everything they could want from a beautiful tropical getaway, including plenty of gorgeous beaches.

While Cancun is relatively new as a tourist destination, it was inhabited by the Maya people for 5,000 years. Many Mayan ruins still stand today and have become popular places for tourists to explore as they look back in time and see how the Maya culture left such a tremendous legacy in Mexico.

## The Local Weather

Cancun offers a lovely tropical climate. During the dry season, which goes from December through April, expect the average temperature to be around 74 degrees. The rainy season goes from May through November. During this time, the average temperature will be around 95 degrees.

## Getting to Cancun

If you'll be vacationing in Cancun and arriving by air, the closest international airport is the Cancun International Airport. It's located between ten and twenty minutes from the majority of the hotels and resorts located in Cancun's hotel zone.

Most major airlines fly to Cancun, typically with nonstop flights from major hubs and U.S. cities. It may, however, be necessary to book a connecting flight to Cancun, depending on your airline of choice and the city you're flying from. Some of the major airlines that offer direct or connecting flights from many U.S. cities to Cancun include these:

- **AeroMexico**: ☏800-237-6639, ✎*www.aeromexico.com*
- **American Airlines**: ☏800-433-7300, ✎*www.aa.com*
- **Continental Airlines**: ☏800-231-0856, ✎*www.continental.com*
- **Delta Airlines**: ☏800-241-4141, ✎*www.delta.com*
- **Northwest Airlines**: ☏800-900-0800, ✎*www.northwest.com*
- **United Airlines**: ☏800-241-6522, ✎*www.united.com*
- **US Airways**: ☏800-748-1070, ✎*www.usairways.com*

## Cancun International Airport

Before your family boards your flight or during the flight to Cancun, each of you will be given a tourist card to fill out. This card must be completed prior to landing in Cancun and should be kept with your airline tickets at all times during your travels. On this form, you'll need to write your name, address, passport number, where you'll be staying in Mexico, your arrival and departure dates, and other information that's relevant to your trip. Ultimately, you will need to present this card upon entering and exiting the country. More information about Cancun International Airport can be found online at ✐*www.cancun-airport.com.*

Also during your flight from the United States to Cancun, you'll be provided with a customs form to fill out prior to landing. This completed form will be handed to the customs agent when you arrive in Cancun. To avoid unnecessary delays, be sure the form is fully and accurately completed. If you need assistance, ask your flight attendant.

United States citizens can enter into Cancun without a U.S. passport as long as they present a birth certificate *and* a government-issued photo ID (such as a valid driver's license). Ideally, a passport should be presented as you go through immigration at the airport upon your arrival to Cancun. A visa is not required for American citizens to enter into Cancun (or any part of Mexico). As you go through immigration, you may be asked several questions, such as the purpose of your trip and how long you'll be staying.

Once you've gone through immigration, you will be directed to baggage claim to collect your luggage. It's important to have your luggage claim tags ready. (These are provided when you check it at the airport prior to your departure.) With your luggage in hand, you'll then go through customs and ultimately be directed to the area of the airport where you can meet ground transportation to take you to your hotel or resort. The length of this whole process ranges from thirty to ninety minutes, depending on crowds.

## ≡FAST FACT

Your airfare or travel package probably includes a $21 per-person departure tax from Cancun. Be sure to determine in advance if this tax will has already been paid or if you should be ready to pay it before you leave the Cancun airport.

# Getting Around Cancun

Navigating your way around Cancun is easy, since almost everything you'll want to see and do on the island is located along Kukulcan Boulevard. There are, however, a handful of exciting day trips you can plan, which are most easily reached via rental car or by signing up for a tour.

Rental cars are readily available on the island, but taxis are probably the most convenient way to get around, especially if you'll be experiencing the local nightlife. Bus service is also available to take you up and down Kukulcan Boulevard, but this can be a time-consuming process and isn't convenient if you're traveling with young children.

### Taking Taxis

If your travel package does not include ground transportation and/ or airport transfers, you'll need to pay for a shuttle bus, taxi, or private car service to take you to and from the airport to your hotel or resort.

Transportation can be reserved in advance by calling ✆866-922-6286 between 9:00 A.M. and 9:00 P.M. (EST). You can also make reservations from the Cancun Shuttle Web site (✐*www.cancunshuttle.com*).

As you'll see from the following table, a public shuttle bus offers the cheapest transportation option to your hotel. However, plan on making multiple stops and paying a per-person fee. It could take up to two hours to reach your hotel via the public shuttle bus, depending on the location of your hotel and the route the bus takes. For a family, it makes much more sense to hire a taxi or private car service.

TABLE 12-1
**TRANSPORTATION FROM/TO AIRPORT**

| Type of Transportation | Cost (Each Way) | Cost (Roundtrip) |
|---|---|---|
| Public shuttle | $9 to $16 (per person) | $17 to $26.50 (per person) |
| Taxi (1 or 2 people) | $35 | $55 |
| Taxi (3 to 4 people) | $40 | $60 |
| Private car (1 or 2 people) | $40 | $60 |
| Private van (3 to 7 people) | $45 | $70 |
| Private van (8 to 10 people) | $50 | $85 |

To get around the island, taxis are readily available at all resorts, shopping areas, and tourist attractions, Because the taxis do not have meters, it's important to negotiate your rate before departing. All of the hotels will post average rates to popular destinations, so use these suggested rates as your guide when negotiating with the driver. The trip from Cancun to Riviera Maya, for example, will cost between $30 and $35 each way and take about an hour.

## Renting a Car

At the Cancun International Airport, you can rent a car from Alamo (*www.alamo.com*), Avis (*www.avis.com*), Budget (*www.budget.com*), Hertz (*www.hertz.com*), National (*www. nationalcar.com*), Thrifty (*www.thrifty.com*), and several other well-known companies. The customer service counters for the rental car companies can be found in Terminal #2 at the airport. It is, however, an excellent idea to reserve your rental car in advance by contacting the company of your choice before leaving home. Many of the popular resorts also have rental car counters in their lobbies. Their staff can assist you in renting a car which can be picked up and dropped off at your resort, as opposed to the airport. This is ideal if you want to rent a car for a single day, for example.

## ≡FAST FACT

Gasoline in Cancun is sold by the liter. There are 3.78 liters to a gallon. Look for "Magna Sin" green gas pumps for unleaded gasoline. The prices are about the same as in the United States; however, at most gas stations, only cash is accepted and there are only full-service pumps. Many gas stations close at 10:00 P.M.

# Island-Hopping Made Easy

If you drive south from Cancun for about forty miles, you'll reach Riviera Maya, one of the ancient homes of the Mayans, which has become a popular tourist and resort destination. By taking a short boat or airplane ride, you can visit nearby Cozumel, another beautiful island that attracts scuba divers and vacationers from around the world.

### Riviera Maya

For a more upscale and less nightlife-oriented vacation experience than what's offered in Cancun, Riviera Maya features plenty of beaches, numerous resort hotels, three golf courses, easy access to many Mayan ruins, plus both Xcaret and Xel-Ha (two popular ecological parks that families shouldn't miss visiting).

Additional information about Riviera Maya can be found by going online to *www.rivieramaya.com* or by calling the Riviera Maya Tourism Board at 877-746-6292.

### Cozumel

In addition to offering a few all-inclusive resorts and other top-notch accommodations, Cozumel offers some of the best scuba diving in the world, thanks to underwater visibility of up to 200 feet and over 200 varieties of colorful fish. The land that makes up this island is also a wonderful place to explore if you want to see Mayan ruins, like El Cedral, San Gervasio, and the Castillo Ruins.

For people who aren't attracted to Cancun's famous nightlife and all-night party atmosphere, Cozumel offers a more tranquil vacation experience. Some travel packages offer a several-night stay in both Cancun and Cozumel, which is a great way to experience both popular islands. If you're staying in Cancun, however, a trip to Cozumel by airplane or boat makes for a fun and memorable day trip. While the two islands are geographically close together, they offer somewhat different experiences. Cozumel offers a more Caribbean flair, while Cancun offers a taste of Mexico. Cozumel is also a port of call for several cruise lines.

A ferry makes multiple trips daily, between 5:00 A.M. and 11:00 P.M., back and forth between Cozumel and Playa del Carmen (Riviera Maya). The forty-five-minute journey costs between $15 and $18 per person for a round-trip ticket.

# Where to Stay: Understanding Your Options

What's nice about Cancun is that everything is relatively nearby. Also, all of the resorts offer their own variety of land- and water-based activities, so you never have to travel far to have fun. If you choose to venture outside of your resort, there's plenty of nearby shopping, activities at neighboring resorts, and a handful of other things for the entire family to see and do.

All of the popular resorts and hotels in Cancun are located right on the beach, although the quality of guestroom accommodations and the types of amenities offered vary greatly. Price doesn't necessarily directly correlate with the quality of accommodations, service, and amenities, so it's best to use a travel agent, get referrals from friends, or contact the Cancun Tourism Department/Mexico Tourism Board (✆800-44-MEXICO, ✐www.visitmexico.com) to help you pinpoint suitable resort accommodations. Of course, you can't go wrong making reservations at a well-known luxury resort like the Ritz-Carlton. Resorts rated "moderate" or "economy" are the ones you need to research carefully to ensure they offer what you're looking for.

As you're choosing your resort accommodations, make sure you'll be situated near the beach and that the reservations department confirms the type of room or suite accommodations you need. Since much of your time, at least during the day, will probably be spent participating in beach- or water-based activities, make sure that the resort you choose offers the activities you're most interested in.

To save money, an all-inclusive resort is definitely worthwhile. This way you won't have to pay each time you want to rent anything such as a lounge chair, sailboat, or boogie board. Plus, with an all-inclusive package, the majority of your meals will be included in the price. There are over forty all-inclusive resorts in Cancun, plus dozens of traditional hotels to choose from. Most offer comfortable-sized guestrooms or multibedroom suites that will accommodate families.

## Calling Home and Surfing the Web

Using one of the major U.S. long-distance carriers (and a calling card from one of them), calling home to the U.S. from Cancun is relatively easy. Using an AT&T calling card, for example, you'd first dial the AT&T access number (✆01-800-288-2872), then follow the detailed directions provided. When placing a call to the U.S. from a public phone, look for one that's marked Ladatel or Telmex.

If you're using a calling card provided by the company that provides your long-distance service at home (such as AT&T, Sprint, MCI, or IDT), be sure to contact the phone company before leaving to ensure that international calling privileges are activated on your calling card.

One company that offers prepaid calling cards specifically for calling from Mexico to the U.S. is Creative Calling Solutions International (✐*www.creativecalling.com*). A twenty-four-minute prepaid calling card (for calls from Mexico to the United States) is priced at $10, while a fifty-one-minute prepaid calling card is priced at $20. When purchasing one of these calling cards from the company's Web site, you'll be provided with the access phone number (✆01-800-088-5383) and a special PIN. Upon calling the access number, follow the recording prompts to make calls. Keep in mind that many hotels and resorts charge a connection fee, even for calling toll-free phone numbers (such as access numbers for calling cards).

## Enjoying Your Time in Cancun

The following is just a sampling of the popular water-based activities you'll find along the beaches in Cancun. Keep in mind that if these activities aren't part of an all-inclusive travel package offered at the resort where you're staying, you'll definitely find these and other activities nearby simply by taking a stroll down the beach.

Each resort offers its own activities, many of which are available to nonguests. Plus, you'll find many independent companies operating on the beach that offer popular activities and tours. You can often negotiate prices. Popular water-based sports and activities include the following:

- Deep-sea fishing
- Parasailing
- Snorkeling
- Water-skiing

- Jet Ski rentals
- Sailboat rentals
- Surfing
- Windsurfing

For information about companies that offer these activities, as well as tours in Cancun, visit the Discovery Mexico Web site (*http://tours.discoverymexico.com*).

## Dining Options

There are over 1,200 restaurants in Cancun. In addition to the many restaurants you'll find situated within Cancun's hotel zone, the shopping and tourist areas offer an abundance of restaurants, cafés, and bars. Here, you'll find popular restaurant chains, such as Outback Steak House (011-52-998-883-3350), Margaritaville (011-52-998-885-2375) and Pat O'Brien's (011-52-998-883-0832). Popular fast-food dining options, like McDonald's, are also plentiful, plus you'll find a selection of independently opened and operated restaurants.

As a general rule, the restaurants found in the hotel zone offer more Americanized menus, featuring a blander array of entrees. They also prepare their foods using purified water. The local restaurants in the downtown area, on the other hand, are more apt to offer traditional local cuisine and Mexican dishes.

Throughout Mexico, including Cancun, tourists sometimes fall prey to traveler's diarrhea, which can be caught by eating contaminated fruit and vegetables or by drinking contaminated water. As a general rule, unless you're eating at a hotel or resort (or in a well-known chain restaurant), avoid eating uncooked foods, enjoying drinks with ice, or drinking unpasteurized milk products.

It's a good strategy to drink only bottled water (or tap water that has been boiled for at least ten minutes). If someone in your family becomes mildly ill as a result of the water or local food, Pepto-Bismol usually works well. Drinking purified water is the best strategy to avoid this illness.

# Must-See Activities and Attractions

At many of the resorts, you'll find a wide range of popular water-based activities and sports, plus other traditional resort activities. If you're looking to parasail, for example, but your resort doesn't offer it, simply take a short walk along the beach to a neighboring resort. You'll almost always find the activities you're looking for.

Aside from traditional beach-related activities, Cancun offers an abundance of other things to see and do, whether you're interested in experiencing outdoor adventures, checking out ancient Mayan ruins, shopping, or taking a tour of the area.

Within a short drive from Cancun, you'll also find several other extremely popular and extremely beautiful vacation destinations, such as Riviera Maya, XCaret, and Xel-Ha. You can visit these places by renting a car or taking an organized bus tour. By boat, Cozumel is a short distance away and makes for a fun-filled day trip.

 **TRAVEL TIP**

One of the best views you'll find in Cancun is from atop La Torre Cancun. This is a rotating tower that's located at El Embarcadero Park. The attraction is priced at $9 per ride or $14 for a day pass. It's open daily from 9:00 A.M. to 11:00 P.M. Call ☏011-52-998-889-7777 for information. This attraction offers great photo opportunities.

### Experience a High-Speed Boat Tour

Shotover Jet motorboat rides take you on a forty-five-minute high-speed tour along the beaches of Cancun, around the mangroves, and through several nearby lagoons. This ride is turbulent and involves many quick turns. The boats hold twelve passengers, including a highly trained driver. Plan on wearing a life jacket for the duration of this exciting and memorable trip. If you're going to bring along a camera, make sure it's waterproof and disposable.

This is a popular tour, so be sure to book your reservation at least two days in advance. The price includes a one-day admission ticket to the Wet 'n Wild water park. Tours depart daily from Nizuc park at 11:00 A.M. and 1:00 P.M. To ride this boat, passengers must be at least four feet tall. Prices start at $45 per person for this unforgettable adventure. You can make reservations through the activities desk at your resort.

**BOAT TOUR**

| Ages up to 5 | Ages 6–15 | Ages 16–20 | Adult | Senior Citizens |
|:---:|:---:|:---:|:---:|:---:|
| N.S. | ★★★ | ★★★ | ★★★ | ★ |

## Experience a Genuine Bullfight

Every Wednesday afternoon, starting at around 3:30 P.M. in the Plaza de Toros (☎011-52-998-884-8372), tourists can witness a traditional sport that is a popular part of Mexico's culture—a genuine bullfight. Unlike bullfights of the past, however, this one is a bit less bloody and offers more of a festive presentation, complete with a folkloric dance exhibition and a performance by Mexican *charros* (cowboys).

The bullfights presented in Cancun are definitely more suitable for a teen and adult crowd, and not for kids. Tickets for this weekly event cost $35 per person. All major credit cards are accepted. The Plaza de Toros is easy to find. It's located on the north end of Kukulcan Boulevard.

**BULLFIGHTS**

| Ages up to 5 | Ages 6–15 | Ages 16–20 | Adult | Senior Citizens |
|:---:|:---:|:---:|:---:|:---:|
| N.S. | N.S. | ★★ | ★★ | ★★ |

## See the Mayan Ruins

You don't have to be an archeologist to appreciate the Mayan ruins. The region of Mexico where Cancun is located contains at least 3,000 architectural sites originally created by the Mayans.

Either as a half-day or full-day trip, it's easy to book a tour that'll take you to some of the more famous ruins, such as El Rey and El Meco. From Cancun, some of the most famous Mayan ruins, like Coba, Tulum, and Xel-Ha, are located between one and three hours away by car. If you're a history buff, the trip is well worth it.

When you explore the ancient ruins, you'll see pyramids and other structures which were created as far back as A.D. 1200. Don't forget to bring your camera.

**THE MAYAN RUINS**

| Ages up to 5 | Ages 6–15 | Ages 16–20 | Adult | Senior Citizens |
|:---:|:---:|:---:|:---:|:---:|
| N.S. | ★ | ★★ | ★★ | ★★★ |

## Scuba Diving

Scuba diving is an extremely popular activity among tourists in Cancun and nearby Cozumel, which offers some of the best scuba diving in the world. If you're a certified diver, you'll find a wide range of scuba-diving tours available through the resorts and nearby dive shops.

Plenty of introductory programs and dive tours are available for novice divers. This includes instruction on land, time to become familiar with the scuba equipment in shallow water (or in a swimming pool), and an introductory dive.

When diving near Cancun or Cozumel, you'll see spectacular underwater sights, like coral reefs, exotic fish, and perhaps even a sunken ship or two. The Great Mesoamerican Reef (El Gran Arrecife Maya) is the largest reef in the Western Hemisphere. It's one that scuba divers come from all over the world to see firsthand.

# ≡ FAST FACT

While in Cancun, you can become a certified scuba diver by participating in a four- to five-day course, which costs between $300 and $400.

Many resorts work with certified dive masters to offer introductory scuba programs on the property. There are also several independent dive centers that offer training, equipment rentals, and dive tours, including Scuba Cancun (☎011-52-998-849-7508, *www.scubacancun.com.mx*) and AquaWorld (☎011-52-998-885-2288, *www.aquaworld.com.mx*).

If you're not a scuba diver and not interested in giving this sport a try, many of the dive centers also offer snorkeling tours to some of the best dive sites around Cancun and Cozumel. All equipment and training is provided. Cancun Mermaid (☎011-52-998-843-6517, *www.cancunmermaid.com*), for example, offers family-oriented snorkeling tours, with round-trip transportation from your resort provided.

### SCUBA DIVING

| Ages up to 5 | Ages 6–15 | Ages 16–20 | Adult | Senior Citizens |
|:---:|:---:|:---:|:---:|:---:|
| N.S. | N.S. | ★★★ | ★★★ | ★ |

## Swim with Dolphins

Swimming with dolphins can be a fun and memorable experience for people of all ages, even those who are not strong swimmers. In and around Cancun, several places offer dolphin interaction programs.

Dolphin Discovery (☎011-52-998-849-4757, *www.dolphindiscovery.com*) is located on Isla Mujeres. Here, the dolphin interaction program lasts about one hour (which includes about thirty minutes of actual swim time with the dolphins.) The price is about $120 per person. Transportation from any Cancun resort is available for an additional fee. Advance reservations are definitely required. Programs begin daily at 9:00 A.M., 11:00 A.M., 1:00 P.M., and 3:00 P.M. Space is limited.

Parque Nizuc (☎011-52-998-881-3030) is a Cancun marine park that also offers a chance to swim with dolphins. This experience is priced at about $135 per person and includes admission to the aquarium and park, which also offers water slides, several swimming pools, and a few rides for the kids. For older visitors, Parque Nizuc offers snorkeling, where you're virtually guaranteed to see manta rays, tropical fish, and tame sharks. Parque Nizuc is open daily from 10:00 A.M. to 5:30 P.M. General admission is priced at $33 (adults) and $25 (children, ages three to eleven).

The Interactive Aquarium (☎011-52-998-883-0436) at the La Isla Shopping Center offers a dolphin swim experience, with prices starting at around $110 per person. Guests can also feed sharks and see a wide range of exotic sea creatures at this popular aquarium. It's an ideal place to visit with kids and teens.

### SWIMMING WITH DOLPHINS

| Ages up to 5 | Ages 6–15 | Ages 16–20 | Adult | Senior Citizens |
| --- | --- | --- | --- | --- |
| N.S. | ★★ | ★★★ | ★★★ | ★★ |

## Go Horseback Riding

There are several equestrian centers and ranches in and around Cancun that offer horseback-riding tours. Rancho Loma Bonita (☎011-52-998-887-5465), for example, is a popular ranch located about thirty minutes away from the popular resorts. Here, several different riding tours are available based on skill level and length. One popular tour involves a two-hour ride through the mangrove swamp that ends at a beach, where you can then spend several hours swimming or sunbathing.

This tour costs $72 (adults) and $65 (kids, ages six to twelve). This fee includes round-trip transportation from your resort to the ranch, soft drinks, lunch, the tour guide, and instruction. No previous riding experience is required. Contact Rancho Loma Bonita for details about what to bring and wear when riding the horses, in addition to sunscreen and beach attire.

**HORSEBACK RIDING**

| Ages up to 5 | Ages 6–15 | Ages 16–20 | Adult | Senior Citizens |
|:---:|:---:|:---:|:---:|:---:|
| N.S. | ★ | ★★★ | ★★★ | ★ |

## Visit the Interactive Aquarium

Located within La Isla Shopping Center in the hotel zone of Cancun, this large, interactive aquarium offers many interesting and interactive exhibits that showcase exotic marine life. Within the aquarium itself, you'll see hundreds of species of fish and marine life on display. Some of the exhibits are truly interactive, allowing visitors to touch the animals.

One of the popular activities, offered every half hour between 11:00 A.M. and 8:30 P.M., is the opportunity to feed sharks. This is a totally safe activity that requires no swimming. You won't even get wet! For an additional fee, there's a swimming with dolphins program that's suitable for anyone over the age of eight.

**THE INTERACTIVE AQUARIUM**

| Ages up to 5 | Ages 6–15 | Ages 16–20 | Adult | Senior Citizens |
|:---:|:---:|:---:|:---:|:---:|
| N.S. | ★★★ | ★★★ | ★★ | ★★ |

## Take a Day Trip to Xel-Ha

No trip to Cancun is complete without taking a day trip to Xel-Ha, a park located in Riviera Maya about seventy-six miles south of Cancun. Xel-Ha offers a wide range of activities for people of all ages and easily provides a full day's worth of memorable adventure and entertainment. This beautiful, all-natural paradise is open daily.

While many activities at Xel-Ha are included in the price of admission, some activities, like swimming with the dolphins, visiting the day spa, snuba diving, and the underwater Sea Trek experience cost extra.

Throughout the day, you are free to enjoy a wide range of water- and land-based activities, such as hiking, snorkeling, swimming, relaxing in a hammock, floating down the Xel-Ha River on a tube, experiencing an eco-tour to learn about the local wildlife and environment, exploring the tree nursery, experiencing the Path of Conscience, or allowing your kids to enjoy the playground.

The best deal for families is to purchase the all-inclusive admission, which includes use of all amenities within the park, including showers, bathrooms, floats, life jackets, hammocks, snorkeling equipment, towels, family-size lockers, meals, and soft drinks. Prices are $56 per day for adults and $28 per day for kids (ages 5 to eleven).

## ≡FAST FACT

Xel-Ha offers a variety of water-based activities for those who don't swim. The park's Aquatic Institute offers Sea Trek, for example, which allows you to explore the underwater sights without actually getting in the water. Lifejackets and other safety gear are readily available.

Basic weekday admission is $29 for adults and $15 for kids. On weekends, basic admission is priced at $22 per adult and $11 per child. With basic admission, you'll pay extra for things like locker rentals, towels, and the use of snorkeling equipment.

The park is open every day, from 9:00 A.M. until 6:00 P.M. You can reach this park easily by rental car or the public bus system. Take the bus downtown, then take another bus toward Tulum. Request to be dropped off at the entrance of Xel-Ha, and expect to walk about five minutes to the main gate.

Make sure you wear comfortable shoes, as you'll be doing considerable walking. Beach shoes will also be useful. Also pack bathing suits, sunscreen, and sunglasses for everyone. When not engaged in water-based activities, cool, comfortable clothing (shorts and a T-shirt) are a must while visiting this park.

**XEL-HA PARK**

| Ages up to 5 | Ages 6–15 | Ages 16–20 | Adult | Senior Citizens |
|:---:|:---:|:---:|:---:|:---:|
| N.S. | ★★★ | ★★★ | ★★★ | ★★ |

## Day Trip to XCaret Ecological and Archaeological Park

Located forty-five minutes from Cancun, XCaret, like Xel-Ha, offers at least a full day's worth of outdoor fun and activities. Many of the activities are suitable for people of all ages, making this the perfect family attraction.

XCaret opened to the public in 1990 and has been expanding ever since. The park now offers dozens of different activities, including an aquarium, beach, swimming with dolphins, a wild bird aviary, jungle walk, zoo (with crocodiles, deer, monkeys, sea turtles, butterfly pavilion, and more), ecological walking tours, wading pools, scuba-diving tours, snorkeling, Sea Trek expeditions, snuba diving, swimming, hiking, sunbathing, and tours to archeological sites, such as a Mayan village. Live entertainment is also offered throughout the day and evening.

Many activities are included in the price of admission to XCaret, although there is an extra fee to participate in certain activities, like swimming with the dolphins. Basic admission is priced at $49 per day for adults and $25 per day for children (ages five to twelve). Round-trip transportation from your hotel can be arranged for an additional fee.

The park is open daily from 9:00 A.M. to 9:00 P.M. (10:00 P.M. in the summer). Free parking is available. Public bus transportation and scheduled bus tours are available from Cancun. For information, call ☎011-52-998-883-3144 or visit the attraction's Web site at ⌘*www.xcaret.com*.

**XCARET'S ECOLOGICAL AND ARCHAEOLOGICAL PARK**

| Ages up to 5 | Ages 6–15 | Ages 16–20 | Adult | Senior Citizens |
|:---:|:---:|:---:|:---:|:---:|
| N.S. | ★★★ | ★★★ | ★★★ | ★★★ |

### See Cancun by Helicopter

Several companies offer short and relatively inexpensive helicopter tours of Cancun that allow you to see the island from a bird's eye perspective. If you and your kids have never experienced a helicopter flight, this is an opportunity for a grand adventure, topped off with the opportunity to see some incredibly beautiful places.

Daytime and nighttime flights are available, as are tours to the Mayan ruins and along the Riviera Maya coastline. Several different tour routes are available. You can, however, charter the helicopter by the hour and have a tour customized just for your family. An introductory fifteen-minute flight that'll take you over the Cancun hotel zone is priced around $80 per person.

During the tour, your pilot will also act as your guide. Be sure to bring along a camera! For more information or to make a reservation, contact Heli Data (☎011-52-998-883-3104) or HeliTours (☎011-52-998-849-4222).

**HELICOPTER TOURS**

| Ages up to 5 | Ages 6–15 | Ages 16–20 | Adult | Senior Citizens |
|:---:|:---:|:---:|:---:|:---:|
| N.S. | ★★★ | ★★★ | ★★★ | ★★ |

# Shopping in Cancun

While in Cancun, you'll definitely want to spend time exploring the shopping areas, where you'll find everything from locally made crafts to designer fashions from around the world. Expect to find several outdoor marketplaces, plus a handful of modern, indoor malls. You'll also discover an array of duty-free shops, offering significant discounts on European goods, as well as jewelry, designer watches, liquor, tobacco products, and perfumes. The U.S. dollar, along with traveler's checks and major credit cards, is accepted virtually everywhere.

## ≡FAST FACT

The prices in the shops located downtown, especially in the duty-free shops, tend to be slightly lower than what you'll find elsewhere on the island. UltraFemme (☎011-52-998-884-1402) is a popular duty-free shop with locations in downtown Cancun and in several shopping areas throughout the island.

Cancun is first and foremost a tourist destination. You can find locally made crafts and items, but prices will be higher than in other parts of Mexico. The Mexican crafts are not actually created in Cancun, so you wind up paying a premium for them. Near the hotel zone, for example, you'll find the open-air crafts market known as Coral Negro, which is open daily from 7:00 A.M. to 11:00 P.M. This is just one of the popular and conveniently located markets where you'll find locally made souvenirs, art, and various types of crafts.

Along Kukulcan Boulevard, several indoor malls can be found. You'll find a wide range of items, from designer fashions to jewelry and crystal. Many of the malls also contain multiple restaurants and nightclubs. The stores are typically open daily from 10:00 A.M. until 10:00 P.M., but the restaurants and clubs stay open much later. Unlike those in many U.S. cities, the clubs in Cancun don't have a designated closing time.

One of the largest indoor malls in Cancun is the Plaza Kukulcan (☎011-52-998-885-2200, ✐www.kukulcanplaza.com). This popular mall is comprised of more than 300 shops and restaurants. In terms of fine dining, you'll be pleased to find the famous Ruth's Chris Steak House. Kids will love engaging in a fun-filled game of laser tag at the Q-Zar laser game pavilion and video game arcade in the mall.

Within Cancun, you'll also find many themed dining experiences. Planet Hollywood (✐www.planethollywood.com), for example, is located within Plaza Flamingo. The Hard Rock Café and the Rainforest

Café are located in the Forum by the Sea mall. All three of these restaurants offer American food and a wonderful family-oriented atmosphere.

If you're looking for an indoor mall with a selection of stores similar to what you'd find in the United States, check out La Isla Shopping Village (☎011-52-998-883-5025, ✎*www.cancunmalls.com*). In addition to great shopping, there's a movie theater here that shows the latest Hollywood blockbusters (in English).

## Golfing in Cancun

There are three eighteen-hole golf courses in Cancun and several more in Riviera Maya. Each offers equipment rentals, instruction, and caddies for hire. Greens fees start at around $120 for eighteen holes. Contact the golf course directly to reserve tee times and for information. Here is contact information for those three courses:

- **Hilton Cancun Beach & Golf Resort**: ☎011-52-998-881-8016. Open from 6:00 a.m. to 6:00 p.m. daily.
- **Pok-Ta-Pok Club (also known as Club de Golf Cancún)**: ☎011-52-998-883-0871. Offers an eighteen-hole course designed by Robert Trent Jones, Sr. Open daily, with hours varying by season.
- **Meliá Cancún**: ☎011-52-998-881-1100. Open daily from 8:00 a.m. until 4:00 p.m.

## Cancun Nightlife

To describe Cancun's nightlife as exciting would be an understatement. On this tropical island, you'll find literally dozens of restaurants, bars, lounges, and nightclubs that are open until the early hours of the morning. Drinking, dancing, and partying are the norm here. Clubbing is one of the few nighttime activities on the island and is definitely the most popular. This scene is definitely not for kids or teens. The drinking age in Cancun is eighteen but tends to be loosely enforced.

One of the most famous nightclubs and bars in Cancun is Carlos 'n Charlies (☎011-52-998-849-4052). In addition to offering a full menu, this club has a fully stocked bar, large dance floor, and live musical performances nightly (starting around 8:30 P.M.).

## Making Cancun Your Vacation Destination

As you're planning your Cancun vacation, visit the following informative Web sites to help you find the best resorts and money-saving package deals, which include airfare, all-inclusive resort accommodations, and ground transfers:

- **Cancun Today**: *www.cancuntoday.net*
- **Discovery Cancun**: *www.discoverycancun.com*
- **Go 2 Cancun**: *www.go2cancun.com*
- **Visit Mexico**: *www.visitmexico.com*

Cancun is a wonderful vacation destination because it was built from the ground up specifically for vacationers. From a convenience and cost standpoint, Cancun also offers one of the best vacation deals in the Caribbean. From a budgeting standpoint, a wide range of accommodations are available. Because Cancun is located so close to other exciting places, like Cozumel and Riviera Maya, for example, there's never a shortage of places to go, things to see, or activities to experience.

Cayman Islands

Lesser Caymans
(U.K.)

Spot Bay

Cayman
Brac

West End

Blossom Village

Little
Cayman

Caribbean Sea

Parish Center

Airport

Road

0        25 Miles

0        25 Kilometers

West
Bay

West
Bay

North
Sound

Georgetown

Owens
Roberts Airport

North Side
Village

Old Man Village

Boddentown

East End

Grand Cayman
(U.K.)

# CHAPTER 13

# *The Cayman Islands*

THE CAYMAN ISLANDS CONSIST of three popular islands: Grand Cayman, Cayman Brac, and Little Cayman. All three islands offer wonderful vacation opportunities, and it's easy to travel between islands to experience everything this region of the Caribbean has to offer. Whether you're traveling by air or will only have a day on your cruise ship itinerary, the Cayman Islands offer an abundance of activities and attractions and plenty of duty-free shopping.

## The Scoop on the Cayman Islands

The Cayman Islands are relatively small. All three islands combined have a land mass of only 100 square miles. Grand Cayman, the largest of the three islands, is about twenty-two miles long by eight miles wide, while Cayman Brac is only twelve miles long by just over one mile wide. The smallest of the islands, Little Cayman, is ten miles long by one mile wide.

All three islands are surrounded by large coral reefs, which offer incredible snorkeling and scuba-diving opportunities. Between the Cayman Islands and Jamaica, however, you'll find some of the deepest waters in the Caribbean Sea (in some places, up to four miles deep).

 **TRAVEL TIP**

The Cayman Islands are located about 480 miles south of Miami, Florida, allowing visitors to reach Grand Cayman Island by air in about seventy minutes from Miami.

The official language throughout the Cayman Islands is English, although many of the Caymanian people speak with a strong accent, with Welsh, Scottish, Jamaican, and Central American influences. The local population is estimated at just over 40,000, with Georgetown, Grand Cayman Island, being the most heavily populated district. In addition to the locals, the workforce on these islands come from Jamaica, the United States, Canada, and the United Kingdom. In Georgetown, for example, you'll find an abundance of international banks, investment firms, and financial institutions interspersed between the shops and tourist areas.

Several areas of the Cayman Islands, particularly Georgetown and the rest of Grand Cayman, are particularly tourist friendly. You will find an abundance of fine-dining restaurants, nightclubs, and modern resorts and hotels, but there are no casinos on these islands. The legal drinking age is eighteen.

Whether you're shopping, dining, or enjoying the local attractions, the U.S. dollar is widely accepted everywhere throughout the three islands. Since 1972, the Cayman Islands have had their own currency, the CI, which is also based on the dollar. Cayman Island currency has a fixed exchange rate to the U.S. dollar, with $1 CI being equal to $1.25 U.S. (or $1 U.S. equaling $.80 CI). While the exchange rate remains constant, if you're using a currency exchange service, you will need to pay fees to exchange currency.

You'll find over 150 restaurants and cafés on Grand Cayman Island, so whatever your taste or budget, there are plenty of dining options. Many restaurants here offer kid's menus. You'll also find a number of popular fast-food chain restaurants, which your kids will definitely appreciate.

In terms of electricity, throughout all three islands, you'll find standard 110-volt outlets, identical to those in the United States.

The Cayman Islands are definitely a tourist destination that's more suited to adults. If you're traveling with kids or teens, however, there are enough activities and attractions here to keep families entertained for several days, providing you select the right resort accommodations (one that offers numerous activities). For scuba divers, people who enjoy snorkeling, and shoppers, however, the Cayman Islands is a perfect vacation spot.

# A Bit of Cayman Islands History

The modern history of the Cayman Islands began back in 1503, when Christopher Columbus reached Little Cayman and Cayman Brac during his fourth voyage to the New World. He happened upon the islands when the local winds blew his ships slightly off course. From the sixteenth to eighteenth centuries, the Cayman Islands were a popular port for English, Dutch, French, and Spanish ships that needed to replenish supplies. The islands came under British control in 1655. For almost 300 years after that, the three islands were ruled as a dependency of Jamaica.

## ≡FAST FACT

During the eighteenth century, the Cayman Islands were occupied by pirates like Blackbeard. It's believed that these pirates left buried treasures throughout the islands that have yet to be found.

Throughout the twentieth century, the people of the Caymans relied on the waters surrounding their islands to support their economy. In 1962, when Jamaica won its independence, the Cayman Islands maintained their ties to the British by remaining a British Crown colony. Today, the islands' economy is supported by tourism and the international financial industry.

## The Local Weather

During the winter months (November through April), the average daytime temperature throughout the Cayman Islands is between 72 and 85 degrees. At night, the temperature drops to between 65 and 72 degrees. The average water temperature is between 78 and 82 degrees, which makes it ideal for swimming and participating in a wide range of water sports.

The summer months (May through October) are considered the rainy season. Daytime temperatures average between 85 and 90 degrees, while at night the temperature might drop to between 72 and 85 degrees. The average water temperature is between 81 and 85 degrees. It's not uncommon to experience a rain shower in the afternoon, which will often quickly pass and be replaced by sunshine.

While you can generally expect to experience nearly perfect weather during your visit, the time between June 1 and November 31 is considered hurricane season. If you'll be traveling to the Cayman Islands during this period, you might encounter a tropical storm or two, and perhaps a hurricane. These storms, however, are forecasted well in advance. If necessary, an evacuation plan will be implemented, although this is seldom necessary. It is, however, a good idea to purchase optional travel or hurricane insurance for your trip if you'll be traveling during hurricane season.

 **TRAVEL TIP**

Especially during the rainy season, be sure to pack a lightweight, waterproof jacket and extra shoes/sneakers to ensure that you stay comfortable if you get caught in a rain shower.

## Getting to the Cayman Islands

Many people visit the Cayman Islands while cruising the Caribbean, but this is also a wonderful stand-alone vacation destination. From the United States, several major airlines, including Air Jamaica, American Airlines, British Airways, Delta Airlines, Northwest Airlines, US Airways, Island Air, and Cayman Airways offer nonstop or connecting flights from many major U.S. airports.

Cayman Airways (✆800-4-CAYMAN, ✆011-345-949-8200, *www. caymanairways.com*) offers nonstop flights between Grand Cayman and Miami, Ft. Lauderdale, Tampa, Chicago, and Houston, plus connecting service from several other Caribbean islands, including Jamaica.

The main international airport on Grand Cayman Island is the Owen Roberts International Airport. Cayman Brac, however, also has a smaller international airport, called the Gerrard Smith International Airport. Little Cayman can only be reached by boat or via a small aircraft offering an interisland flight. There are more than 180 flights to the Caymans per week, including seventy flights per week from Miami, Florida, to one of the Cayman Islands' two international airports.

## ═══FAST FACT

Upon leaving the Cayman Islands, visitors must pay a $25 per-person departure tax, which is usually, but not always, included in the price of airline tickets. Determine in advance if this fee has been prepaid to avoid accidentally paying it twice.

To enter into the Cayman Islands, American tourists must have a valid passport and a return or continuing airline ticket (if arriving by air). A birth certificate and government-issued ID (such as a driver's license) can also be used if a passport isn't available. If you have questions about entering the Cayman Islands from the United States or another country, contact the Cayman Islands' Department of Immigration at ✆011-345-949-8052.

Upon arriving in the Cayman Islands, the immigration department will provide visitors with a pink immigration card. This card should be kept with your passport until your departure.

# Island-Hopping Made Easy

From Grand Cayman, you can either fly or take a boat to the other islands. Island Air (☎011-345-949-5252, ✎*www.islandaircayman.com*) and Cayman Airways (☎800-327-8777, ☎011-345-949-8200, ✎*www.caymanairways.com*) both offer regularly scheduled air service between the three islands on 19-passenger turboprop Twin Otter and nine-passenger Navajo Chieftain aircrafts. The flight between Grand Cayman and Cayman Brac or Little Cayman takes about 40 minutes.

## Cayman Island

If you're visiting the Cayman Islands to experience the shopping and local attractions, and to participate in a wide range of land- and water-based activities, much of your time will most likely be spent on Grand Cayman. Georgetown is the capital city of the Cayman Islands. Here, you'll find a wide range of modern hotels and resorts, countless restaurants, plenty of bars and nightclubs, and enough duty-free shopping to tire out the most energetic shopaholics.

For people who enjoy wildlife and nature, Grand Cayman is famous for its Seven Mile Beach, considered to be one of the most beautiful in all of the Caribbean, as well as the sixty-five-acre Queen Elizabeth II Botanic Park and the National Trust's Mystic Trail.

Out of the three islands that comprise the Cayman Islands, this one is the most suitable for family vacationers because of the abundance of activities offered here.

## Cayman Brac

The local population living on Cayman Brac (called Brackers) is fewer than 1,400. This island is comprised of a series of small towns, where beautiful landscapes are the norm. World-famous scuba diving, and snorkeling sites and fishing are what attract many visitors to this relatively small Caribbean getaway.

On land, this island offers a network of caves to explore, as well as hiking trails that allows tourists to experience much of the island's natural beauty and wildlife. For those who don't scuba dive, Cayman

Brac offers a nice half-day or full-day side trip if you're staying on Cayman Island.

### Little Cayman

This is the least developed of the Cayman Islands. Most of this island is uninhabited. What this island offers vacationers is the ultimate in privacy and the opportunity to experience total relaxation, since there are few actual activities or attractions on this island aside from the beaches.

Scuba diving is an extremely popular activity on Little Cayman, where you can get instruction and find introductory dives. Right off the coastline, you'll find Bloody Bay and Jackson Point, where the coral formations, starting at just twenty feet, are a sight to behold. Another popular activity on this island is fishing. The fifteen-acre Tarpon Pond is a popular spot for catching gamefish.

The animals and wildlife on Little Cayman are diverse and plentiful. Visitors will see everything from rare and exotic birds to a population of well over 2,000 iguanas. Throughout the island, you'll find several hiking trails.

# Getting Around the Cayman Islands

On Grand Cayman, rental cars, taxis, and public buses are all popular forms of transportation. The public bus system runs from 6:00 a.m. until midnight. Service runs throughout Georgetown and from Georgetown to West Bay, Boddentown, the East End, and the North Side. The easiest way to get around Georgetown, however, is either on foot or by taxi.

### Taking Taxis

From the airport on Grand Cayman Island, the taxis work on a fixed rate to all hotel and resort destinations. You'll find taxis readily available at all hotels and resorts, as well as at all popular tourist destinations and throughout Georgetown.

### Renting a Car

Rental cars are available on Grand Cayman Island. Cars here drive on the left side of the road. A local (temporary) driver's license is required before renting a car. This can be obtained from the police station or from any rental car company. The fee is $7.50, and the driver must present a valid driver's license from their home country.

Most of the major car-rental companies all have offices in the Caymans, including Avis (*www.avis.com*) and Hertz (*www.hertz.com*). The minimum age to rent a car is twenty-one for drivers who have their own insurance. To purchase daily rental car insurance in conjunction with the rental car, drivers must be at least twenty-five years old. Local rental-car companies in the Caymans include the following:

- **Andy's Rent A Car:** ☏011-345-949-5579 (Grand Cayman)
- **Buccaneer Rentals:** ☏011-345-948-2020 (Little Cayman)
- **Economy Car Rental:** ☏011-345-949-9550 (Grand Cayman)
- **McLaughlin's Enterprises:** ☏011-345-948-1000 (Little Cayman)
- **Soto's Jeep and Car Rentals:** ☏011-345-945-2424, ☏800-625-6174 (Grand Cayman)
- **Sunshine Car Rental:** ☏011-345-949-3858 (Grand Cayman)

Throughout Grand Cayman and Cayman Brac, motorized scooters and mopeds are readily available for rent. The average daily rental fee is $25. Both riders and passengers must wear helmets (provided) at all times. Also, drivers of scooters and mopeds must adhere to local driving laws.

# Where to Stay: Understanding Your Options

Grand Cayman Island offers a great selection of full-service resorts, featuring plenty of modern amenities, on-property activities, and top-notch service. You'll also find guestrooms and suites in a wide range of configurations, so finding ideal accommodations for families and extended families is relatively easy.

Resorts like the Hyatt Regency Grand Cayman, Westin Casuarina Resort, Marriott Cayman Beach Resort, and the new Ritz-Carlton Resort (slated to open in October 2005), all offer upscale accommodations and everything you'd expect from a full-service resort, including organized activities for kids and teens. Grand Cayman also offers a selection of smaller low-rise hotels, as well as villas and cottages for rent. On Cayman Brac and Little Cayman, you'll find more inns, guesthouses, and rental cottages and villas, as opposed to full-service resort properties. To find an agency that specializes in villa or guesthouse rentals, using any Internet search engine, enter the search phrase "Grand Cayman Island villa rental."

If you're looking to truly get away and simply relax at the beach (or go scuba diving or snorkeling) during your vacation, staying on Cayman Brac or Little Cayman makes sense. If, however, you're more interested in a wide range of land- and water-based activities that are suitable for the entire family, you'll definitely find more to see and do on Grand Cayman, so staying on this island is recommended.

## ≡FAST FACT

If you're interested in renting a condo or villa during your stay in the Cayman Islands, contact the Cayman Islands Condominium Service at ☎877-722-2114, ✉www.caymancondoservice.com. Many condos and villas offer multiple bedrooms and a full kitchen. Rates vary dramatically by season.

## Calling Home and Surfing the Web

On Grand Cayman, you'll find modern phone service and high-speed Internet access available at several Internet cafés as well as at popular hotels and resorts. On Cayman Brac and Little Cayman, however, both phone service and Internet service are limited.

One of the cheapest ways to call the United States is using a prepaid phone card, which you can purchase at stores, the post office, and hotels throughout the islands. Limited cellular phone service is available on the islands, except in and around Georgetown, where your existing cell phone will work if you have an international roaming plan compatible with the services offered by Cable & Wireless, Ltd., the local phone company.

Dial-up Internet access is available from any telephone for under $.12 per minute. Simply dial the local access number, which is ☎345-976-4638. No password is required.

# What to See and Do

Activities and attractions are somewhat limited on Cayman Brac and Little Cayman, but you'll have no trouble finding a wide range of land- and water-based activities on Grand Cayman, especially if you're staying in or near Georgetown. On this island, you'll find virtually all of the activities you read about in Chapter 5, plus a handful of attractions that are exclusive to the Cayman Islands.

If you want to enjoy any activities without your kids, private baby-sitting services are available at many of the resorts. You can also call Baby-Sitting & More (☎345-949-1509) to arrange for private in-room baby-sitting services wherever you're staying.

### Enjoy the Beaches

Although you'll find many beaches along the coastline of Grand Cayman, Cayman Brac, and Little Cayman, the most famous beach (and the one that people travel from around the world to experience) is Seven Mile Beach, located on Grand Cayman, just outside of Georgetown. Along Seven Mile Beach, you'll encounter many tour operators that offer boat rentals and various activities. Parasailing, for example, is a popular activity here. Plan on spending about $50 per person for a parasailing adventure.

The following is a list of water-sport tour operators you'll find along Seven Mile Beach. Many of these companies offer parasailing and other water sports and activities:

- **Abank's Watersports & Tours, Ltd.:** ☏011-345-945-1444
- **Agua Delights:** ☏011-345-945-4786
- **Beach Club Watersports:** ☏800-482-3483
- **Bob Soto's Diving, Ltd.:** ☏800-262-7686
- **Cayman Skyriders:** ☏011-345-949-8745
- **Kirk Sea Tours and Watersports:** ☏011-345-949-6986

### Golfing in the Cayman Islands

On Grand Cayman Island, you'll find several championship nine- and eighteen-hole golf courses that offer immaculate landscaping and breathtaking views. The Links at Safehaven (☏344-949-5988) is located about five miles outside of George Town and meets all USGA standards. A clubhouse, locker rooms, bar, pro shop, and putting green are available here.

Located near Seven Mile Beach at the Hyatt Regency Grand Cayman is The Britannia (☏345-949-8020, ✐*www.britanniagolfclub. com*), a Jack Nicklaus–designed eighteen-hole course. In addition to local tournaments that are held regularly, this course offers special programs for young golfers.

The Sunrise Family Golf Center (☏345-947-4653, ✐*www. sunrisecayman.com*) is a nine-hole course that's located about fifteen minutes outside of Georgetown. This walking course was designed specifically for young golfers, novice players, and families. Equipment can be rented here from the pro shop, and both private as well as group instruction is available.

# Dining Options

There are over 100 restaurants throughout the Cayman Islands, including many popular fast-food chain establishments, like McDonald's, Wendy's, Burger King, Domino's Pizza, and Subway.

For families, mid-priced dining options are also plentiful, particularly on Grand Cayman, where you'll find European, Italian, Japanese, Thai, German, Mexican, and American cuisines. Popular menu items at mid-priced family-friendly restaurants include hamburgers, chicken, pizza, salads, and subs. The local cuisine, however, has a strong Jamaican influence, which uses jerk, curry, and other seasonings.

# Must-See Activities and Attractions

In addition to spending days at the beach enjoying all of the various water sports, not to mention the sunshine, Grand Cayman offers several family-friendly attractions that are well worth experiencing, whether you're visiting this island for a day or spending a week.

The following sections describe the top ten must-see attractions and family-friendly activities in the Cayman Islands.

### Explore the Cayman Turtle Farm

The Cayman Turtle Farm is the only attraction of its kind in the world. You can see over 16,000 endangered green sea turtles being raised in their natural habitat. Some of these turtles weigh only a few ounces, while others have grown to weigh over 600 pounds.

Guests are invited to explore this attraction at their own pace. Plan on spending at least thirty minutes exploring this farm and the many tanks which house the turtles. Hours of operation are from 8:30 A.M. to 5:00 P.M. daily. Admission is $6 per adult and $3 per child.

The farm is located about eight miles outside of Georgetown in the West Bay area. For more information, call ☎345-949-3894, or go online to ✐*www.turtle.ky*. This is both an entertaining and educational attraction.

**THE TURTLE FARM**

| Ages up to 5 | Ages 6–15 | Ages 16–20 | Adult | Senior Citizens |
| --- | --- | --- | --- | --- |
| ★ | ★★★ | ★★★ | ★★ | ★ |

### Atlantis Submarine Ride

Prepare to take a unique and exotic submarine adventure as you dive 800 to 1,000 feet toward the ocean floor. You'll see incredible ocean life, coral reefs, and several sunken ships through the submarine's portals. Alternatively, you can experience the Seaworld Explorer (operated by Atlantis Adventures), a unique semi-submarine, which offers a less expensive, one-hour tour allowing passengers to get a glimpse under the sea.

The undersea journey in the Atlantis submarine is surprisingly smooth, although if you're claustrophobic, being enclosed within the submarine may not hold much appeal. Also, there are no restrooms available on the actual submarine, so plan accordingly.

Either the Atlantis submarine ride or the Seaworld Explorer ride provides a memorable and exciting experience for people over the age of four. Depending on the depth and length of the dive adventure, the cost is between $32 and $450 per adult, with discounts offered for kids.

This is a much more elaborate and longer submarine ride experience than what Atlantis Adventures offers on other Caribbean islands. Advance reservations are definitely required and can be made online at ✍www.atlantisadventures.com. This is an extremely popular attraction, and it books up quickly. For more information, call ☎345-949-7700.

**ATLANTIS SUBMARINE RIDE**

| Ages up to 5 | Ages 6–15 | Ages 16–20 | Adult | Senior Citizens |
|:---:|:---:|:---:|:---:|:---:|
| N.S. | ★★★ | ★★★ | ★★★ | ★★★ |

### Visit Stingray City

This underwater zoo is home to thousands of stingrays. These big flat sea creatures are generally very friendly and can be touched and fed by visitors. Guests are invited to scuba dive, snorkel, swim or take a glass-bottomed boat ride through the shallow water areas where the stingrays live, then interact with these wondrous sea creatures in their natural habitat.

No matter how you decide to interact with the stingrays, you'll need to take a short boat trip to the area right off the coast of Grand Cayman where these animals can be found. This is one of the most unique water-based attractions you'll find anywhere in the Caribbean. It's also one of the most popular attractions in the Cayman Islands.

**STINGRAY CITY**

| Ages up to 5 | Ages 6–15 | Ages 16–20 | Adult | Senior Citizens |
|:---:|:---:|:---:|:---:|:---:|
| N.S. | ★★★ | ★★★ | ★★★ | ★★ |

## Take a Glass-Bottomed Boat Ride

Between the coral reefs and exotic sea life that live just off the coast of the Cayman Islands, there's a lot for people to see and experience. For people who aren't certified scuba divers and who don't enjoy snorkeling, one of the best ways to see this sea life is to take a glass-bottomed boat ride.

As the name suggests, passengers ride in a 100-foot motorized boat whose bottom (hull) has been replaced by glass viewing portals. This lets passengers look down into the depths of the sea without getting wet.

Glass bottom boat tours are available throughout the islands from several tour operators. They're generally inexpensive (under $30 per person) and last anywhere from one to three hours. Contact your hotel's concierge or your cruise line's land excursion desk for details about how to sign up for one of these memorable tours.

**GLASS-BOTTOMED BOAT RIDE**

| Ages up to 5 | Ages 6–15 | Ages 16–20 | Adult | Senior Citizens |
|:---:|:---:|:---:|:---:|:---:|
| N.S. | ★★ | ★★★ | ★★ | ★★ |

## Visit Cardinal D's Park

Located about five miles from Georgetown, this unique zoo will be of interest primarily to kids. Here, visitors can see over sixty species of exotic birds, iguanas, turtles, ducks, emus, miniature ponies, and an assortment of other animals native to the Cayman Islands. There's also a petting zoo area. For more information, call ✆345-949-8855. The zoo is open seven days a week. Hours of operation vary by season. Plan on spending between one and three hours visiting this zoo.

**CARDINAL D'S PARK**

| Ages up to 5 | Ages 6–15 | Ages 16–20 | Adult | Senior Citizens |
|---|---|---|---|---|
| ★★★ | ★★★ | ★ | ★ | ★ |

## Go Bowling

The Stingray Bowling Center is a relatively new, ten-lane bowling center offering traditional bowling, glow-in-the-dark bowling, and disco bowling, all with computerized scoring. Instruction is available. Call ✆011-345-945-4444 for information. This bowling alley is open every day and is suitable for people of all ages. A snack shop is available on the premises. Bowling balls and shoes can be rented.

**BOWLING**

| Ages up to 5 | Ages 6–15 | Ages 16–20 | Adult | Senior Citizens |
|---|---|---|---|---|
| N.S. | ★★ | ★★ | ★★ | ★★ |

## Sail Aboard the Jolly Roger

Climb aboard a replica seventeenth-century Spanish galleon and prepare to experience life as a pirate. Afternoon sailings are of particular interest to kids and teens, who will be able to fire the ship's cannons and participate in other activities while aboard this eighty-foot-long vessel.

The crew members take on the roles of authentic pirates, guiding passengers through their high-seas adventure. During your journey, the ship will make a stop that enables passengers to go snorkeling or swimming. Advance reservations are recommended. The cruise itself lasts about two hours.

The cost is $35 per adult and $25 per child for an afternoon cruise. Evening and dinner cruises are also available, although the evening sailings are more adult oriented. Transportation from your hotel can be arranged for a small additional fee. For information, contact Jolly Rogers Cruises at ☎345- 945-SAIL, *www.jollyrogercayman.com*.

**THE JOLLY ROGER**

| Ages up to 5 | Ages 6–15 | Ages 16–20 | Adult | Senior Citizens |
|:---:|:---:|:---:|:---:|:---:|
| N.S. | ★★★ | ★★ | ★★ | ★ |

## Visit Grand Cayman's Queen Elizabeth II Botanic Park

Of interest more to adults and older children, the Queen Elizabeth II Botanic Park is open daily, from 9:00 A.M. until 6:00 P.M. This sixty-five-acre park offers thousands of tropical plants and trees, a handful of walking trails, and an iguana breeding and reintroduction facility (which younger people will enjoy).

More than forty acres of this park remain in their natural state. In the visitor's center, you can view exhibits, purchase souvenirs at the gift shop, enjoy a snack at the café, or participate in an introduction and orientation program. The Floral Color Garden features almost three acres of flowers in a rainbow of vibrant colors. The lake area is a wonderful spot for bird-watching.

Admission is $6 for adults and $3.50 for children (ages six to twelve). Guided tours are offered throughout the day. For more information, call ☎345-947-3558 or go online to *www.botanic-park.ky*.

**GRAND CAYMAN'S QUEEN ELIZABETH II BOTANIC PARK**

| Ages up to 5 | Ages 6–15 | Ages 16–20 | Adult | Senior Citizens |
|:---:|:---:|:---:|:---:|:---:|
| N.S. | ★ | ★★ | ★★ | ★★★ |

## Hike the Mastic Trail

The Mastic Reserve and Trail is an area of natural dry forest that is fully protected by the National Trust and is the largest contiguous area of untouched dry, subtropical forest on Grand Cayman. Here, you'll find a wide variety of local plants and wildlife. The Mastic Trail offers a two-mile hiking expedition that's unique and beautiful. Guided walks are offered and take between two and three hours to complete. Comfortable walking/hiking shoes and proper attire is an absolute must. This is a great way to experience the outdoors and is an alternative to the many water-based activities available on Grand Cayman.

As you explore the Mastic Trail, you'll encounter several unique habitats, including the Black Mangrove Wetland, stands of royal palms and silver thatch palms, abandoned agricultural land, and extensive ancient dry forest. As you're hiking, you'll be able to see rare trees, such as cedar and mahogany, plus many mastic trees, which inspired this region's name.

If you visit this area in June, you'll see the wild banana orchid (the national flower of the Cayman Islands) as you walk along the trails. Throughout the year, you'll see an abundance of birds that inhabit the forest areas. One bird that makes its home in this region is the native Cayman parrot, although you'll also see West Indian woodpeckers and perhaps the Caribbean dove, only seen in undisturbed areas.

In terms of other wildlife, expect to encounter butterflies, lizards, snakes (nonpoisonous), frogs, large hermit crabs, and the carton nests of termites as you hike.

For more information about the Mastic Trail, visit the National Trust's Web site at ✐*www.nationaltrust.org.ky*. To take a guided walking tour, call ✆345-945-6588 for reservations. This hike is not suitable for people under the age of six or anyone who isn't physically fit.

### MASTIC TRAIL

| Ages up to 5 | Ages 6–15 | Ages 16–20 | Adult | Senior Citizens |
|:---:|:---:|:---:|:---:|:---:|
| N.S. | ★ | ★★ | ★★★ | ★ |

### Duty-Free Shopping At Its Best

Located in the heart of Georgetown, you'll find an abundance of upscale duty-free shops selling fine jewelry, diamonds, designer watches, perfumes, tobacco products, liquor, china, crystal, designer clothes, and other items at discounted prices. If you're a smart shopper, you can often shave between 30 and 50 percent off of suggested retail prices in the United States. Americans are given a duty-free allowance of $800 per person. (See page 33 for more information on duty-free shopping.)

In addition to the large selection of duty-free shops, where negotiating your best price is the way to get the best deals, you'll find many locally owned shops selling souvenirs, artwork, and a nice selection of handcrafted gift items. For a directory of duty-free stores in the Cayman Islands, go online to ✑*www.dutyfreecayman.com*.

**DUTY-FREE SHOPPING**

| Ages up to 5 | Ages 6–15 | Ages 16–20 | Adult | Senior Citizens |
|---|---|---|---|---|
| N.S. | ★ | ★ | ★★★ | ★★★ |

# Making the Cayman Islands Your Vacation Destination

If you're arriving by cruise ship and have only the afternoon to spend here, choose one or two activities, such as a visit to Seven Mile Beach and/or the Turtle Farm, then enjoy the rest of your time strolling through Georgetown.

For families making the Cayman Islands their vacation destination, plan on spending several days enjoying the beaches and the activities offered at your resort. Set aside one to three full days to go sightseeing (depending on your budget), and experience some of the attractions that are unique to these islands. For these sightseeing days, consider renting a car.

To help you plan your vacation to the Cayman Islands, visit the Cayman Islands Department of Tourism's Web site (✑*www.*

*caymanislands.ky*), which offers detailed information about resorts, hotels, activities, and attractions. You can also request free full-color brochures. Another useful Web site about the Cayman Islands can be found at ✐*www.caymanislands.com.* For an online directory of tour companies, airlines, auto rental agencies, nightclubs, bars, scuba dive shops and other services of interest to tourists, go online to ✐*www.destination.ky.*

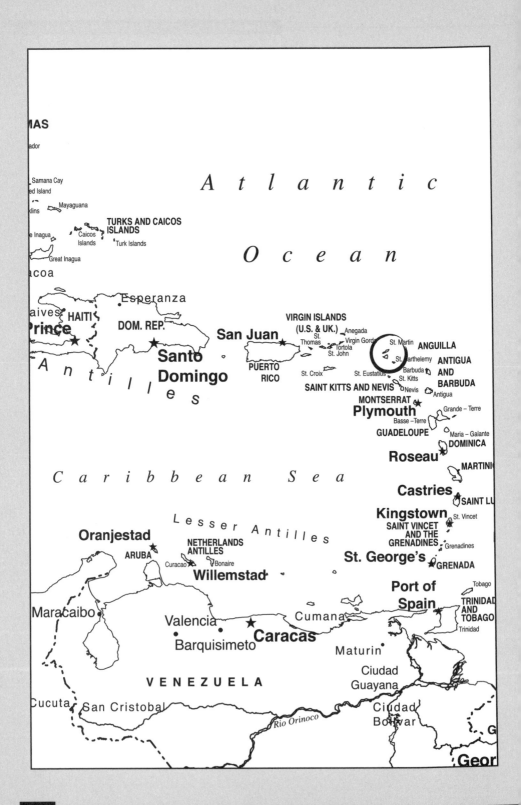

# CHAPTER 14

# St. Maarten (and St. Martin)

ST. MAARTEN/ST. MARTIN OFFERS what many vacationers would consider the ultimate tropical settings. It's far less commercial than most Caribbean islands, and it provides two very different vacation experiences on one island. Divided into two unique sections, there's Dutch St. Maarten on the south side of the island and French St. Martin on the north side. (For convenience, this chapter refers to the island as St. Maarten.) The smallest landmass on the planet that's shared by two separate governments, this island offers vacationers who enjoy the outdoors a wonderful tropical vacation opportunity.

## The Scoop on St. Maarten

The island is located in the Caribbean Sea, approximately 150 miles southeast of Puerto Rico. St. Maarten is contained on a landmass with an area of just thirty-seven square miles, which incorporates Dutch St. Maarten (sixteen square miles, with a population of 41,000) and French St. Martin (twenty-one square miles, with a population of 35,000).

Throughout the island, English is spoken everywhere, although those living here come from over 140 different nationalities. As you'd expect, Dutch is the official language of St. Maarten, while French is the official language of Saint Martin.

This island offers many of the activities you read about in Chapter 5, such as snorkeling, Jet Skiing, windsurfing, parasailing, kite-surfing, deep-sea fishing, tennis, golf, and hiking, but one of the most popular activities for tourists is the St. Maarten 12-Metre Challenge in Philipsburg. Ordinary people, even those with no sailing experience, have a chance to experience the thrill of participating in a scaled-down version of the America's Cup race, while riding aboard ships like Dennis Conner's *Stars & Stripes, Canada II, True North,* or *True North IV.*

In terms of driving, motorists drive on the right side of the street (just like in the United States). While U.S. dollars, major credit cards, and traveler's checks are readily accepted throughout the island, the official currency on the Dutch side of the island is the Netherlands Antilles florin or guilder (NAF). The Euro is the official currency on the French side of the island. Prices in stores, however, are typically displayed in U.S. dollars.

You'll find full-service banks and ATM machines located through-out the island. Not all ATM machines dispense U.S. dollars, however. Be sure to read the signs on the machine to determine what currency that particular machine dispenses.

St. Maarten goes by Atlantic Standard Time, which is one hour ahead of Eastern Standard Time, and observes Daylight Saving Time. All hotels and resorts on the Dutch side of the island use 110-volt electricity (the same as in the United States); however, the French side uses 220-volt power and European outlets. That means you need power adapters or converters to plug in your personal electronics or appliances brought from home, such as laptop computers, camcorders, or electric shavers. Contact your hotel or resort in advance to determine what type of electrical power is available and what special adapters will be required.

## ══FAST FACT

When it comes to dining, St. Maarten features more than 300 restaurants, offering a wide range of Caribbean, Dutch, French, Italian, Chinese, Indonesian, and Creole cuisine. In addition to mid-priced, family-friendly dining, you'll find many fine-dining establishments.

# A Bit of St. Maarten History

For years, the local Indians, known as the Arawaks, were the primary inhabitants of this island, which they referred to as Soualiga ("Land of Salt"). By the time Christopher Columbus "discovered" the island in November 1493, few of the Arawaks had survived an invasion by the Caribs.

The Dutch arrived on the island in 1631. The Spanish stepped in and temporarily drove the Dutch out in 1633. In 1648, after the Eight Years' War between Spain and the Netherlands, the Dutch took possession of the island. At around the same time, the French also claimed the island as their own.

In March 1648, after a skirmish, a settlement was reached and the island was divided between the Dutch and French. This agreement is still in place today. In 1943, the Princess Juliana International Airport was built, and by 1947, when the first hotel opened, tourism had become a prominent part of the island's economy.

By the 1960s, tourism had expanded dramatically. By the mid-1990s, over a million tourists per year were visiting the island, arriving either by air or cruise ship.

# The Local Weather

How can you go wrong when the weather on this island is sunny and warm year-round? There's often a tropical breeze that blows. The average temperature during the winter season is 80 degrees. In the summer, it gets even warmer and a bit more humid. Late summer and early fall is the island's rainy season.

# Getting to St. Maarten

St. Maarten is readily accessible by air, with many airlines offering connecting service from San Juan, Puerto Rico. Airlines that service this island include American Airlines (✍*www.aa.com*) , Continental Airlines (✍*www.continental.com*), Delta Airlines (✍*www.delta.com*), and US Airways (✍*www.usairways.com*). These airlines fly into and out of Princess Juliana Airport, an international airport that's located at Simpson Bay, on the Dutch side of the island. For flight information relating to this airport, call ☎011-599-545-5757. The French side of the island has a smaller regional airport. It offers numerous interisland connecting flights.

## ≡FAST FACT

As you leave St. Maarten by air, be prepared to pay a $20 per-person departure tax. This fee isn't typically included with your airline ticket or travel package.

To enter into St. Maarten, a valid passport along with a return airline ticket is required. (If you're visiting via cruise ship, you need only a passport.) Many of the popular cruise-ship lines that sail throughout the Caribbean offer St. Maarten as a port of call.

## Getting Around St. Maarten

Due to the small size of the island, navigation here is simple, although the roads aren't always of the quality you'd find in the United States. Thus, many vacationers rely on taxis to get around. Rental cars, however, are readily available. You'll also find some public bus transportation available for traveling between popular destinations on the island. While less expensive than taxis or a rental car, the local bus system takes considerably longer, and you have to modify your travel to fit to the posted bus schedules.

### Taking Taxis

Throughout the island, taxis can be found at the airport, at all hotels/resorts, and at taxi stands. The taxis have no fare meters. Instead, drivers are required to charge the official, government-sanctioned rates. As you enter the taxi, agree to the fare in advance. It's also a good idea to consult your hotel's concierge to determine what the rate should be for your destination.

Between 10:00 P.M. and midnight, taxis raise their rates by 25 percent. Between midnight and early-morning, rates increase by 50 percent. It's possible to rent a taxi for several hours, a half day, or a full day if you'd like a private tour of the island. Most of the drivers are very knowledgeable and will provide a totally customized, entertaining, and highly informative driving tour of the island, at your own pace.

### Renting a Car

Many rental car companies, including all of the popular companies, like Hertz (*www.hertz.com*), Avis (*www.avis.com*), and Budget (*www.budget.com*) are available on the island, allowing for rental-car pickup at the airport as well as at many of the larger resorts/hotels. In addition to traditional cars, SUVs, four-wheel-drives, and even motorcycles are available for rent.

When renting a car, you'll usually need a major credit card. If no credit card is available, a refundable cash deposit of at least $350 will be required to pick up your car once a reservation is made. A valid driver's license is required. Motorists drive on the right side of the street throughout the island.

Plan on spending between $35 and $55 per day for a standard rental car. Rates vary based on the size of the vehicle, the time of year, and the rental car company. Prices for specialty vehicles such as four-wheel-drives will be higher. Unlimited mileage is offered with virtually all car rentals. In some cases, if a rental car company isn't offered at your hotel or resort, pickup and delivery service is available.

# Island-Hopping Made Easy

If you want to enjoy a day trip to a nearby Caribbean island, you can either fly or take a ferry. From Philipsburg, Marigot, Anse Marcel, Oyster Pond, and Pelican, for example, there's regular ferry service to Anguilla, St. Barth's, Saba, St. Kitts, and Statia. For information about inter-island boat transportation, call Infos Voyagers at ☎011-599-542-4096.

TRAVEL TIP

To learn what's available on the nearby island of Saba in the Dutch Caribbean, contact the Saba Tourism Bureau at ☎011-599-416-2231 (🖱www.sabatourism.com). This island is an hour away by ferry or fifteen minutes away by air. Ferry transportation costs $57 per person (roundtrip) from St. Maarten, while round-trip airfare will cost around $100 per person.

The Edge Ferry Service (☎011-599-544-2640) and The Voyager (☎011-599-542-4096) offer regularly scheduled trips to several nearby islands.

If you're interested in island-hopping via airplane, Caribbean Star Airlines (☎011-599-545-4234) and WINAIR (☎011-599-545-2568) offers regularly scheduled flights between St. Maarten and many of the Caribbean islands. St. Barth Commuter (☎011-599-545-3651) is a small airline offering flights between St. Maarten and St. Barth's.

# Where to Stay: Understanding Your Options

While you'll find an assortment of large, full-service resorts on the islands, it's much more common for people to stay in rental condominiums or villas, smaller inns, guesthouses, or fully-equipped rental apartments. This alternate method of accommodation offers comfort and convenience, a less commercial and more homey environment, and a chance to better experience the local culture and dining options.

It's important to choose accommodations that offer guestroom configurations that are best suited to your family. You also want to choose a place that's conveniently located near the beach, restaurants, and activities, especially if you don't plan on renting a car.

### Villa Rentals

A villa is a stand-alone house that's equipped with multiple bedrooms, a full kitchen, several bathrooms, and many comforts of home.

Most are equipped with their own laundry facilities and can be rented by the week. For larger families, families traveling with a nanny, or extended families traveling together, you'd probably want multiple (adjoining) bedrooms within a resort or hotel. Renting a villa or condo, however, is a financially viable and extremely convenient option.

Remax Island Properties (☎800-738-9444) can assist you in finding the perfect rental villa or apartment for your vacation. Another local rental agency is Jennifer's Vacation Villas (☎011-599-544-3107).

## ≡FAST FACT

Just twenty minutes away by ferry (or ten minutes by air), Anguilla is a beautiful tropical island with thirty-three beaches. The round-trip ferry ride costs about $25 per person, while round-trip airfare costs around $66 per person, plus taxes. St. Barth's most popular area is Gustavia (a lovely harbor town). It's located about forty-five minutes from Dutch St. Maarten by ferry, a trip that costs under $60 per person (roundtrip).

### Popular Hotels and Guesthouses

The following are some of the popular hotels and guesthouses you'll find on the island. Keep in mind, some of the guesthouses do not allow kids, so be sure to contact the guesthouse directly to discuss your required accommodations before booking a prepaid and non-refundable reservation. Additional information about these and other hotels, resorts, inns and guesthouses can be found at the official St. Maarten Web site (✐www.st-maarten.com) operated by the St. Martin Tourist Office. You can also visit any of the popular travel-related Web sites, such as Hotwire.com, Orbitz.com or Travelocity.com.

One of the things you'll notice as you begin researching accommodations is that the majority of the resorts, hotels, and guesthouses are not affiliated with major name-brand hotel or resort chains. The commercialism on this island is limited, offering vacationers an added feeling of truly getting away.

## HOTELS, RESORTS, AND GUESTHOUSES ON ST. MAARTEN

| Hotel/Resort Name | Location | Phone Number | Web Site |
|---|---|---|---|
| Atrium Beach Resort | Simpson Bay | 011-599-544-2126 | www.atrium-resort.com |
| Beachside Villas | Simpson Bay | 011-313-844-7706 | www.beach-sidevillas.com |
| Belair Beach Resort | Little Bay | 877-523-5247 | www.belairbeach.com |
| Buena Vista Vacation Resort | Cole Bay | 800-732-9480 | www.princessresortandcasino.com |
| Calypso Guesthouse | Simpson Bay | 011-599-545-4233 | |
| Caribbean Hotel | Philipsburg | 011-599-542-2028 | |
| Carl's Unique Inn | Cole Bay | 011-599-544-2812 | |
| Delta Hotel | Philipsburg | 011-599-542-2682 | |
| Divi Little Bay Beach Resort | Little Bay | 800-367-3484 | www.diviresorts.com |
| Earnest Hotel | Cul-de-Sac | 011-599-542-2003 | |
| George's Guesthouse | Philipsburg | 011-599-542-2126 | |
| Great Bay Beach Hotel & Casino | Great Bay | 800-223-0757 | www.greatbayhotel.com |
| Holland House Beach Hotel | Philipsburg | 800-223-9815 | www.hhbh.com |
| Horizon View Beach Hotel | Philipsburg | 011-599-543-2121 | |
| Horny Toad Guesthouse | Simpson Bay | 800-417-9361 | www.thehornytoadguesthouse.com |
| Hotel La Chatelaine | Simpson Bay | 011-599-545-4269 | www.chatelainehotel.com |
| Joshua Rose Guest House | Philipsburg | 011-599-542-4317 | |
| La Vista Resort | Pelican Bay | 011-599-544-3005 | www.lavistaresort.com |
| L'Esperance Hotel | Cay Bay | 011-599-542-5355 | www.lesperancehotel.com |
| Maho Beach Resort & Casino | Maho Bay | 800-223-0757 | www.mahobeach.com |
| Mary's Boon Beach Plantation | Simpson Bay | 011-599-545-4235 | |

| Hotel/Resort Name | Location | Phone Number | Web Site |
|---|---|---|---|
| Midtown Hotel II | Philipsburg | 011-599-542-0590 | |
| Oyster Bay Beach Resort | Oyster Bay | 877-478-6669 | *www.oysterbaybeachresort.com* |
| Paula's Country Inn | South Reward | 011-599-548-3777 | |
| Pasanggrahan Royal Guesthouse | Philipsburg | 011-599-542-3588 | |
| Pelican Resort Club | Pelican Key | 800-550-7088 | *www.pelicanresort.com* |
| Pitusa Hotel | Over-The-Pond | 011-599-542-5926 | |
| Princess Heights | Oyster Bay | 800-441-7227 | *www.princessheights.com* |
| Radisson Vacation Villas | Oyster Bay | 877-478-6669 | |
| Rama Hotel Apartments | Pointe Blanche | 011-599-543-2286 | |
| Royal Islander Club | Maho Bay | 011-599-545-2388 | *www.royalislander.com* |
| Sea Breeze Hotel | Philipsburg | 011-599-542-6054 | |
| Sea Palace Resort | Philipsburg | 011-599-542-2700 | *www.seapalace.net* |
| Sea View Hotel | Philipsburg | 011-599-542-2323 | |
| Silvia Guesthouse | Cayhill | 011-599-542-3389 | |
| Summit Resort Hotel | Lowlands | 800-622-7836 | *www.thesummitresort.com* |
| Sunset Inn | Cole Bay | 011-599-544-5077 | |
| Sunterra Resorts Flamingo Beach | Pelican Key | 011-599-544-3900 | *www.sunterra.com* |
| Sunterra Resorts Royal Palm Beach | Simpson Bay | 011-599-544-3737 | *www.sunterra.com* |
| Tamarind Hotel | Point Blanche | 011-599-542-4359 | *www.tamarindhotel.com* |
| Travel Inn | Simpson Bay | 011-599-545-3353 | |
| Turquoise Shell Residence Hotel | Simpson Bay | 011-599-545-5642 | |
| Wyndham Sapphire Beach Club & Resort | Cupecoy | 800-WYNDHAM | *www.wyndham.com* |

# Calling Home and Surfing the Web

The phone service in St. Maarten is a bit confusing, because calling from one side of the island to the other is considered an international call. One of the easiest and least expensive ways to make calls is to purchase a prepaid calling card once you arrive on the island, then use it from any public pay phone. As you'd expect, there's typically a hefty surcharge for making calls from your hotel or resort guestroom.

In terms of cellular phone service, a few of the U.S.-based cellular service providers offer international roaming here; however, the per-minute fees are relatively high. A cheaper alternative if you want a cell phone on the island is to rent one from B.T. Electronics (☎011-590-878-198, ✐*www.b-t-electronics.com*) on the Dutch side of the island. Yet another option is to purchase a prepaid SIM chip (for a cost of approximately 15 Euros) for your unlocked GSM cell phone through Amigo Reseau GSM (☎011-590-290-077, ✐*www.amigo-gsm. com*). Low prepaid local and international rates are available.

To surf the Web, the least expensive option is to visit a local Internet café. Some hotels offer in-room high-speed Internet connections or computer workstations in their lobby or business centers (for which you'll pay either a flat daily or per-minute connection fee).

## ═══FAST FACT

To call the Dutch side of the island from the French side, dial ☎00-599-54, followed by the five-digit local phone number. To call the French side of the island from the Dutch side, dial ☎00-590-590, followed by the six-digit local phone number.

# Dining Options

The more than 300 dining options available throughout St. Maarten are influenced by cuisine from around the world. You'll find restaurants along the beaches and waterfront, in the tourist and shopping areas, and in the hotels and resorts.

In Philipsburg, for example, Harbor View Restaurant (Frontstreet 89, ☎011-599-542-5200) is the most popular restaurant in the area, serving breakfast, lunch, and dinner every day but Sunday. Serving mainly Caribbean-style cuisine, this is a casual dining experience offering a wonderful sea view.

Joe's Grill & Ribs at Simpson Bay (☎011-599-577-9954) is known for its enjoyable locally influenced menu, featuring rib platters. On Tuesdays and Saturdays, enjoy an all-you-can-eat-ribs special for under $13 per person. Fajitas, kabobs, burgers, and even chicken nuggets for the kids can be found on the mid-priced menu.

Kids, in particular, will enjoy Pizza Galley (☎011-599-557-7416 (*www.pizzagalley.com*) on Airport Road at Simpson Bay. Open daily, this casual dining establishment offers delicious pizza and a great view. Prices are very reasonable. If you're looking for a family-friendly restaurant that's a bit more upscale, check out the Green House Restaurant, Bar & Nightclub at Bobby's Marina in Philipsburg (☎011-599 542-2941). You'll find an extensive menu featuring many local and Americanized dishes. Every Friday, lobster is the house special.

## What to See and Do

St. Maarten has become a wonderful tourist destination for those who love the beach, boating, and water sports. These are the primary activities offered throughout the island although, as you'll discover from this section, you'll also find a handful of fun land-based activities.

 **TRAVEL TIP**

Scuba diving, like snorkeling, is an extremely popular sport in St. Maarten. To schedule introductory training and a dive, a few of the companies you can contact include Octoplus Dive Center (☎590-87-20-62) and Scuba Fun Dive Center (☎011-599-557-0505, *www.scubafun.com*).

Activities such as golf, horseback riding, hiking, and the St. Maarten Park all take full advantage of the island's natural beauty. To further enhance your relaxation and enjoyment of the island, several upscale day spas are available to help you pamper yourself, while at night, adults can enjoy any of the casinos, nightclubs, bars, and lounges.

For such a small island, St. Maarten offers a lot to see and do, but first and foremost, this is a wonderful place to get away and just relax.

# Must-See Activities and Attractions

The following sections describe the top ten must-see attractions and family-friendly activities in St. Maarten.

### Visit St. Maarten Park

Especially if you're traveling with kids and teens, St. Maarten Park in Philipsburg offers a wide range of outdoor activities, including a zoo that feature more than eighty species of mammals, exotic birds, reptiles, and other creatures.

Unlike most zoos, this one offers a tropical garden setting as opposed to lots of metal cages. This layout is visually appealing for guests and more comfortable for the animals. It also allows guests to get extra close to the animals. The park offers a large playground facility, gift shop, and dining options. Hours of operation are 9:30 A.M. to 6:00 P.M. daily. For more information, call ☎011-599-543-2030.

**ST. MAARTEN PARK**

| Ages up to 5 | Ages 6–15 | Ages 16–20 | Adult | Senior Citizens |
|:---:|:---:|:---:|:---:|:---:|
| ★★★ | ★★★ | ★★★ | ★★ | ★★ |

### Enjoy a Day-Long Cruise

Whether you choose to participate in a sunset cruise or a day-long cruise, there are many companies in St. Maarten offering charters and organized group cruises aboard yachts, sailboats, glass-bottomed boats, and other vessels. Some cruises offer snorkeling off the back of the boat, fishing, or scuba-diving opportunities.

**DAY-LONG CRUISE**

| Ages up to 5 | Ages 6–15 | Ages 16–20 | Adult | Senior Citizens |
|:---:|:---:|:---:|:---:|:---:|
| ★ | ★★ | ★★★ | ★★★ | ★★ |

## Experience the Beaches

First and foremost, St. Maarten is the place to come if you enjoy the beach. Throughout the thirty-seven-square-mile island, you'll find thirty-seven beautiful beaches. That's at least one beach per square mile of property on the island. On many of these pristine beaches you'll find a wide range of activities available, including many popular water sports, such as snorkeling, parasailing, Jet Skiing, sailing, and surfing. There are, however, less busy beaches, where the main activity is simply swimming and basking in the sunshine.

On the Dutch side of the island, Mullet Bay and Maho Bay offer more family-friendly beaches with plenty of activities offered.

**EXPERIENCE THE BEACHES**

| Ages up to 5 | Ages 6–15 | Ages 16–20 | Adult | Senior Citizens |
|:---:|:---:|:---:|:---:|:---:|
| ★★ | ★★★ | ★★★ | ★★★ | ★★★ |

## Ride an Atlantis Submarine

Prepare to take a unique and exotic submarine adventure as you dive 150 feet toward the ocean floor. You'll see incredible ocean life, plus several sunken ships through the submarine's portals. Your journey begins by taking a short boat ride to the submarine. Upon boarding the submarine, your undersea journey will last about one hour. The entire adventure is about ninety minutes long and includes live narration by the sub's copilot.

Built at a cost of $3.6 million, each Atlantis submarine holds forty-eight passengers and makes up to nine dives per day. The undersea journey is surprisingly smooth. There are no restrooms available on the actual submarine, however, so plan accordingly.

An Atlantis submarine ride provides a memorable and exciting experience for people over the age of four. The cost is $84 per adult and $34 per child (ages four to sixteen). To save $10 per adult ticket, make your reservations online at ✑*www.atlantisadventures.net*. Advance reservations are definitely required. This is an extremely popular attraction, and it books up quickly.

To make a reservation or for additional information, call ✆011-590-542-4078 or ✆011-599-542-4078.

**ATLANTIS SUBMARINE RIDE**

| Ages up to 5 | Ages 6–15 | Ages 16–20 | Adult | Senior Citizens |
|:---:|:---:|:---:|:---:|:---:|
| N.S. | ★★★ | ★★★ | ★★★ | ★★★ |

## Visit the Butterfly Farm (La Ferme des Papillons)

While young people will enjoy seeing and interacting with hundreds of exotic and colorful butterflies and learning all about them, adults will appreciate the exquisite landscaping and tranquil surroundings that make up the butterfly farm. Colorful flowers, tropical plants, and tranquil waterfalls found along the windy paths of this attraction create a lovely environment to stroll through.

Admission to the Butterfly Farm allows you to return as often as you wish during your stay in St. Maarten. Hours of operation are from 9:00 A.M. until just after 3:00 P.M. Guided tours are offered throughout the day. For more information, call ✆001-590-87-31-21 or e-mail *info@butterflyfarm. com*. A small café and gift shop (featuring butterfly-themed merchandise and souvenirs) can be found just outside the farm area.

**THE BUTTERFLY FARM**

| Ages up to 5 | Ages 6–15 | Ages 16–20 | Adult | Senior Citizens |
|:---:|:---:|:---:|:---:|:---:|
| ★★ | ★★★ | ★★★ | ★★ | ★★ |

## Experience a Sport-Fishing Excursion

Deep-sea fishing and sport fishing are popular activities along the coast of St. Maarten. You'll find many half-day and full-day fishing excursions available. Contact the activities desk at your hotel for details about fishing trips. The catch of the day might be marlin, tuna, snapper, grouper, or jewfish (which can be up to five feet in length).

**SPORT FISHING**

| Ages up to 5 | Ages 6–15 | Ages 16–20 | Adult | Senior Citizens |
|:---:|:---:|:---:|:---:|:---:|
| N.S. | N.S | ★★ | ★★ | ★★ |

## Take a Kayak Tour

One reason that kayaking is a popular water sport among tourists is that it's easy to learn and lots of fun. After just a few minutes of instruction, even someone who has never set foot in a boat will find themselves maneuvering a kayak with relative ease. St. Maarten offers an array of lagoons, swamps, and winding canals that offer perfect kayaking opportunities, complete with beautiful scenery. The Simpson Bay Lagoon, for example, offers several unique routes for kayakers. Plenty of different guided tours are available, some of which incorporate snorkeling.

Tri Sport (☎011-599-545-4384) is just one of the companies on the island that offers kayak rentals and guided tours. Keep in mind when you embark on a kayaking adventure that you'll be exposed to the sun. Be sure to wear protective clothing and sunscreen to avoid getting burned.

**KAYAKING TOUR**

| Ages up to 5 | Ages 6–15 | Ages 16–20 | Adult | Senior Citizens |
|:---:|:---:|:---:|:---:|:---:|
| N.S. | N.S | ★★ | ★★★ | ★★ |

### Enjoy a Nature Hike

Throughout the island, you'll find over twenty-five miles of hiking trails catering to novice and experienced hikers alike. Hiking is one of the best ways to enjoy the various terrain types the island has to offer. Before embarking on an unfamiliar trail, make sure it caters to someone at your skill level and physical abilities. Comfortable hiking shoes or boots, along with appropriate protection from the sun, are an absolute must.

Guided hiking tours are available. These tours are recommended for beginners.

**HIKING**

| Ages up to 5 | Ages 6–15 | Ages 16–20 | Adult | Senior Citizens |
|---|---|---|---|---|
| N.S. | N.S. | ★★ | ★★ | ★ |

### Go Sailing! Participate in America's Cup 12-Metre Challenge

Throughout the year, experienced sailors and fans of the world-famous America's Cup race can experience what it's like for the crew aboard these beautiful sailing vessels as they strive to reach the finish line.

The extremely popular 12-Metre Challenge allows participants to crew aboard one of several actual America's Cup sailing yachts, such as the *Stars & Stripes, Canada II, True North,* and *True North IV.*

During the shortened races, every participant is given a job aboard the yacht. The actual crew offers training to participants. This is an exciting, half-day experience suitable for people over the age of sixteen. The price is $75 per person, which includes drinks. Since space is limited and this is one of the island's most popular attractions, reservations should be made in advance through your hotel or the shore excursions desk aboard your cruise ship.

## ≡FAST FACT

You don't have to have any previous sailing or boating skills to experience this unique sailing adventure. If you are an experienced sailor, however, you'll truly appreciate the splendor of the America's Cup yacht you'll be sailing.

### AMERICA'S CUP 12-METRE CHALLENGE

| Ages up to 5 | Ages 6–15 | Ages 16–20 | Adult | Senior Citizens |
|---|---|---|---|---|
| N.S. | N.S. | ★★★ | ★★★ | ★★★ |

## Duty-Free Shopping

Shopping is a popular activity among tourists visiting this island, and with good reason. The duty-free shopping here offers excellent savings on a wide range of designer watches, fine jewelry, perfumes, cashmere, Chinese embroidery, Japanese-made cameras and electronics, crystal, linens, porcelain, and liquor.

The duty-free shops are typically open from 9:00 A.M. until 6:00 P.M.; however, on days when cruise ships are in the port, some of the shops, including those in Maho, stay open until 10:00 P.M. (or later).

One reason that St. Maarten is so popular among shopaholics is that the retailers themselves are able to import items on a duty-free basis and pass those savings along to customers. To find the best deals, be sure to research what you're looking for before leaving home (in terms of brand names, model numbers, and retail prices), then shop around for the best deals, keeping in mind that you'll need to negotiate.

Front Street and Back Street in Philipsburg offer plenty of shopping opportunities. For local crafts and art, be sure to visit Market Place, an outdoor market in Philipsburg. The Maho area is also a shopper's paradise, offering a selection of high-fashion boutiques, jewelry stores, and perfume shops. The Maho area also offers an abundance of restaurants, nightclubs, and several casinos.

### DUTY-FREE SHOPPING

| Ages up to 5 | Ages 6–15 | Ages 16–20 | Adult | Senior Citizens |
|:---:|:---:|:---:|:---:|:---:|
| ★ | ★ | ★★ | ★★★ | ★★★ |

# Making St. Maarten Your Vacation Destination

Because of its lack of commercialism and incredible beauty, St. Maarten offers a wonderful and very different vacation opportunity than many islands in the Caribbean. Between the Dutch and French sides of the island, vacationers have a chance to experience two very different cultures, while enjoying the beaches and participating in the countless water sports and land-based activities that are available.

This island is best experienced by staying at a smaller resort or by renting a villa or condo, as opposed to staying in a larger, more commercial hotel or resort. For assistance in finding the perfect accommodations or planning a vacation to this unique tropical island, contact the St. Maarten Tourist Office (675 Third Avenue, New York, NY 10017, ✆800-786-2278, ✐www.st-maarten.com).

 **JUST FOR PARENTS**

The island of St. Maarten may be small, but when it comes to night-time entertainment and gambling, you'll find a dozen casinos on the Dutch side of the island. These casinos are typically open daily, from noon until 2:00 A.M.

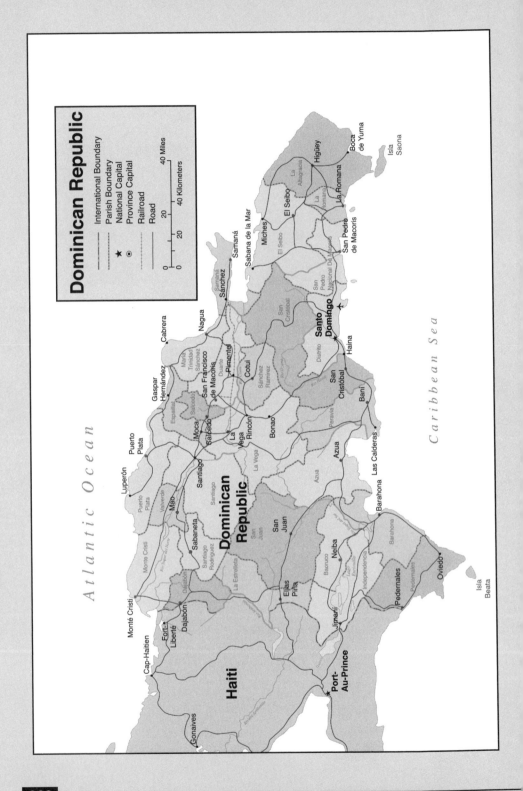

# Dominican Republic

International Boundary
Parish Boundary
★ National Capital
◉ Province Capital
Railroad
Road

40 Miles
40 Kilometers
20
20
0
0

Atlantic Ocean

Caribbean Sea

Haiti

Dominican Republic

Santo Domingo

Cap-Haïtien
Gonaïves
Fort-Liberté
Port-Au-Prince
Monte Cristi
Dajabón
Sabaneta
Mao
Santiago Rodríguez
Santiago
Valverde
Puerto Plata
Luperón
Puerto Plata
Monte Cristi
La Estrelleta
San Juan
San Juan
Elías Piña
Jimaní
Neiba
Baoruco
Independencia
Pedernales
Oviedo
Isla Beata
Barahona
Barahona
Azua
Azua
Peravia
Las Calderas
Baní
San Cristóbal
San Cristóbal
Distrito Nacional
Haina
Bonao
La Vega
La Vega
Rincón
Salcedo
Moca
Espaillat
Gaspar Hernández
Cabrera
Nagua
María Trinidad Sánchez
Duarte
San Francisco de Macorís
Pimentel
Sánchez Ramírez
Cotuí
Monseñor Nouel
Samaná
Samaná
Sabana de la Mar
Sánchez
Miches
El Seibo
El Seibo
San Pedro de Macorís
San Pedro de Macorís
La Romana
La Romana
Higüey
La Altagracia
Boca de Yuma
Isla Saona

# CHAPTER 15

# The Dominican Republic

IN 2004, ALMOST 3.5 million tourists visited the Dominican Republic, making it one of the most popular vacation destinations in the Caribbean. Perhaps this is because of the pristine white-sand beaches found throughout the Dominican Republic's 1,000 miles of coastline. The popular beach areas in this region include Playa Grande, Punta Cana, and Saona Island. You'll find a wide range of water-based activities, such as windsurfing, snorkeling, sailing, scuba diving, and deep-sea fishing. Even if you're just looking to relax in the sunshine, there's plenty for families to see and experience here.

With the exception of an occasional hurricane (which could hit during hurricane season, between July and October), the weather throughout the Dominican Republic is typically warm, sunny, and utterly enjoyable. The temperature seldom drops below 60 degrees or rises above 90.

Most of the hotels, resorts, and tourist attractions can be found on the northern Atlantic side of the republic, along a forty-mile zone that stretches between Puerto Plata and Cabarete. You will also want to explore the other parts of the island to see many of its historical sites.

By airplane, the Dominican Republic is a three-hour flight from New York, less than two hours from Miami, and a mere forty-five minutes from San Juan, Puerto Rico. The population of the Dominican Republic is about 8 million.

# The Scoop on the Dominican Republic

One reason that the Dominican Republic is so popular among tourists, particularly during the winter holiday season, is because this region has the largest number of all-inclusive resorts in the world. They are often the most economical as well. For one package price, vacationers receive round-trip airfare, resort accommodations, meals, and plenty of activities. No matter what your travel budget, chances are you'll discover a vacation package your family can afford. This is one of the most economical places in the Caribbean to visit, although if you have a large budget, it's easy to find luxurious accommodations. This is also a relatively noncommercial place to vacation. Unlike other Caribbean islands, you won't find too many franchise stores or popular fast-food chains in the Dominican Republic. Plus, if you're staying at an all-inclusive, full-service resort, most of your time will be spent on the resort's property.

Encompassing about 30,000 square miles, the landmass that makes up the Dominican Republic is comprised of lowlands, rainforest, swamps, desert, and mountains. Combine these landscapes with beautiful coastal surroundings, and virtually any type of warm weather, outdoor activity, or sport can be experienced here.

In the summer, the average temperature remains in the low 80s, while in the winter, the temperature will dip to the mid 70s. Thanks to the year-round warmth of the water temperature, not only is the climate ideal for water sports like scuba diving, swimming, and snorkeling, but it appeals to aquatic wildlife as well. Every year, tourists can witness over 3,000 humpback whales travel to the coast of Bahia de Samana, where they mate, give birth, and play.

The official language of the Dominican Republic is Spanish, yet most of the locals speak fluent English as well. The official currency is the Dominican peso. The exchange rate fluctuates daily but averages about 16 to 17 pesos to one U.S. dollar. Currency can be exchanged at banks, at many hotels/resorts, and at currency exchange services located throughout the Dominican Republic. Throughout the island, you'll find standard, 110-volt electricity (the same as used in the United States).

## 🧳 TRAVEL TIP

Refrain from drinking the tap water in the Dominican Republic. You're much better off drinking only bottled water or tap water that has been boiled. Almost all of the resorts have purified water coming through their taps. The time to exercise caution is when you're exploring the island and dining at independent restaurants.

The Dominican Republic is about the size of Scotland, although it occupies only about half of the island of Hispaniola. If you're looking for an all-inclusive resort vacation, chances are you'll find it in either Bavaro or Punta Cana. Puerto Plata is also an extremely popular tourist destination, while Santo Domingo has appeal from a historical perspective.

Santo Domingo is one of the largest cities in the Dominican Republic. You'll find Aeropuerto Internacional Las Americas, the largest international airport in the country, in Santo Domingo. This area of the country is far less tropical in terms of being a vacation getaway, but it does offer many historical landmarks and tourist attractions, plus more traditional, high-rise hotels.

If you're looking for beaches and beauty, the Samana Peninsula and the Silver Coast are the places to visit. In the Silver Coast region, you'll find Puerto Plata and Playa Dorada, the unofficial tourism capitals of the country.

While many Caribbean islands generate much of their tourism traffic from American visitors, the Dominican Republic is different. The majority of tourists visiting this country come from Europe and other parts of the world.

## A Bit of Dominican Republic History

Before Christopher Columbus visited the Dominican Republic back in 1492, the region was inhabited by the Tainos, who had occupied the land for hundreds of years. Ultimately, Spanish settlers came in and began taking over territory, using the Tainos as slaves. Around

1629, the French began staking its claim on the region. It took until 1843 for the Spanish colonists to force the invaders out, allowing the Dominican Republic to be established as an independent country. This wasn't without tremendous struggle, however.

 **TRAVEL TIP**

If you're traveling with an infant or young kids, be sure to pack plenty of disposable diapers and prepackaged foods and snacks that your kids enjoy. These items are not readily available in the Dominican Republic. When they can be found, you'll pay a hefty premium for popular American brands.

In the early twentieth century, the United States began developing an interest in the Dominican Republic, paving the way for a U.S. occupation between 1916 and 1924. After World War I, however, public opinion relating to the occupation changed, and the Harding Plan, was drafted in 1921 to outline the U.S. plan for withdrawal. It wasn't until 1924, however, that the republic was returned to Dominican hands. Internal political turmoil persisted until a military coup took place in September 1963, causing a civil war. In 1965, the United States again intervened in an effort to restore order.

Currently, the government of the Dominican Republic is a representative democracy, run by a president and congress (comprised of thirty senators and 149 house representatives). The population of the Dominican Republic exceeds 7 million. The official language of the region is Spanish, and not everyone speaks English, so be sure to pack a English-Spanish dictionary or phrase book.

As in many areas of the Caribbean, tourism is the country's primary industry, with over 2 million tourists visiting the region annually.

# The Local Weather

The Dominican Republic enjoys a tropical climate, but the weather varies dramatically depending on where you're staying and whether you're near the coast or inland. In general, you can count on "partly sunny weather with the possibility of a brief shower" almost daily. In the cooler months (December through April), the temperature can drop to 66 degrees, although you can generally count on the temperature to be in the low- to mid-80s. Between August and September, temperatures will reach the low 90s in certain regions.

In addition to packing bathing suits, you should definitely plan to pack sunscreen, a hat, sunglasses, and other clothing to help protect you from getting a sunburn. At night and when it does rain, you'll definitely want a jacket to stay warm and dry.

# Getting to the Dominican Republic

The Dominican Republic has seven international airports. To enter the Dominican Republic by air, American tourists will need a passport, a return or continuing airline ticket, and a tourist card, which will be provided at the airport for a fee of $10. There's also a $10 per-person departure tax, which is often included in the price of an airline ticket.

Airlines that offer nonstop or connecting service from the United States to one of the Dominican Republic's airports include American Airlines (*www.aa.com*), American Eagle (*www.aa.com*), Continental Airlines (*www.continental.com*), and US Airways (*www.usairways.com*). Many charter companies and tour operators offer direct flights from major U.S. cities.

## ≡FAST FACT

The peak travel periods in the Dominican Republic are the summer months (July and August), as well as during the winter (December, January, and February).

# Getting Around the Dominican Republic

Public buses offer an inexpensive and efficient way to get around the country. Caribe Tours (✆809-221-4422) offers an extensive bus network, while the Metro bus network (✆809-566-7126) can be used to travel between cities within the Dominican Republic. There's also a network of smaller vans (called gauguas) that can be used to navigate your way around the island inexpensively. These mini buses do tend to get overcrowded.

## ≡FAST FACT

The speed limit is usually no higher than 50 miles per hour and is strictly enforced, especially in the major cities.

If you're staying in a particular city, taxis are a much more convenient, albeit a more expensive, option than buses for getting around. Rental cars are also readily available.

### Renting a Car

Many rental car agencies are available in the Dominican Republic. You can rent a standard car or a more exotic (and fun to drive) four-wheel-drive or Jeep. Rates for a rental car start at $50 per day, plus gas and insurance.

Cars drive on the right side of the road throughout the Dominican Republic, which makes it easy for American drivers to acclimate themselves, although many of the road signs are in Spanish. The roads themselves aren't always in top-notch shape, especially outside of the main cities, so be prepared.

Also, gas stations aren't as commonplace as they are in the United States. Don't set off on a long journey without a full tank of gas, especially in the evening or at night. In addition, gas isn't cheap in the Dominican Republic, so take this into consideration when planning your driving routes and travel budget. Plan on spending at least $88.70 pesos per liter for regular unleaded gas. That's over $3.34 per liter (more than $10 a gallon), based in April 2005 exchange rates and gas prices.

You will find most major U.S. car-rental agencies have offices in the Dominican Republic, including Avis (*www.avis.com*), Budget (*www.budget.com*), Hertz (*www.hertz.com*), and National (*www.nationalcar.com*).

### Island-Hopping Made Easy

Because the Dominican Republic is so large, many tourists opt to fly between cities instead of driving. Air Santo Domingo (809-683-8006) offers regularly scheduled domestic flights between cities within the Dominican Republic.

# Where to Stay: Understanding Your Options

For families, staying at the nicest all-inclusive resort you can afford is typically the best option, but there are also stand-alone hotels and smaller beachfront resorts, as well as guesthouses that can be rented. Prices for stand-alone accommodations vary greatly, depending on time of the year, occupancy rates, location, and the type of guestroom. You're most apt to find the best deals by booking an all-inclusive resort or complete travel package online, either by working with a travel agent or by traveling with a major tour operator.

 **TRAVEL TIP**

When choosing an all-inclusive resort, begin your quest with reputable resort operators you know, like Club Med (809-686-5500, *www.clubmed.com*). GWV Vacations (866-797-0038, *www.gwvvacations.com*) is an independent tour operator that offers a wide range of all-inclusive travel packages. Some packages include accommodations at popular resorts, such as Iberostar Costa Dorada (in Puerto Plata).

## Club Med in Punta Cana

Club Med is known throughout the world as offering a top-notch, all-inclusive resort experience in over 100 locations. The seventy-four-acre property in Punta Cana is no exception. Here, you'll find a half mile of pristine beach, two swimming pools, a children's activities center, two restaurants, two bars, 518 guest rooms and suites, live entertainment nightly, and plenty of activities included in the package price. This property, which recently underwent a $35-million renovation project, is located just ten minutes from the Punta Cana Airport.

Just some of the activities guests can participate in on the property include tennis (with private lessons available), scuba diving, archery, trapeze, soccer, in-line skating, windsurfing, water polo, sailing, kayaking, basketball, and volleyball.

Three different activity programs are available for kids, according to what age range they fall into. A teen program is also available during peak holiday seasons.

For more information about Club Med, call ✆888-WEB-CLUB or ✆809-686-5500 (from the Dominican Republic). You can also go online to ✐*www.clubmed.com.*

## ≡FAST FACT

SuperClubs (✆877-467-8737, ✐*www.superclubs.com*) operates two, all-inclusive Breezes Resorts in the Dominican Republic. Both are family friendly and offer a wide range of mid-priced accommodations and amenities. These properties have their own private beaches, day spas, and casinos.

## Iberostar in Punta Cana

Located along Bavaro Beach in Punta Cana, about forty minutes from the Punta Cana airport, is another family-friendly, all-inclusive resort operated by Iberostar (✆809-221-65-00 ✐*www.ibersostar. com*). You'll find luxurious rooms and suites, each featuring either one large double bed or two single beds and an array of amenities, including cable television and an in-room telephone.

As you'd expect, this resort offers multiple dining options, including a beachfront restaurant and four other specialty dining rooms (with a steakhouse and buffets). The resort itself is comprised of 346 rooms and junior suites, housed in two- or four-story buildings or bungalows.

In addition to multiple dining options, the Iberostar resort features an on-property casino, fitness center, tennis courts, day spa, multiple swimming pools, and plenty of beach access. In addition to a wide range of water-sport activities for the entire family, the resort features a special kids program for guests between the ages of three and twelve.

Like all all-inclusive resorts, this one offers just about everything you'd need or want from a vacation property, making it virtually unnecessary to leave the resort during your stay unless you want to go sightseeing.

## Calling Home and Surfing the Web

Finding a public pay phone to call home from while visiting the Dominican Republic won't be hard. However, finding a phone with an affordable per-minute rates will definitely be a challenge. Even from a public pay phone, you could wind up paying up to several dollars per minute to call the United States. A slightly cheaper option is to use a prepaid calling card from Codetel or Tricom, which come in several different denominations.

 **TRAVEL TIP**

For laptop computer users hoping to access America Online via a dial-up number (and a 56K modem), the access number is ☎809-533-9181. There is a surcharge of $12 per hour, plus local phone charges, to use this access number.

The cheapest and easiest way to access the Internet is to use one of the computer workstations you'll find in many hotel/resort lobbies. You'll pay a flat per-minute fee to access the Internet. There are also many Internet cafés throughout the island.

Throughout the country, mobile phone service is available. The cheapest option is to rent a local cell phone and pay the per-minute usage fees. For information, call Codetel Telecommunications at ☎809-549-0448. If you have a cell phone, you may be able to use international roaming to make or receive calls while in the Dominican Republic. Another relatively inexpensive option is to purchase a prepaid SIM chip for your unlocked GSM cell phone. These per-minute fees for calling the United States are reasonable.

## Dining Options

Throughout the Dominican Republic, you'll find a wide range of restaurants in every price range, serving a vast selection of international cuisine. Seafood is a popular dining option, with places like Bucanero (☎809-592-2202), El Calamar (☎809-532-8876), La Llave del Mar (☎809-686-7076), and Sully (☎809-562-3389) offering upscale, family-friendly options.

Aside from the many restaurants found within the hotels and resorts, you'll also find over a dozen upscale steak houses and over thirty restaurants serving Dominican and Caribbean food. Contact your hotel's concierge for dining recommendations based on your location and budget. For a mid-priced dining experience, plan on spending anywhere from $8 to $20 per person for lunch or dinner. Fine-dining restaurants will range from $20 to $35 or more per person for lunch or dinner.

If you're staying at an all-inclusive resort, however, you'll save money dining on the resort property, since your meals are already paid for as part of your vacation package. Within the Dominican Republic, all-inclusive resorts offer the all-around best vacation deals on food, lodging, and activities.

# What to See and Do

Boating, sailing, and yachting are all popular activities throughout the Dominican Republic. Depending on which beaches you visit, you'll also find a wide range of water sports and beach-related activities. Fishing, windsurfing, hiking, golf, horseback riding, cycling, scuba diving, and tennis are all activities available throughout the island and at many of the resorts.

When it comes to shopping, you'll find duty-free shops galore, offering a wide range of jewelry, designer watches, liquor, and tobacco products. Throughout the Dominican Republic, locally made and Cuban cigars and locally grown Dominican coffee are popular items among tourists.

Locally made crafts and artwork are the perfect souvenirs to bring home. Jewelry created from amber and a locally mined semipre-cious stone, called larimar, are also popular. If you're buying jewelry, however, be sure to make your purchases from a reputable store, where you can be certain in the authenticity of the item, as opposed to a street merchant.

# Must-See Activities and Attractions

Unlike many Caribbean destinations, the Dominican Republic doesn't offer a whole lot of activities and attractions for kids that are outside of the resorts. Many of the resorts, particularly the all-inclusive resorts, offer an ideal selection of organized, supervised activities for kids and teens .

The following are ten of the must-see attractions and activities in the Dominican Republic. Keep in mind that not all of these are suit-able for kids or teens.

### Explore the Many Historical Sites

Throughout the country, you'll find literally hundreds of historical buildings and sites worth visiting. Many are open to the public and offer guided tours. For example, in Santo Domingo, there's Alcazar de Colon, the castle of Don Diego Colon, that was built in 1517. Casa del Cordon, built in 1503, is the oldest stone house in the Western

Hemisphere. Christopher Columbus's son, Diego Colon, lived here with his wife for several years.

El Faro a Colon (☎809-591-1492) is a lighthouse and monument that pays tribute to Christopher Columbus. The complex is home to several museums and the tomb of Columbus.

From your resort or hotel, you can register to participate in half-day or full-day sightseeing tours that will take you to many historical sites in the region of the country where you're staying. These cultural and historical tours, however, are typically of interest to adults who are history buffs, not to kids or teens.

**THE HISTORICAL SITES**

| Ages up to 5 | Ages 6–15 | Ages 16–20 | Adult | Senior Citizens |
|:---:|:---:|:---:|:---:|:---:|
| N.S. | ★ | ★★ | ★★★ | ★★★ |

## Golfing

There are several golf courses in the Dominican Republic, most of which are open to the public and offer full-service pro shops and equipment rentals. Greens fees are relatively inexpensive at many of the courses, starting as low as $35 for nine holes.

Some of the more popular golf courses include the following:

- **Barcelo Bavaro Beach Golf & Casino Resort**: ☎809-686-5797
- **Casa de Campo**: ☎809-523-3333
- **The Metro Country Club**: ☎809-526-3315
- **Playa Grande Golf Course**: ☎809-582-0860
- **Punta Cana Resort & Club**: ☎809-688-1561
- **Santa Domingo Country Club**: ☎809-530-6606

**GOLF**

| Ages up to 5 | Ages 6–15 | Ages 16–20 | Adult | Senior Citizens |
|:---:|:---:|:---:|:---:|:---:|
| N.S. | ★ | ★★ | ★★★ | ★★★ |

## Horseback Riding

Kids, teens, and adults alike will enjoy exploring the Dominican Republic on horseback. Guided tours are available along the beach, through the forests, and across several other types of terrain. Tours can last anywhere from an hour to an entire day. The full-day tours include multiple stops for swimming, lunch, and other activities.

Tours are available for riders at different skill levels, so make sure you select a tour that's suitable for your family. Some of the ranches and equestrian centers offering horseback riding tours include the following:

- **Alonzo Horse Ranch**: ☎809-523-3503
- **The Equestrian Center in Casa de Campo**: ☎809-523-3333
- **The Equestrian Center at Punta Cana Resort & Club**: ☎809-688-1561
- **Rancho Isabella**: ☎809-847-4849
- **Sea Horse Ranch**: ☎809-571-3880

**HORSEBACK RIDING**

| Ages up to 5 | Ages 6–15 | Ages 16–20 | Adult | Senior Citizens |
|:---:|:---:|:---:|:---:|:---:|
| N.S. | ★★ | ★★★ | ★★★ | ★ |

## Scuba Diving

Corel reefs and many sunken galleons offer an abundance of exciting dive sites off the coast of the Dominican Republic. Many dive-tour operators offer introductory dives and training for beginners. For certified divers, there's no shortage of places to explore. On Sosua Beach alone, you'll find no fewer than ten dive schools and centers offering scuba diving and snorkeling tours.

**SCUBA DIVING**

| Ages up to 5 | Ages 6–15 | Ages 16–20 | Adult | Senior Citizens |
|:---:|:---:|:---:|:---:|:---:|
| N.S. | N.S. | ★★ | ★★★ | ★ |

### Gamble at a Local Casino

Throughout the Dominican Republic you'll find many independent casinos, as well as casinos affiliated with some of the major resorts. Most offer traditional table games, like craps, roulette, blackjack, and poker, along with slot machines. The gambling and drinking age in the Dominican Republic is eighteen, although this isn't always strictly enforced. Visiting the casinos to gamble is a popular nighttime activity for adults. You don't have to gamble big dollar amounts, however, to have several hours of fun.

**CASINOS**

| Ages up to 5 | Ages 6–15 | Ages 16–20 | Adult | Senior Citizens |
|---|---|---|---|---|
| N.S. | N.S. | N.S. | ★★★ | ★★★ |

### Visit Fun City Action Park

Located about ten minutes outside of Puerto Plata, you'll find two popular, family-friendly attractions. The Fun City Action Park (✑*www.funcity-gocarts.com*) features activities like go-karts and bumper cars, plus a kiddy playground. The "unlimited racing pass" is priced at $15 per adult and $10 per child. This wristband allows you to experience all of the activities here, as often as you like, throughout the day.

The Columbus Water Park is a water-based park that features water slides and other activities. It's located nearby and offers an additional family-friendly activity.

**FUN CITY ACTION PARK**

| Ages up to 5 | Ages 6–15 | Ages 16–20 | Adult | Senior Citizens |
|---|---|---|---|---|
| N.S. | ★★★ | ★★★ | ★★ | ★ |

### Visit the Santo Domingo Botanical Garden and Park

The Santo Domingo Botanical Garden offers the largest attraction of its kind in the Caribbean. Visitors can explore much of the park by taking a train tour, although walking tours and self-paced exploration are also options. The park is divided into sections, which showcase various types of flowers and plant life. The Japanese garden is one of the most popular areas of the park.

### SANTO DOMINGO BOTANICAL GARDEN

| Ages up to 5 | Ages 6–15 | Ages 16–20 | Adult | Senior Citizens |
|:---:|:---:|:---:|:---:|:---:|
| N.S. | ★ | ★★ | ★★★ | ★★★ |

## An Afternoon at the Racetrack

Santo Domingo is where you'll find the V Centenario Horse Race Track, which overlooks the sea. Each day, thoroughbred horse races are held before up to 15,000 spectators. It's a one-mile track that offers plenty of excitement outside of the casinos. This is a spectator sport (which involves gambling) that's suitable for adults only.

### V CENTENARIO HORSE RACE TRACK

| Ages up to 5 | Ages 6–15 | Ages 16–20 | Adult | Senior Citizens |
|:---:|:---:|:---:|:---:|:---:|
| N.S. | N.S | N.S | ★★ | ★★ |

## Spend Time at the Beach

Sunbathing, swimming, building sand castles, and kite-flying are just some of the activities you'll find tourists engaging in as they take full advantage of the Dominican Republic's lovely beaches. Being able to spend time at the beach is one of the main reasons why people choose to visit the Dominican Republic. If you're not an avid beach-goer, you might consider choosing another island.

Depending on where you're staying, chances are your resort will be located right on a beach. If not, ask your hotel's concierge to recommend a nearby beach. The beach you choose should offer the activities you're looking for. While some beaches offer solitude and serenity, others are more suitable for families looking for plenty of water-based activities. These tend to be the more crowded beaches.

As you're searching for the perfect beach, make Punta Cana your first stop. The east-coast beach strip offers a wonderful selection of family-friendly beaches. You'll find beautiful beaches in Boca Chica, about fifteen miles east of Santa Domingo, for example. In addition to enjoying the sand and sun, on weekends, you'll find peddlers selling a wide range of goods along the beach. Juan Dolio is also a lovely beach area.

Beaches, along with resorts, are plentiful in Puerto Plata. In the Playa Dorado region, you'll find almost twenty resorts, each with its own incredible beaches.

**THE BEACHES**

| Ages up to 5 | Ages 6–15 | Ages 16–20 | Adult | Senior Citizens |
|:---:|:---:|:---:|:---:|:---:|
| N.S. | ★★★ | ★★★ | ★★★ | ★★★ |

## Experience an Off-Road Safari Adventure

Taking a traditional bus tour to see a Caribbean island can get boring, especially for kids and teens. What families will enjoy more is a four-wheel-drive, off-road safari adventure. These all-terrain vehicles will take you not just on the main roads, but allow you to explore places not readily accessible by car. You might find yourself driving through shallow streams or through sugar cane plantations. These tours are fast-paced, typically a bit bumpy, and definitely exciting. They generally last between three to five hours and will cost anywhere from $50 to $75 per person. Off-road tours are available throughout the country. Consult with your resort's tour desk for assistance in finding a tour operator offering four-wheel-drive safari or off-road tours.

**OFF-ROAD SAFARI ADVENTURE**

| Ages up to 5 | Ages 6–15 | Ages 16–20 | Adult | Senior Citizens |
|:---:|:---:|:---:|:---:|:---:|
| N.S. | ★★★ | ★★★ | ★★★ | ★ |

# Making the Dominican Republic Your Vacation Destination

As you're planning your vacation to the Dominican Republic, keep in mind that the least expensive and easiest option is to purchase a travel package that includes airfare and all-inclusive resort accommodations (so meals and activities are also included.) While staying at your resort, you can engage in a wide range of activities offered on the property, then set off on single-day sightseeing excursions or tours that you can coordinate through the resort's tour desk or concierge. This will make your vacation planning easy. Remember, shopping around for the best travel deals is a must. Also, if a travel deal seems too good to be true, chances are it is. Before paying for your vacation, research exactly where you'll be staying and what's included in the package. Confirm that the quality of the accommodations you're reserving, for example, is what you're looking for. You don't want to get stuck staying at no-frills resort when you could have afforded a three- or four-star luxury resort in a more convenient part of the island that offers more amenities and included activities.

For additional information about the Dominican Republic, contact the tourism office at ✆888-374-6361 (⌨*www.drl.com/travel*). While in the Dominican Republic, call ✆809-221-4660 or ✆809-586-3676.

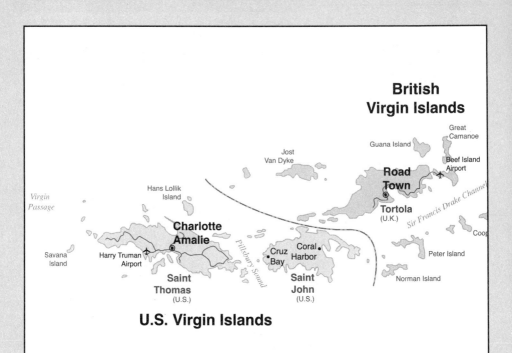

British
Virgin Islands

Great
Camanoe

Guana Island

Beef Island
Airport

Jost
Van Dyke

Road
Town

Virgin
Passage

Hans Lollik
Island

Tortola
(U.K.)

Sir Francis Drake Channel

Coop

Charlotte
Amalie

Pillsbury Sound

Coral
Harbor

Cruz
Bay

Peter Island

Savana
Island

Harry Truman
Airport

Saint
Thomas
(U.S.)

Saint
John
(U.S.)

Norman Island

U.S. Virgin Islands

Caribbean Sea

Buck Island

East Point

Saint Croix
(U.S.)

Christiansted

Frederiksted

Southwest
Cape

Alexander Hamilton
Airport

# CHAPTER 16

# U.S. Virgin Islands

ST. CROIX, ST. JOHN, AND ST. THOMAS are the three Caribbean islands that make up the U.S. Virgin Islands. As the name suggests, these islands are part of the United States' territory, which makes traveling to and between these islands very easy for U.S. citizens. As you'll discover from this chapter, each of the three islands offers something slightly different to families planning a Caribbean getaway.

## The Scoop on the U.S. Virgin Islands

One of the best reasons to visit the U.S. Virgin Islands (USVI) for your Caribbean vacation is that you get to experience virtually everything the Caribbean has to offer without leaving U.S. territory. This means getting into and departing from the USVI is relatively easy, whether you're traveling by air or cruise ship.

The economy here is based exclusively on the U.S. dollar, the phone service and electricity throughout the islands are identical to those used in the United States, and you'll find that the hotels and resorts offer many modern amenities. The islands themselves, however, have a rich and long history that goes back thousands of years.

The USVI is located in the Lesser Antilles of the Caribbean, between the Atlantic Ocean and the Caribbean Sea. The USVI is comprised of more than fifty small islands, although the three largest and most popular among tourists are St. Croix (eighty-four square miles), St. John (nineteen square miles) and St. Thomas (thirty-two square miles).

The USVI goes by the Atlantic Standard Time zone, which is one hour ahead of Eastern Standard Time (except during Daylight Saving Time). One thing tourists will quickly notice when visiting here is that the cars drive on the left side of the street, although all U.S. traffic laws and driving regulations apply.

While the official language of the USVI is English, approximately 45 percent of the local inhabitants (of St. Croix, for example) also speak Spanish. The USVI is governed by U.S. laws.

When visiting the USVI, U.S. citizens are not required to carry a U.S. passport, although a government-issued photo ID is required. As a vacation destination, these islands offer a large array of land- and water-based activities and sports for guests to experience.

Those who arrive in the USVI by air and plan to spend their entire vacation here often opt to stay in a traditional hotel or a full-service resort, but the islands also offer rentable houses and villas, small inns and guesthouses, and several time-share properties. Traditional full-service resorts are more popular here than all-inclusive resorts, so plan on paying for your guestroom accommodations, meals and activities separately, unless you purchase a special travel package.

## ≡FAST FACT

If you need to mail postcards or letters home, you'll find U.S. post offices (✍*www.usps.com*) throughout all three of the islands. All rates and available postal services are the same as in the United States. Overnight couriers, such as FedEx, UPS, and DHL, for example, are readily available on these islands.

Many of the popular cruise lines offer one or more of the U.S. Virgin Islands as a port of call. In addition, because these islands are so close to the British Virgin Islands, some vacationers opt to take a day trip to these other islands, which offer a very different vacation experience and culture.

# A Bit of U.S. Virgin Islands History

Christopher Columbus "discovered" the USVI in 1493 when he first made a stop on the northern shore of St. Croix. He named the island Santa Cruz. In 1733, Denmark purchased the islands of St. John and St. Thomas, bringing them under Danish rule. During this time, sugar was the primary export; however, cotton, rum, and tobacco were also exported. Through the 1840s, slavery was common in this region as the sugar production increased.

Over the years, however, the Spanish, Dutch, British, French, and Knights of Malta all controlled the islands at some point in the region's history, before the United States purchased St. Croix, St. John, and St. Thomas in 1917 for $25 million in gold. It was then that this region took on the name U.S. Virgin Islands.

Early in the islands' history, the Taino and Carib Indians were the main inhabitants for more than 3,000 years. However, most of the natives were ultimately slaughtered during the European occupation. These days, the local population is comprised of people from Europe, North America, India, the Middle East, and the Orient. Many are West Indians of African decent. Today, Danish heritage continues to be present in the region, both in local traditions as well as the architecture, which makes this an even more desirable place for tourists to visit.

# The Local Weather

As you'd expect from a tropical Caribbean travel destination, the weather is usually beautiful throughout the year. Average temperatures range from the high 70s in the fall and winter to the mid- to high 80s during the spring and summer months.

## 🧳 TRAVEL TIP

If you're booking your travel during hurricane season, be sure to add travel insurance or special hurricane insurance to your travel package. This will ensure you're covered financially if your vacation is cancelled or cut short due to bad weather.

The rainy season in the USVI goes from October to mid-December. Experiencing several days of rainfall in a row is very uncommon, although this region will periodically be exposed to hurricanes and tropical storms during hurricane season.

# Getting to the U.S. Virgin Islands

From the U.S. mainland, getting to the USVI by air is as easy as traveling to any other U.S. city. There are several international airports in the region, all of which are relatively small. The Cyril E. King Airport on St. Thomas is where the majority of flights originating from the United States land. There's also the Henry E. Rohlsen Airport on St. Croix. For details about these airports, go online to *www.viport. com/aviation.html*. Visitors to St. John can fly into and out of the St. John's International Airport (*www.stjohnsairport.com*).

Several major airlines, including American Airlines (*www. aa.com*), Continental Airlines (*www.continental.com*), Delta Air Lines (*www.delta.com*), United Airlines (*www.united.com*) and US Airways (*www.usairways.com*) offer nonstop or connecting service from major U.S. cities to the USVI.

From within the Caribbean, Air St. Thomas (📞340-776-2722), Air Sunshine (📞340-776-7900), American Eagle (📞800-474-4884) and Cape Air (📞800-352-0714) offer inter-island flights, typically between San Juan, St. Croix, and St. Thomas.

Many of the cruise lines that sail in and around the Caribbean offer St. Croix, St. Thomas, and/or St. John as ports of call. See Chapter 4 for information about Caribbean cruises.

# Getting Around the U.S. Virgin Islands

The easiest way to get around any of the islands is either by taxi or rental car. You'll find the roads easy to navigate and well-maintained (unlike the roads in the British Virgin Islands).

### Taking Taxis

As opposed to traditional taxis, taxi vans are commonplace throughout the USVI. These are full-sized vans that offer shared-ride services, so be prepared to ride with other tourists or local residents.

## ≡FAST FACT

In addition to taking a taxi from one location to the next, taxis associated with the V.I. Taxi Association can be rented for two-hour, three-hour, or full-day private sightseeing tours. To schedule a tour or to learn about rates, call ☎340-774-4550.

Private taxis are also available in the USVI, but the fares are higher. You can reserve a private taxi at any taxi stand or through your hotel or resort. When hiring a taxi, look for vehicles with the Virgin Islands Taxi Commission medallion clearly displayed. This ensures that the taxi is properly licensed and that you will be charged based on distance traveled (not on time).

The maximum fare to reach any destination on any one of the islands should be well under $20 each way. The average taxi fare will be closer to between $5 and $10 each way, depending on the distance you travel.

 **TRAVEL TIP**

For a fun-filled, relatively inexpensive, and exciting island tour of St. Thomas, be sure to experience Air Force 1 Taxi Tours. Rates start at $40 per person. The taxi service will pick you up at your hotel (or cruise-ship port) and take you on a memorable, ninety-minute tour in an open-air covered vehicle. Shopping tours, sightseeing tours, and beach tours are available. For information or to make a reservation, call ✆800-501-0122.

### Renting a Car

Many rental car companies are available in the USVI. The thing to remember, however, is that cars drive on the left side of the road (the opposite of U.S. traffic). Aside from that, all traffic laws and driving customs are identical to those in the United States. A valid U.S. driver's license or international driver's license is required to drive within the USVI. Also, the driver and passenger sitting in the front seat of any car are required by law to wear a seatbelt.

You'll find all the popular rental car companies in the USVI. Budget Rent-A-Car (✆800-626-4516, ✍www.budget.com) offers a particularly large selection of Jeeps, SUVs, vans, and four-wheel-drive vehicles. When you rent a car for more than two days from Budget, you'll receive a coupon book full of over $1,000 in savings on attractions, shopping, restaurants, and activities.

## Island-Hopping Made Easy

Traveling is relatively easy between islands within the U.S. Virgin Islands and the nearby British Virgin Islands, as well as to and from San Juan, Puerto Rico. You can take a high-speed ferry or fly between islands. Cape Air Airlines (✆800-352-0714, ✍www.flycapeair.com) offers twelve daily flights between St. Thomas and San Juan (a thirty-three-minute flight) and between San Juan and St. Thomas.

Seven flights per day are also offered between St. Thomas and St. Croix and back (a twenty-five-minute flight each way). Cape Air also offers nine daily flights between St. Croix and San Juan and back.

## Seaplane Island-Hopping

For a more memorable island-hopping experience, Seaborne Airlines (☎888-FLY-TOUR/340-773-6442, *✎www.seaborneairlines. com*) offers eighteen-minute seaplane rides/tours between St. Thomas and St. Croix. Up to thirty trips each way are flown daily for a round-trip airfare of $85 per person. The airline also offers multiple flights per day between St. Thomas and Old San Juan, Puerto Rico and between St. Croix and Old San Juan.

## High-Speed Ferry Services

High-speed ferry service is a great option for getting around the islands. The following list provides contact information for high-speed ferry or boat services that offer inter-island transportation.

- **Dohm's Water Taxi**: ☎340-775-6501, *✎www.watertaxi-vi.com*. Transportation between the U.S. Virgin Islands and the British Virgin Islands. Custom chartered day trips can also be arranged. Regularly scheduled ferry service is offered between various places in St. Thomas and St. John, for between $3 and $7 per person (one way).
- **Inter-Island Boat Services**: ☎340-776-6597. Regularly scheduled ferry service between St. Thomas and St. Croix.
- **Native Son, Inc.**: ☎340-774-8685. Regularly scheduled ferry service between St. Thomas and St. Croix.
- **Smith's Ferry Services, Ltd.**: ☎340-775-7292. Regularly scheduled ferry service between St. Thomas and St. Croix.

# Where to Stay: Understanding Your Options

The USVI offers a wide selection of traditional hotels, full-service resorts, a few all-inclusive resorts, many smaller inns and guesthouses, rental homes and villas, and time-share properties at a wide range of prices. Ideally, you'll want to find accommodations that are located on or near a beach and that offer room configurations that meet your needs. Unless you're planning on renting a car, you also want to ensure that where you'll be staying is located near restaurants, activities, and shopping. This will help you avoid the need for many taxi rides.

##  TRAVEL TIP

For information about renting a villa in the USVI, as opposed to staying at a resort or hotel, go online to Caribbean Way Luxury Villa Rentals and Sales' Web site (✎*www.caribbeanway.com*) or call ✆877-953-7400.

For families staying for a week or more, renting a fully equipped townhouse or a villa that's located near a beach is often a cheaper and more convenient option than staying at a resort or hotel. Many full-service resorts, however, offer special family travel packages.

To help you find the perfect accommodations, based on your needs, contact the United States Virgin Islands Hotel & Tourism Association (✆340-774-6835, ✎*www.sttstjhta.com*).

# Calling Home and Surfing the Web

Throughout the USVI, you'll find public pay telephones that can be used to make local or international calls using a credit card, cash (coins), or a prepaid calling card. Collect calls can also be made from all public pay phones.

To call the U.S. mainland, simply dial a 1 followed by the area code and phone number. To place an international call, dial the international access code (011) followed by the country code, area code, and phone number.

Many U.S.-based cellular phone service providers offer seamless roaming throughout the U.S. Virgin Islands, so your existing cell phone and phone number will probably work. It's also possible to purchase a local, prepaid SIM card for your unlocked GSM cellular phone or rent a local cell phone by the day. By renting a phone, you'll pay a daily fee plus the fee for airtime you use.

## ≡FAST FACT

If you'll be making calls home to the U.S. mainland, using a prepaid calling card from a public pay phone is one of the least expensive options. Most hotels and resorts charge a hefty premium for making long-distance calls from your guestroom. IDT (✆800-889-9126, ✑www.idt.net) offers several different prepaid calling card options with extremely low per-minute rates.

To rent a cellular phone in the USVI, call Genesis Communications on St. Thomas at ✆340-776-3811. In St. John, call ✆340-775-5906.

Throughout all of the islands, you'll find many Internet cafés offering high-speed online access for a per-minute fee. These cafés typically offer the least expensive high-speed Internet access. Many hotels and resorts offer in-room high-speed Internet access for a flat daily fee, plus computer workstations in their lobbies or business centers with Internet access available at a per-minute fee.

Many of the U.S.-based dial-up Internet service providers offer local access numbers in the USVI, so you can obtain a dial-up connection using your laptop's modem and by making a local call.

## What to See and Do

Aside from the beauty of the USVI and the convenience of not having to go through customs or immigration to get here, one of the best things about these islands is the abundance of things to see and do that are suitable for all ages.

 **TRAVEL TIP**

In addition to any baby-sitting services or children's programs offered by your resort or hotel, Nannies In Paradise (✆877-768-6699, ✉www.nanniesinparadise.com) is an independent baby-sitting and child-care service providing in-room baby-sitting and other related services on St. Thomas and St. John. These nannies will also come to private rental villas and time-share properties.

Virtually all of the popular activities you read about in Chapter 5 are available on these islands. There are also many activities and attractions that are exclusive to St. John, St. Croix, and St. Thomas, which make these family-friendly destinations well worth visiting.

## Dining Options

All three of the U.S. Virgin Islands offer a selection of restaurants, most within a reasonable price range. Expect to spend between $10 and $30 per person to enjoy a nice lunch or dinner at a restaurant that's not part of an all-inclusive resort.

Continental, American, French, Italian, and Mexican cuisine, along with seafood and vegetarian fare, are all among what you'll find throughout the islands. Virtually all of the restaurants, regardless of whether they're located within a hotel or resort, accept major credit cards. Most are family-friendly, offering special children's menus and Americanized entrees.

On all three islands, you'll find many reasonable dining options where hamburgers, fries, pizza, and chicken dishes are served, making it easy for kids to find entrées they'll enjoy.

# Visiting the USVI's Beaches

White sand, a cool tropical breeze, plenty of sunshine and palm trees swaying in the background are what you can expect when visiting the USVI's many beaches. All beaches on the islands are public, although some beaches located close to resorts and hotels charge guests to take advantage of the beach amenities they provide.

Some of the most popular beaches on St. Thomas are listed in the following sections.

### Bolongo Beach

You'll almost always find beach volleyball games underway on Bolongo Beach, especially on Thursday nights. There are plenty of nearby gift shops, cafés, snack bars, and water-sport rentals offered here.

### Brewer's Bay

This typically peaceful beach tends to be more crowded on weekends. It's located near the University of the Virgin Islands campus.

### Coki Beach

Snack bars selling food and tropical (alcoholic) drinks, plus water-sport rental companies offering snorkeling gear, floats and lounge chairs, for example, are plentiful here. This beach is located near Coral World.

### Great Bay Beach

Once known as Bluebeard's Beach, Great Bay is home to the Ritz-Carlton Club. Windsurfing and kite boarding are popular at this otherwise tranquil beach.

### Hull Bay Beach

Surfers tend to flock to this beach in the mornings, especially in the winter months when the waves are larger. It's generally a quiet place that's popular among sunbathers and those who enjoy fishing. The beach is located west of Magen's Bay.

### Lindbergh Beach

This beach is located near several popular resorts, including the Island Beachcomber and the Emerald Beach Resort, each of which offers its own fee-based beachfront amenities.

### Magen's Bay Beach

This beach has won the reputation of being one of the top ten most beautiful beaches in the world. It's the perfect place to sunbathe, swim, snorkel, and enjoy a lush Caribbean setting. At this famous beach, you'll find picnic tables, changing rooms, lounge-chair rentals, bars, cafés, and water-sport rentals. It's located on St. Thomas' north side, toward the very end of Route 35. There is a small entrance fee for this beach, which is extremely well maintained.

### Morning Star Beach

You can find several places to rent snorkeling gear, participate in a multitude of water sports (such as windsurfing or sailing), enjoy a tropical drink, or be able to rent a comfortable lounge chair in order to relax in the sun.

At many of the beaches throughout the USVI, you'll find popular water sports and activities, plus equipment rentals and expert instructors available for hire. Popular water sports and activities at many of the beaches include the following:

- Kayaking and boating
- Kite boarding
- Parasailing
- Sailing
- Scuba diving

- Snorkeling
- Snuba diving
- Submarine and glass-bottomed boat rides
- Surfing
- Swimming
- Windsurfing

# Must-See Activities and Attractions

Whatever your interests, and no matter what activities you enjoy, there's something for everyone in the USVI! The following sections outline the top ten must-see attractions and family-friendly activities in the U.S. Virgin Islands.

 **TRAVEL TIP**

Need help making reservations for your favorite activities or planning your vacation itinerary? The Concierge VI Activity Desk can help. Call ☎800-808-1654 or ☎340-715-1445 for assistance finding and booking tours, boat rides, scuba-diving excursions, snorkeling trips, and other activities.

### Virgin Islands National Park (St. John)

For eco-tourists and those who love the outdoors, the Virgin Islands National Park on St. John offers a chance to explore more than 7,000 acres on twenty miles of hiking trails and outdoor activities. Within this park, you'll have a chance to explore old Danish plantation roads and several beautiful beaches.

You can explore the park on your own or sign up for a guided tour at the National Park Visitor's Center, which is located at the dock in Cruz Bay. One excellent tour that's offered follows the Reef Bay Trail. It's a guided, three-mile hike that takes several hours to complete.

For information about guided tours within the park, call ☎340-776-6201, ext. 238. There is a $4 entrance fee to access each of several areas and trails within the park, such as the Cinnamon Bay Trail, the Annaberg Sugar Mill Historical Trail, and the Truck Bay Snorkel Trail.

Visiting the Virgin Islands National Park offers at least a full day's worth of outdoor adventures. Make sure you wear comfortable hiking shoes or sneakers, and be prepared to do a lot of walking and mild climbing. Swimming and snorkeling is allowed in certain areas of the park, so bring bathing suits, towels, and related gear.

**THE VIRGIN ISLANDS NATIONAL PARK**

| Ages up to 5 | Ages 6–15 | Ages 16–20 | Adult | Senior Citizens |
|---|---|---|---|---|
| ★ | ★★ | ★★ | ★★ | ★ |

### The World Famous Mountain Top (St. Thomas)

This mountain peak, which marks the island's highest elevation point, at 1,542 feet above the Caribbean Sea, offers an incredible view of Magen's Bay (one of the island's most beautiful beaches). Looking out, you can also see more than twenty other islands from this vantage point. Visiting the World Famous Mountain Top offers a great photo opportunity and is one of the most popular tourist attractions on St. Thomas.

## 💼 TRAVEL TIP

Air Center Helicopters (☎340-775-7335) provides helicopter tours of both St. Thomas and St. John. The average flight time is thirty minutes long and costs $100 per person. The helicopters hold up to six passengers. This is an incredible experience that offers breathtaking views and amazing photo opportunities, so bring a camera!

At the snack shop located here, you can enjoy a famous banana daiquiri. Over 6 million of these drinks have been served to date, so it's become something of a tradition to enjoy a daiquiri while taking in the breathtaking views. While visiting this site, be sure to drop in to some of the popular duty-free shops located nearby.

To preview the view from the mountaintop, go online to ✍*www. greathouse-mountaintop.com.*

### THE WORLD FAMOUS MOUNTAIN TOP

| Ages up to 5 | Ages 6–15 | Ages 16–20 | Adult | Senior Citizens |
|---|---|---|---|---|
| ★ | ★★ | ★★ | ★★ | ★★★ |

## Atlantis Submarine Ride (St. Thomas)

Prepare to take a unique and exotic submarine adventure as you dive 150 feet toward the sea floor. You'll see incredible ocean life and several sunken ships through the submarine's portals. Your journey begins by taking a short boat ride to the submarine. Upon boarding the submarine, your undersea journey lasts about an hour. The entire adventure is about ninety minutes long and includes live narration by the copilot.

Built at a cost of $3.6 million, each Atlantis submarine holds forty-eight passengers and makes up to nine dives per day. The undersea journey is surprisingly smooth. There are no restrooms available on the actual submarine, however, so plan accordingly.

An Atlantis submarine ride provides a memorable and exciting experience for people over the age of four. The cost is $84 per adult and $34 per child (ages four to sixteen). To save $10 per adult ticket, make your reservations online at ✍*www.atlantisadventures.net.* Advance reservations are definitely required. This is an extremely popular attraction, and it books up quickly.

To make a reservation or for additional information, call ✆340-776-5650.

**ATLANTIS SUBMARINE RIDE**

| Ages up to 5 | Ages 6–15 | Ages 16–20 | Adult | Senior Citizens |
|---|---|---|---|---|
| N.S. | ★★★ | ★★★ | ★★★ | ★★★ |

## The St. Thomas Skyride

This enclosed-gondola skyride allows passengers to experience the breathtaking view as they enjoy the smooth, 700-foot ascent to Paradise Point. The seven-minute journey (each way) offers views of Charlotte Amalie Harbor and beyond. Once you reach Paradise Point, you'll enjoy an array of shops and cafés, plus a tropical-bird show and a nature trail. The skyride departs from near the Havensight Mall and cruise-ship dock in St. Thomas.

The tropical-bird show is presented at 10:30 A.M. and 1:30 P.M. daily. The skyride operates from 9:00 A.M. to 5:00 P.M. This is an extremely popular attraction among kids and teens.

**ST. THOMAS SKYRIDE**

| Ages up to 5 | Ages 6–15 | Ages 16–20 | Adult | Senior Citizens |
|---|---|---|---|---|
| ★★ | ★★★ | ★★★ | ★★★ | ★★★ |

## Coral World Ocean Park (St. Thomas)

This kid- and teen-friendly museum and aquarium provides visitors with a unique way to see the world under the sea—without actually getting wet! By stepping into Coral World Ocean Park's underwater observatory and riding in a thirty-passenger submarine, you'll get incredible views of coral gardens, tropical fish, sea turtles, stingrays, and other exotic aquatic life, all from an underwater perspective. Plan on spending several hours visiting this popular attraction.

The underwater observatory (included with the price of admission to Coral World) takes you 100 feet offshore and fifteen feet beneath the sea, where you'll find yourself in the middle of a living coral reef.

The optional Sea Trekin' submarine ride is priced at $68 for adults and $59 for children, and the price includes admission to Coral World.

## ▐ TRAVEL TIP

To learn about full- and half-day bicycle tours offered on St. Croix, which include the bike and safety equipment rentals, plus knowledgeable guides, call ☎340-773-5004. Tours are available for experienced and novice riders.

Hours of operation are 9:00 A.M. to 5:00 P.M. daily. Coral World admission is $18 for adults and $9 for children. For the family rate of $52, two adults and two children will be admitted. If you wish to visit this attraction more than once, purchasing an annual membership for each person is definitely worthwhile. Members also receive a 10-percent discount on food, beverages, and items from the gift shop.

For details, call ☎888-695-2073 or visit the attraction's Web site at ✍www.coralworldvi.com. This is one of the best places in the USVI to visit with kids and teens!

### CORAL WORLD OCEAN PARK

| Ages up to 5 | Ages 6–15 | Ages 16–20 | Adult | Senior Citizens |
|---|---|---|---|---|
| ★★ | ★★★ | ★★★ | ★★ | ★★ |

### Captain Nautica Tour

You and your family can experience a half-day high seas adventure aboard Captain Nautica's thirty-one-foot power-raft. This exciting and at times high-speed cruise is a sightseeing tour with a twist that kids and teens will really enjoy.

In addition to hearing about the history of the Virgin Islands, as you cruise around them in a bright yellow, open-air power boat, the tour guide entertains passengers with exciting pirate tales and upbeat music. You'll also make two stops, during which guests are invited to go snorkeling (with all equipment provided). Drinks and snacks are included.

##  RAINY DAY FUN

If you're looking for land-based activities while visiting the U.S. Virgin Islands, some of what's offered include biking, bowling, casinos, golf, hiking, horseback riding, paintball, shopping, tennis, and day spas. Check with your hotel's concierge or tour desk for details about participating in these and other activities.

Departure times are at 8:30 A.M. and 1:00 P.M. daily. The voyage lasts between three and a half and four hours. Tours depart from the North Cruise Ship dock in Havensight (St. Thomas). This is one of the best boat tours you'll find that's suitable for families.

For details or to make a reservation, call ✆340-715-3379, or visit the company's Web site at *⬦www.captainnautica.com*.

### CAPTAIN NAUTICA TOUR

| Ages up to 5 | Ages 6–15 | Ages 16–20 | Adult | Senior Citizens |
|:---:|:---:|:---:|:---:|:---:|
| ★ | ★★★ | ★★★ | ★★ | ★★ |

## Dolphin Discovery

Located a short boat ride away from the U.S. Virgin Islands are the popular British Virgin Islands (see Chapter 11). You can take a high-speed ferry and go island-hopping in order to spend an afternoon enjoying some of the activities offered within the British Virgin Islands, such as the Dolphin Discovery program, where participants get to swim with bottlenose dolphins and interact with them.

For more information about the Dolphin Discover program offered in nearby Tortola (in the British Virgin Islands), call ✆011-284-494-7675 (*⬦www.dolphindiscovery.com*).

### DOLPHIN DISCOVERY

| Ages up to 5 | Ages 6–15 | Ages 16–20 | Adult | Senior Citizens |
|:---:|:---:|:---:|:---:|:---:|
| ★ | ★★★ | ★★★ | ★★ | ★ |

## St. Croix Heritage Trail

The St. Croix Heritage Trail encompasses a twenty-eight-mile journey across the island. By following this trail (by car) and stopping at designated historical sites and attractions, you'll discover the rich history of this island. You can experience the heritage trail at your own pace by renting a car and following a clearly labeled map. Organized bus and van tours are also offered from a variety of tour operators. Contact your hotel's concierge for details.

This tour will be of greater interest to adults and seniors, since it focuses more on history and culture, as opposed to fun activities for kids or teens. Participating in this tour, however, will provide you with a detailed understanding and appreciation for this island's history.

As you'll discover, there's no start or formal end to the trail. Thus, you can pick it up at any location and visit only those designated stops that are of interest to you and your family. Along the trail, you'll visit full-service attractions (which can be toured and that are fully staffed), visitation sites (with irregular hours and no staff), plus points of interest (which can be viewed from outside, but that are not open to the public.)

Two of the attractions along the trail you won't want to miss if you're traveling with kids or teens are the St. Croix Aquarium (✆340-773-8995) and the Base Array Telescope (✆340-773-0196).

 **TRAVEL TIP**

Are you a golfer? The USVI is home to several championship golf courses designed by people like George and Tom Fazio and Robert Trent Jones. While there are no courses on St. John, you will find several eighteen-hole championship courses on St. Thomas and St. Croix. Golf courses include Mahogany Run (✆800-253-7103, ✐*www.mahoganyrungolf.com*), The Buccaneer (✆340-773-2100), Carambola Golf Club (✆340-778-5638) and the Reef Golf Course (✆340-773-8844).

For information about the St. Croix Heritage Trail, call ☎340-713-8563 or ☎340-772-0598. Be sure to pick up a free copy of *St. Croix Heritage Trail: Your Guide to the History, Culture and Nature of St. Croix, U.S. Virgin Islands*. It's a full-color brochure and guide map available from all of the attractions along the trail, as well as from USVI tourism offices.

**THE ST. CROIX HERITAGE TRAIL**

| Ages up to 5 | Ages 6–15 | Ages 16–20 | Adult | Senior Citizens |
|---|---|---|---|---|
| ★ | ★ | ★★ | ★★★ | ★★★ |

## EcoTours Kayak and Snorkel Tours

Some of the best adventures and most memorable experiences you'll have in the USVI will take place outdoors. The Virgin Island EcoTours will take you on an exciting kayak journey through St. Thomas' Marine Sanctuary and Mangrove Lagoon. Along the way, you'll make several stops to go snorkeling in the crystal-clear waters. Some of the wildlife you'll see when snorkeling here includes barracuda, eagle rays, snapper, angelfish, and octopus. All equipment and a tour guide are provided. Call ☎340-779-2155 for reservations and details.

**ECOTOUR'S KAYAK AND SNORKEL TOURS**

| Ages up to 5 | Ages 6–15 | Ages 16–20 | Adult | Senior Citizens |
|---|---|---|---|---|
| N.S. | ★ | ★★★ | ★★★ | ★★ |

## Duty-Free Shopping

All three major islands that comprise the USVI offer an abundance of duty-free shopping opportunities. You'll find name-brand and designer jewelry, watches, perfumes, liquor, tobacco products, leather goods, cameras, china, and other items available at discounted prices that are also being sold tax-free, allowing for additional savings.

In St. Thomas, for example, some of the popular duty-free jewelry stores worth visiting include Cardow, Little Switzerland, H. Stern Design Center & World Outlet, Tanzanite International, Omni, Royal Caribbean (not to be confused with the cruise line), and Rolex Watches at A.H. Riise.

## ≡FAST FACT

The USVI offers visitors a $1,200 per-person duty-free shopping quota. This means you can spend up to $1,200 on duty-free items without paying any taxes on those items.

The best way to save money when shopping at duty-free stores is to know, in advance, exactly what you're looking for. Before leaving home, do research on those items and have a good understanding of prices, brand names, and model numbers (when applicable). This will allow you to intelligently compare prices when shopping in the USVI and ultimately save more money when you negotiate your best price, especially on items like jewelry and designer watches.

**DUTY-FREE SHOPPING**

| Ages up to 5 | Ages 6–15 | Ages 16–20 | Adult | Senior Citizens |
|:---:|:---:|:---:|:---:|:---:|
| ★ | ★ | ★ | ★★★ | ★★★ |

# Making the U.S. Virgin Islands Your Vacation Destination

Before embarking on your vacation, be sure to visit these informative Web sites:

- **The USVI Tourism Board:** ✐*www.usvitourism.com*
- **U.S. Virgin Islands Tropical Update:** ✐*www.usvi.net*

- **U.S. Virgin Islands Tour Guide:** *www.usvi-info.com*
- **Virtual Guide to St. Thomas:** *www.st-thomas.com*
- **United States Virgin Islands Guide:** *www.usviguide.com*

To learn more about the USVI, contact the USVI Department of Tourism by calling (800-372-USVI. The tourism department has offices and information desks throughout all three USVI islands, as well as in Atlanta, Chicago, Los Angeles, Miami, New York, and Washington, D.C.

# CHAPTER 17

# *Other Exciting Caribbean Destinations*

WHETHER YOU HAVE JUST a few days or you're lucky enough to have a week or more to experience a Caribbean vacation, you have the option to choose one island and enjoy all that it has to offer, or go island-hopping in order to see a lot more of the Caribbean firsthand. Thus far, you have read all about many of the most popular vacation destinations in the Caribbean. There are, however, a few additional islands well worth considering as you plan your vacation itinerary.

## Exploring the Rest of the Caribbean

While the Caribbean itself encompasses more than 7,000 individual islands, not all of them are inhabited and even fewer are considered vacation destinations. In addition to the islands you've already read about, this chapter offers information about a few of the other popular vacation spots in the Caribbean.

To discover more about any of these Caribbean getaways, consider visiting the Web site for each island's department of tourism. You could also contact a travel agent.

### Antigua and Barbuda

Visit the Antigua department of tourism's Web site at *≤www. antigua-barbuda.org*. Antigua (which is pronounced "Ant-EE-ga") and Barbuda are situated in the Eastern Caribbean. English is the official language of these relatively small islands, where the temperature is almost always in the mid 70s to mid 80s. As you'd expect from a tropical paradise, many of the activities you read about in Chapter 5 are available here.

On land, popular activities include hiking, bird watching, tennis, and horseback riding. Cricket, however, is one of the most popular sports on the island, both to watch and participate in.

Water-based activities include boating, fishing, scuba diving, snorkeling, kayaking, windsurfing, and swimming with dolphins. From this island, visitors can also participate in a variety of eco-tours. For details about these educational and adventurous outdoor tours, go online to *www.adventureantigua.com* or *www.antiguaseafaris.com*.

## ≡FAST FACT

On Antigua, you'll find two eighteen-hole golf courses: Jolly Harbor Golf Club (☎ 268-462-7111) and Cedar Valley Golf Course (☎ 268-462-0161).

These are the islands to visit if you and your family are interested in outdoor adventures, as opposed to just laid-back and relaxing tours. For example, the kayak tours offered on the island (*www.antiguapaddles.com*) offer a half-day of kayaking, snorkeling, and/or hiking combined into one adventure. Speedboat tours (☎ 268-774-1810) are also a popular way to go sightseeing as passengers ride in a Glastron GX185 speedboat driven by a professional.

One activity that kids and teens will enjoy is Stingray City Antigua (☎ 268-562-7297). Tourists visit a shallow reef, where they can swim with, feed, and interact with stingrays. Helicopter tours (*www.caribbeanhelicopters.com*) and four-wheel-drive or Jeep tours (*www.estatesafari.com*) are two other fun-filled ways to experience these islands in a manner that'll keep your adrenalin pumping.

Of course, when you're ready to relax, it's easy to find a beautiful beach on Antigua. The island itself encompasses only ten square miles, yet it offers tourists a choice of 365 beaches. That's a different beach, offering a different view, for every single day of the year! All of the beaches are open to the public.

Flying to Antigua takes about four hours from New York, three hours from Miami, and one hour from Puerto Rico. Popular airlines, including: American Airlines (✎*www.aa.com*), Continental Airlines (✎*www.continental.com*), Air Jamaica (✎*www.airjamaica.com*), and US Airways (✎*www.usairways.com*) all offer nonstop or connecting flights to Antigua and Barbuda from the United States. Several popular cruise lines also offer Antigua as a port of call.

Once you're on the island, taxis, rental cars, and public buses are the most popular ways to get around. Antigua and Barbuda are in the Atlantic Standard Time zone, which is one hour ahead of Eastern Standard Time. The islands do not observe Daylight Saving Time. The official currency here is the Eastern Caribbean dollar (EC), which has a fixed exchange rate. One U.S. dollar is equal to $2.70 EC.

##  TRAVEL TIP

High-speed ferryboat service is available between Antigua and Barbuda (as well as to St. John) via the Barbuda Express (✎*www.antiguaferries.com*). The journey takes about ninety minutes.

### Barbados

You can visit the Barbados Department of Tourism's Web site at ✎*http://barbados.org*. Barbados is another relatively small, but extremely beautiful tropical island in the Caribbean. On this island, you'll also find a wide range of activities and tours. Adventure tours (involving off-road vehicles or high-speed boats) are popular with families, while adults and senior citizens might prefer some of the eco, nature, or heritage (historical) tours offered on the island.

Atlantis Adventures offers a memorable submarine ride which is a favorite attraction amongst people of all ages, while Bubbles

Adventure Dive Center (✆246-436-7095) offers a specialized scuba diving and snorkeling instructional program designed for kids (over age eight) as well as adults.

If you're looking to go Jet Skiing or want to take a glass-bottomed boat ride, catamaran cruise, or ride on a banana boat, for example, Free Spirit Watersports (✆246-230-1865) and Just Breezing Watersports (🖮www.justbreezingwatersports.com) both offer a wide selection of adventure-based water sports and activities suitable for the entire family. Each activity is priced separately, although discounted package deals are available.

To see firsthand the natural wildlife in Barbados, the Wildlife Preserve offers a chance to go hiking and see a wide range of animals in their natural habitats. There's also a zoological attraction here, where you'll see more exotic animals. People of all ages will also enjoy exploring Harrison's Cave. Admission to this spectacular attraction is priced at $16 per adult and $7 per child. In addition to being one of the best deals on the island, in terms of activities and attractions, Harrison's Cave is also one of the most memorable. Harrison's Cave is stunningly beautiful and a unique phenomenon of nature. As you walk through the cave complex, you'll see stalactites hanging from overhead and large stalagmites emerging from the ground as streams of crystal-clear water flow around you. Your exploration of the caves begins with a tram ride to the lowest level of the complex, where you're then free to walk around or even swim in the deep pool of underground water. The caves are open daily. Tours operate from 9:00 A.M. until 4:00 P.M. Be sure to bring a camera.

From Miami, the flight to Barbados is about three hours and forty minutes. From New York, it's just under four and a half hours. Air Jamaica, American Airlines, and US Airways all offer nonstop and connecting service from major U.S. cities.

Barbados offers a lot for tourists, not just with water-based activities and land tours, but in terms of its rich culture. There are plenty of dining and shopping opportunities, plus nightclubs and bars to keep adults entertained at night.

## Curacao

Visit Curacao's Department of Tourism's Web site at ✍*www. curacao-tourism.com* or ✍*www.curacoa.com.* Located a hop, skip, and a puddle-jumper flight from Aruba, Curacao offers its own vacation-getaway experience. The average temperature here is in the mid 80s year-round. Dutch is the official language, although most everyone also speaks English, Spanish, and Papiamento. Curacao is a popular port of call for cruise ships (including Royal Caribbean, Holland America, Carnival Cruise Lines, Princess Cruise Lines, and Norwegian Cruise Lines). It's also easy to reach by air from the United States.

American Airlines, Delta Airlines, and Air Jamaica offer regular service from the United States, although a handful of charter companies and tour operators also offer special travel packages to this island. The flight time from Miami to Curacao is approximately two and a half hours.

Like Aruba, Curacao offers a wide range of accommodation options, from full-service and all-inclusive resorts, to time-shares, rentable villas, and smaller inns. For kids, one of the most popular activities here is the Curacao Kids Sea Camp (✆800-433-3483, ✆954-236-6611, ✍*www.kidsseacamp.com*), which is a fully supervised program for kids between the ages of four and fifteen.

Beach lovers will enjoy the Beach Express Tour service, a bus that takes visitors on a tour of the island's most popular beaches and offers a taste of a few lesser-known and more remote beaches. This tour includes drinks, lunch, and the use of floating devices for swimming. The price is $30 per adult and $20 per child for this all-day experience. For an additional fee, the Beach Express Tour will coordinate snorkeling, scuba diving, and other beach activities. For information, go online to ✍*www.islandstyletours.com.* Of course, you can also visit any of the island's thirty public beaches on your own.

Bicycle tours, off-road Jeep safaris, canoe safaris, deep-sea fishing trips, scuba-diving (and snorkeling) tours, and the Willemstad Pleasure Train are all family-friendly ways of experiencing this island.

The Hato Caves (✆011-599-9868-0379) is another visually breathtaking attraction which people of all ages will enjoy. These old coral reefs have naturally transformed into massive caves that can be explored. The caves are open every day except Mondays, between 10:00 A.M. and 5:00 P.M. Admission is $6.25 per adult and $4.75 per child. Tours are offered throughout the day.

Curacao also offers a swimming-with-dolphins experience at the Curacao Sea Aquarium (☎011-599-9465-8300, ✍*www.dolphin-academy. com*), as well as a wide range of other activities both on land and that relate to the water.

While rental cars are readily available, taxis are the most popular way of getting around the island. The taxis here have no meters, so it's important to agree on a fare before departing. You can also hire a taxi driver as a private tour guide for $20 per hour.

## Martinique

You can visit the Martinique Department of Tourism's Web site at ✍*www.martinique.org*. Martinique, like many of the Caribbean islands, has a rich and interesting history. The island became a Region of France in 1974. Fort-de-France is the administrative and commercial capital of the island, which maintains a near-perfect temperature in the high 70s throughout the year.

This is one of the islands that can be found in the heart of the Caribbean Archipelago. It is part of the cluster of islands referred to as the "breezy islands," because of the near-constant trade winds. Martinique is just under 2,000 miles from New York City, about 1,500 miles from Miami and 425 miles from San Juan. The island itself encompasses about 426 square miles.

When visitors arrive to Martinique by air, they'll find themselves at the International Lamentin Airport, an ultramodern airport that's located near Fort-de-France. Regular flights from the United States are available from American Airlines (✍*www.aa.com*), Air France (✍*www.airfrance.com*) and BWee Express or BWIA (✍*www. bwee.com*). If you're looking for a complete vacation package, TNT Vacations (☎617-262-9200, ✍*www.tntvacations.com*) is a tour operator based in Boston that offers several different charters and travel packages to this island.

# ═FAST FACT

From Guadeloupe, St. Lucia, Dominica, and Les Saintes, ferryboat service allows for easy island-hopping. Contact Express de Illes (✆ 767-448-2181, ✉www.whitchurch.com/express.htm or Brudey Freres (✉www.brudey-freres.fr).

In terms of accommodations in Martinique, your options are diverse. The island offers large, full-service resorts, as well as much smaller resorts and inns offering between ten and 100 rooms and suites. The larger hotels and resorts all have restaurants, a wide range of activities, and entertainment right on the property. For adults traveling without kids, the island offers more than 200 country guesthouses, many of which offer apartments, studios, and guestrooms. For families, a more viable alternative to staying at a full-service resort is to rent a villa.

For information about renting a villa in Martinique, contact the Villa Rental Service of the Martinique Tourist Office (✆011-596-61-61-77). Villas can be rented by the week or by the month. Most offer multiple bedrooms, a living room, and a full kitchen.

Martinique, like most Caribbean islands, offers a lot in terms of activities and attractions. In addition to a wide range of land and water sports (which you read about in Chapter 5), one of the family-friendly attractions worth experiencing is the Seaquarium (✆011-596-73-02-29). Tropical Adventures (✆011-596-64-58-49), for example, is a tour operator offering catamaran sailing, scuba diving, mountain biking, and a wide range of other activities. There are also off-road vehicle safari tours, cycling tours, and canoeing tours, any of which will be of interest to more athletic families looking for adventure.

Tennis, golf, sailing, deep-sea fishing, hiking, scuba diving, mountain biking, horseback riding, windsurfing, and yachting are among the other popular activities offered on the island. Taking a helicopter tour (ACF Aviation, ✆011-596-51-07-17) is also a fun and memorable way to go sightseeing.

One way to experience the local culture of Martinique is to visit one of the craft centers. Morne-des-Esses (✆011-596-69-83-74), for example, is open Monday through Saturday, and it offers dozens of local artists and craftspeople showcasing and selling their works. This is the perfect opportunity to pick up a few unique souvenirs.

To get around Martinique, rental cars and taxi service are readily available. All taxis use meters. You can pick up a taxi at most hotels or at designated taxi stands throughout the island and near virtually all tourist areas. Taxis can also be ordered by phone. Dial ✆63-63-62 or ✆63-10-10 from any local phone. The public bus system is the least expensive way to travel throughout the island. They only operate until around 6:00 P.M., however. In terms of rental cars, Avis (⌨www.avis.com), Budget (⌨www.budget.com), Hertz (⌨www.hertz.com), National (⌨www.nationalcar.com) and a handful of local rental-car agencies are available. Cars can be picked up at the airport or at some major resorts and hotels.

## St. Lucia

You can visit the St. Lucia Department of Tourism's Web site at ⌨www.stlucia.org. St. Lucia is another relatively popular vacation destination in the Caribbean that has recently become more family friendly. Many of the resort hotels now offer kids' clubs, special kids' menus, and adjoining guestrooms. There are also a handful of tours and activities designed to appeal to entire families.

The island is located in the Eastern Caribbean, about twenty-one miles south of Martinique and ninety miles northwest of Barbados. The official language in St. Lucia is English, but you'll find that Spanish and French are common languages here as well. One unique aspect of this island is that it offers very varied terrain. The 238-square-mile island has its own mountain range, rainforest, and volcanoes.

The temperature throughout the year ranges from 70 to 90 degrees, with the rainy season going from June to November.

From the United States, St. Lucia is about three and a half hours by air from Miami and four hours from New York. American Airlines, US Airways, Delta, and BWIA are among the airlines offering nonstop and connecting service to this island. International flights arriving to St. Lucia land at Hewanorra International Airport. A second, smaller airport, called Charles Inter Island Airport, is used primarily by a handful of airlines offering island-hopping opportunities and for private aviation. St. Lucia is also a popular port of call among cruise ships that sail the Caribbean.

The official currency of St. Lucia is the Eastern Caribbean dollar, which has a fixed exchange rate with the U.S. dollar. One U.S. dollar equals $2.70 EC. U.S. dollars are widely accepted throughout the island, as are major credit cards.

The electricity available throughout the island is 220 volts, although a few hotels and resorts offer 110-volt electricity (identical to that in the United States). If you'll be bringing personal electronics, such as a laptop computer, camcorder, or electric shaver, for example, make sure you have the appropriate electrical adapters.

In terms of accommodations, all-inclusive resorts are often chosen by families, although villas can also be rented. Guesthouses, hotels, and inns provide for a very different vacation experience than a full-service resort, giving visitors additional options when it comes to deciding where to stay.

To get around the island, rental cars are available from Avis, Budget, Hertz, Economy, and a handful of local car-rental agencies. Taxis, however, are readily available throughout the island.

In terms of things to see and do that are unique to St. Lucia, there's Marigot Bay, which is a natural harbor that once served as a secret hideout for pirates. From the coastline or via boat, whale watching is a popular pastime. Over twenty species of whales, as well as dolphins, can often be seen swimming in the ocean.

Water sports such as windsurfing, snorkeling, scuba diving, parasailing, and water-skiing are all offered on the island, which is also famous for its beautiful beaches. For people who enjoy hiking and experiencing nature, the Tropical Islands Rainforest in St. Lucia offers 19,000 acres of rainforest with twenty-nine miles of marked trails running through it. In the rainforest, tourists will encounter tropical birds and other wildlife. Guided tours are offered for hikers with various levels of experience.

From an historical standpoint, St. Lucia offers a handful of places to visit and explore, like several plantations and the botanical gardens. These attractions, however, tend to appeal more to adults. For more adventurous travelers, all-terrain vehicle tours, biking tours, and horseback riding tours provide a fun way to experience this island.

One nice thing about St. Lucia is that it's located close to other Caribbean islands. Short flights on Caribbean Express (✆758-452-2211) or high-speed ferryboats will take you to Martinique, Dominica, and Guadeloupe, for example, with relative ease. This makes planning a day trip to another island extremely easy.

# The Caribbean Awaits

Now that you've read an overview of what the various islands in the Caribbean have to offer in terms of a memorable vacation experience for you and your family, it's time to do your homework, pack your bags, and get ready for your vacation.

As you've read multiple times throughout this book, the best way to ensure you'll have a wonderful vacation is to invest time and effort in proper planning before you leave. Researching the best deals and planning much of your itinerary will help ensure that your vacation will be fun, memorable, and within your travel budget. One of the most disappointing vacation-related experiences is arriving at a lovely Caribbean resort and beginning to enjoy your vacation only to discover, after speaking with another vacationing family, that you overpaid for your trip by hundreds of dollars because you didn't shop around for the best deals. Be sure to take full advantage of the online travel-related Web sites, as well as the Web sites sponsored by the department of tourism for each of the Caribbean islands as you're deciding where to go and what to experience.

Once you arrive in the Caribbean, be open to new experiences and to trying new things. A wide range of foods, drinks, cultural experiences, activities, and attractions await, the likes of which you've probably never experienced living anywhere in the United States.

## 🧳 TRAVEL TIP

On the other hand, you don't want to exhaust yourself surfing the Internet at 3:00 A.M. to save a few dollars. Find a deal you're comfortable with, and then stop looking.

Finally, to ensure that you and your family enjoy the most stress-free vacation possible, choose accommodations that are best suited to your needs. If you're traveling with multiple kids or teens, or members of your extended family, multiple bedrooms, connecting guestrooms, or separate guestrooms or suites might be most appropriate. It's never a good idea to save money by cramming too many people into a tiny hotel room or cabin aboard a cruise ship.

The experience you're about to have will create memories that'll last a lifetime. Don't forget to pack a camera and plenty of batteries and film. You'll pay a premium to buy film and batteries (or disposable cameras) in the Caribbean. No matter where in the Caribbean you travel, there will be countless photo opportunities! Before leaving the Caribbean, either have your film developed or pack your undeveloped film in your carry-on, and don't allow it to be X-rayed by airport security.

One Web site that offers useful information about virtually all of the Caribbean Islands is Caribbean Online (✐ *www.caribbean-on-line. com*). On this Web site, you'll find maps, travel tips, details about discounted travel packages, plus additional information about each Caribbean island.

# APPENDIX A

# *Travel Itinerary Worksheet*

THIS WORKSHEET WILL HELP you keep track of all your flight information, hotel reservations, rental-car reservations, and other travel-related information. Photocopy this form and fill it out, as applicable, for each person you're traveling with. Keep the completed forms with your passport(s), photo IDs, airline tickets, and other travel documents.

Traveler's name: _____

Passport number: _____

## **Primary Departure Flight Information**

Airline: _____

Airline phone number: _____

Ticket confirmation/reservation number: _____

Flight number: _____

Departure date: _____

Departure time: _____

Departure city: _____

Arrival city: _____

Arrival time: _____

## Connecting Flight Information (If Applicable)

Connecting flight number: _____

Connecting flight city: _____

Connecting flight departure time: _____

Connecting flight arrival time: _____


Connecting flight number: _____

Connecting flight city: _____

Connecting flight departure time: _____

Connecting flight arrival time: _____

## Primary Return Flight Information

Airline: _____

Airline phone number: _____

Ticket confirmation/reservation number: _____


Flight number: _____

Departure date: _____

Departure time: _____

Departure city: _____

Arrival city: _____

Arrival time: _____

## Connecting Flight Information (If Applicable)

Connecting flight number: _____

Connecting flight city: _____

Connecting flight departure time: _____

Connecting flight arrival time: _____


Connecting flight number: _____

Connecting flight city: _____

Connecting flight departure time: _____

Connecting flight arrival: _____

## Home City Airport Parking Information

Parking lot name, color, or number: _____
Space number/location:_____
Daily or weekly parking rate: _____

## Rental Car Information

Rental car company:_____
Phone number: _____
Reservation number: _____
Daily or weekly rate: _____
Type of vehicle: _____
Pick-up date/time: _____
Drop-off date/time: _____

## Hotel/Resort Information

Hotel/resort name: _____
Address: _____
_____
Toll-free phone number: _____
Local phone number:_____
Reservation number(s): _____
Number and type of room(s) reserved: _____
Check-in date: _____
Check-out date: _____
Nightly rate: _____

## Ground Transportation Information

Taxi, limo, or shuttle-bus company:_____
Phone number: _____

Reservation number: _____

Pick-up date/time: _____

Pick-up location: _____

## Tour/Activity Reservation Information

Tour name/activity description: _____

Tour operator: _____

Phone number: _____

Web site/e-mail address: _____

Reservation/confirmation number: _____

Tour date/time: _____

Duration: _____

Price per person: _____


Tour name/activity description: _____

Tour operator: _____

Phone number: _____

Web site/e-mail address: _____

Reservation/confirmation number: _____

Tour date/time: _____

Duration: _____

Price per person: _____


Tour name/activity description: _____

Tour operator: _____

Phone number: _____

Web site/e-mail address: _____

Reservation/confirmation number: _____

Tour date/time: _____

Duration: _____

Price per person: _____


Tour name/activity description: _____

Tour operator: _____

Phone number: _____

Web site/e-mail address:_____

Reservation/confirmation number:_____

Tour date/time: _____

Duration: _____

Price per person:_____

Tour name/activity description:_____

Tour operator: _____

Phone number: _____

Web site/e-mail address:_____

Reservation/confirmation number:_____

Tour date/time: _____

Duration: _____

Price per person:_____

## Dining Reservation Information

Restaurant name: _____

Address: _____

Phone number: _____

Reservation date/time: _____

Meal (breakfast/lunch/dinner/brunch): _____

Number of people: _____

Confirmation # (if applicable):_____

Restaurant name: _____

Address: _____

Phone number: _____

Reservation date/time: _____

Meal (breakfast/lunch/dinner/brunch): _____

Number of people: _____

Confirmation # (if applicable):_____

Restaurant name: _____

Address: _____

Phone number: _____

Reservation date/time: _____

Meal (breakfast/lunch/dinner/brunch): _____

Number of people: _____

Confirmation # (if applicable):_____


Restaurant name: _____

Address: _____

Phone number: _____

Reservation date/time: _____

Meal (breakfast/lunch/dinner/brunch): _____

Number of people: _____

Confirmation # (if applicable):_____


Restaurant name: _____

Address: _____

Phone number: _____

Reservation date/time: _____

Meal (breakfast/lunch/dinner/brunch): _____

Number of people: _____

Confirmation # (if applicable):_____


Restaurant name: _____

Address: _____

Phone number:_____

Reservation date/time: _____

Meal (breakfast/lunch/dinner/brunch):_____

Number of people:_____

Confirmation # (if applicable):_____

# Appendix B

# *Making the Conversion*

ALL OF THE CARIBBEAN islands use the metric system. For example, speed limit signs are in kilometers per hour, gasoline is sold by the liter, and temperatures are measured on the Celsius scale. Also, unless you're staying at an all-inclusive resort, chances are you'll need to tip people who assist you, including the waiters and waitresses in restaurants and taxi drivers. This section offers a series of conversion charts that'll help you while traveling throughout the Caribbean.

# Convert Kilometers to Miles

To convert kilometers to miles, simply multiple the number of kilometers by .62. To convert miles to kilometers, multiple the number of miles by 1.61. The following chart will help you make conversions quickly.

TABLE B-1

**DISTANCE CONVERSION: KILOMETERS TO MILES**

| Kilometers | Miles |
| --- | --- |
| 1 | 0.62 |
| 2 | 1.24 |
| 3 | 1.86 |
| 4 | 2.48 |
| 5 | 3.10 |
| 6 | 3.72 |
| 7 | 4.34 |
| 8 | 4.96 |
| 9 | 5.58 |
| 10 | 6.20 |
| 20 | 12.40 |
| 30 | 18.60 |
| 40 | 24.80 |
| 50 | 31.00 |
| 60 | 37.20 |
| 70 | 43.40 |
| 80 | 49.60 |
| 90 | 55.80 |
| 100 | 62.00 |
| 125 | 77.50 |
| 150 | 93.00 |
| 175 | 108.50 |
| 200 | 124.00 |

# Temperature Conversions: Celsius to Fahrenheit

To convert Celsius to Fahrenheit, multiply the Celsius temperature by 1.8 and then add 32. To convert Fahrenheit to Celsius, subtract 32, then multiple by .555. The following chart will help you make the conversions quickly.

TABLE B-2
**TEMPERATURE CONVERSION: CELSIUS TO FAHRENHEIT**

| Celsius (Degrees) | Fahrenheit (Degrees) |
|---|---|
| 0 | 32 |
| 5 | 41 |
| 10 | 50 |
| 15 | 59 |
| 20 | 68 |
| 25 | 77 |
| 30 | 86 |
| 35 | 95 |
| 40 | 105 |

# Liters to Gallons Conversion

To convert liters to gallons, multiply the number of liters by .264. To convert gallons to liters, multiple the number of gallons by 3.79. The following chart will help you make the conversion quickly.

**TABLE B-3**
**LITERS TO GALLONS CONVERSION**

| Liters | Gallons |
|--------|---------|
| 1 | 0.264 |
| 2 | 0.528 |
| 3 | 0.792 |
| 4 | 1.05 |
| 5 | 1.32 |
| 6 | 1.58 |
| 7 | 1.85 |
| 8 | 2.11 |
| 9 | 2.38 |
| 10 | 2.64 |
| 15 | 3.95 |
| 20 | 5.28 |
| 25 | 6.60 |
| 30 | 7.92 |
| 35 | 9.24 |
| 40 | 10.56 |
| 45 | 11.88 |
| 50 | 13.20 |
| 75 | 19.80 |
| 100 | 26.40 |
| 125 | 33.00 |
| 150 | 39.60 |
| 175 | 46.20 |
| 200 | 52.80 |

# Tipping Made Easy

This chart will help you quickly calculate tips, based on whether it's appropriate to leave a 10-percent, 15-percent, 18-percent, or 20-percent tip.

**TABLE B-4**
**CALCULATING TIPS**

| Dollar Amount | 10% | 15% | 18% | 20% |
|---|---|---|---|---|
| $1.00 | $0.10 | $0.15 | $0.18 | $0.20 |
| $2.00 | $0.20 | $0.30 | $0.36 | $0.40 |
| $3.00 | $0.30 | $0.45 | $0.54 | $0.60 |
| $4.00 | $0.40 | $0.60 | $0.72 | $0.80 |
| $5.00 | $0.50 | $0.75 | $0.90 | $1.00 |
| $6.00 | $0.60 | $0.90 | $1.08 | $1.20 |
| $7.00 | $0.70 | $1.05 | $1.26 | $1.40 |
| $8.00 | $0.80 | $1.20 | $1.44 | $1.60 |
| $9.00 | $0.90 | $1.35 | $1.62 | $1.80 |
| $10.00 | $1.00 | $1.50 | $1.80 | $2.00 |
| $15.00 | $1.50 | $2.25 | $2.70 | $3.00 |
| $20.00 | $2.00 | $3.00 | $3.60 | $4.00 |
| $25.00 | $2.50 | $3.75 | $4.50 | $5.00 |
| $30.00 | $3.00 | $4.50 | $5.40 | $6.00 |
| $40.00 | $4.00 | $6.00 | $7.20 | $8.00 |
| $50.00 | $5.00 | $7.50 | $9.00 | $10.00 |
| $60.00 | $6.00 | $9.00 | $10.80 | $12.00 |
| $70.00 | $7.00 | $10.50 | $12.60 | $14.00 |
| $80.00 | $8.00 | $12.00 | $14.40 | $16.00 |
| $90.00 | $9.00 | $13.50 | $16.20 | $18.00 |
| $100.00 | $10.00 | $15.00 | $18.00 | $20.00 |
| $125.00 | $12.50 | $18.75 | $22.50 | $25.00 |
| $150.00 | $15.00 | $22.50 | $27.00 | $30.00 |
| $175.00 | $17.50 | $26.25 | $31.50 | $35.00 |
| $200.00 | $20.00 | $30.00 | $36.00 | $40.00 |
| $500.00 | $50.00 | $75.00 | $90.00 | $100.00 |
| $1,00.00 | $100.00 | $150.00 | $180.00 | $200.00 |

# Currency Conversion

While the U.S. dollar is readily accepted throughout the Caribbean, many of the islands have their own currency. You can purchase a currency conversion program for your Palm PDA. From the Palm Source Web site (*www.palmsource.com*), do a keyword search for "Currency" or "Currency Converter." Another option is to use a standard calculator, once you determine the exchange rate between the U.S. dollar and the foreign currency.

The following Web sites can be used to convert currency.

- *http://finance.yahoo.com/currency*
- *www.flash-db.com/Currency*
- *www.oanda.com/convert/classic*
- *www.xe.com*
- *www.x-rates.com*

# Resources for Popular Caribbean Islands

The following is a listing of Web sites operated by the tourism offices for the popular Caribbean islands:

**Aruba**
✎ *www.aruba.com*

**Bahamas**
✎ *www.bahamas.com*

**Barbados**
✎ *http://barbados.org*

**Bermuda**
✎ *www.bermudatourism.com*

**British Virgin Islands**
✎ *www.bvitouristboard.com*

**Cancun**
✎ *www.mexico-travel.com* or
*www.visitmexico.com*

**Cayman Islands**
✎ *www.caymanislands.ky*

**Dominican Republic**
✎ *www.dominicana.com.do*

**Jamaica**
✎ *www.visitjamaica.com*

**Martinique**
✎ *www.martinique.org*

**Puerto Rico**
✎ *www.gotopuertorico.com*

**St. Lucia**
✎ *www.stlucia.org*

**St. Maarten (St. Martin)**
✎ *www.st-martin.com* or
*www.st-maarten.com*

**U.S. Virgin Islands**
✎ *www.usvitourism.vi*

**Directory of other Tourism Offices**
✎ *www.towd.com*

# *Index*

# Everything® Family Travel Guides from Adams Media

This accessible, informative series contains all the
information a family needs to plan a vacation
that every member will enjoy!

The Everything® Family Guide to Hawaii
1-59337-054-7, $14.95

The Everything® Family Guide to New York City, 2nd Ed.
1-59337-136-5, $14.95

The Everything® Family Guide to RV Travel & Campgrounds
1-59337-301-5, $14.95

The Everything® Family Guide to Las Vegas, Completely Updated!
1-59337-359-7, $14.95

The Everything® Family Guide to Cruise Vacations
1-59337-428-3, $14.95

The Everything® Family Guide to the Walt Disney World Resort®,
Universal Studios®, and Greater Orlando, 4th Ed.
1-59337-179-9, $14.95

The Everything® Family Guide to Washington D.C., 2nd Ed.
1-59337-137-3, $14.95

The Everything® Guide to New England
1-58062-589-4, $14.95

The Everything® Travel Guide to the Disneyland Resort®, California
Adventure®, Universal Studios®, and the Anaheim Area
1-58062-742-0, $14.95

Available wherever books are sold.
Or call 1-800-258-0929 or visit us at *www.adamsmedia.com*.